WRITING
VOYAGE

TITLES OF RELATED INTEREST

COLLEGE WRITING BASICS: A PROGRESSIVE APPROACH, Third Edition, by Thomas E. Tyner (1993)

COMPOSING THROUGH READING, Second Edition, by Peter Elias Sotiriou (1994)

DEVELOPING WRITERS: A DIALOGIC APPROACH, by Pamela Gay (1992)

INSIDE WRITING: A WRITER'S WORKBOOK, FORM A, Second Edition, by William Salomone, Stephen McDonald, and Mark Edelstein (1993)

INSIDE WRITING: A WRITER'S WORKBOOK, FORM B, Second Edition, by William Salomone, Stephen McDonald, and Mark Edelstein (1994)

THE LANGUAGE OF LEARNING: VOCABULARY FOR COLLEGE SUCCESS, Second Edition, by Jane N. Hopper and JoAnn Carter-Wells (1994)

MAKING CONNECTIONS THROUGH READING AND WRITING, by Maria Valeri-Gold and Mary P. Deming (1994)

THE MOUNTAIN IS HIGH UNLESS YOU TAKE THE ELEVATOR: SUCCESS STRATEGIES FOR ADULT LEARNERS, by Laurence N. Smith and Timothy L. Walter (1992)

PATTERNS AND THEMES: A BASIC ENGLISH READER, by Judy R. Rogers and Glenn C. Rogers (1993)

RIGHT WORDS, RIGHT PLACES, by Scott Rice (1993)

TEXTS AND CONTEXTS: A CONTEMPORARY APPROACH TO COLLEGE WRITING, by William S. Robinson and Stephanie Tucker (1991)

VARIATIONS: A RHETORIC AND READER FOR COLLEGE WRITING, by Judy R. Rogers and Glenn C. Rogers (1991)

WRITING AS A LIFE-LONG SKILL, by Sanford Kaye (1994)

WRITING PARAGRAPHS AND ESSAYS: INTEGRATING READING, WRITING, AND GRAMMAR SKILLS, by Joy Wingersky, Jan Boerner, and Diana Holguin-Balogh (1992)

FOURTH EDITION

WRITING VOYAGE

A Process Approach
to Basic Writing

Thomas E. Tyner
Kings River College

Wadsworth Publishing Company
Belmont, California
A Division of Wadsworth, Inc.

English Editor: Angela Gantner
Senior Editorial Assistant: Lisa Timbrell
Production: Del Mar Associates
Print Buyer: Barbara Britton
Permissions Editor: Robert Kauser
Designer: Juan Vargas
Copy Editor: Robin Witkin
Cover Designer: Harry Voigt
Cover Photo: J. A. Kraulis/Masterfile
Compositor: Graphic World, Inc.
Printer: Arcata Graphics/Fairfield

*This book is printed on
acid-free recycled paper.*

I**T**P™

International Thomson Publishing
The trademark ITP is used under license.

Printed in the United States of America

1 2 3 4 5 6 7 8 9 10—97 96 95 94

Library of Congress Cataloging-in-Publication Data

Tyner, Thomas E., 1944–
    Writing voyage : a process approach to basic writing / Thomas E.
  Tyner.—4th ed.
      p.   cm.
    Includes index.
    ISBN 0-534-21270-0
    1. English language—Rhetoric.   2. English language—Grammar.
I. Title.
PE1408.T96 1994
808′.042—dc20   93-25560
                                                  CIP

Contents

vi   Contents

UNIT SIX
CONVINCING OTHERS   163

FINAL EDITING 199

Preface

The purpose of this text is to provide an integrated writing experience for students. Textbooks often isolate basic elements of writing from the developmental process itself. Students are left with a fragmented approach to writing, in which connections between textbook work and real writing are difficult to see.

Writing Voyage, Fourth Edition, folds these writing elements into the process so that students write papers and work concurrently on specific writing skills to apply at different stages of the drafting process. Students learn what elements of writing are most important at each stage of the process, and they understand that a mastery of a variety of skills is crucial to the effective communication of the writer's ideas.

The following eight features help make *Writing Voyage* an effective writing text.

Focus on Process

In each unit, students are taken through the process of prewriting, drafting, revising, and proofreading their papers. The text emphasizes that writing is a process that develops in general stages that most writers go through. As students progress through the book, they tailor the process to their needs and preferences. By the book's end they are well versed in the basic elements of effective writing and in command of a process that works for them.

Content Orientation

Throughout the text, the primary emphasis is on writing content: what the writer wants to communicate to his or her readers. All other elements of effective writing—organization of ideas, paragraphing, wording, correctness—are addressed as a *means* to communicate a writer's ideas most effectively. Substance is always emphasized before structure, and structure is evaluated by how it contributes to the reader's appreciation of the substance.

Rotating Format

Writing texts frequently introduce a subject in one unit and then virtually abandon it. From my teaching experience, students who have been taught parallel construction in the first unit may have forgotten what they learned by the third or fourth unit unless the topic has been regularly reinforced. Therefore, this text is designed so the basic elements of writing—prewriting, audience/purpose consideration, paragraphing, sentence structure, organization—are covered in every unit. Many students in basic writing courses have problems that cannot be solved with the traditional block-coverage textbook approach. *Writing Voyage* provides reinforcement of basic writing skills throughout the book.

Emphasis on Writing

Assuming that students cannot learn to write well without writing often, the text provides constant writing opportunities: free writing, drafting essays, paragraph writing, copying exercises, sentence combining exercises, and a variety of sentence writing activities. In addition to the major assignments that students take through the writing process in each unit, there are numerous shorter writing assignments, each emphasizing a particular aspect of the process. Most of these assignments are light in nature and require some invention by students.

Student Writing Samples

Throughout the text, students will find student writing samples that relate to the kinds of writing they are doing. The writing samples are interesting to read, provide realistic models for students, and supply material to be analyzed from a number of angles: thesis development, purpose, audience consideration, organization, paragraphing, style, originality, and overall effectiveness. Each unit also contains first-draft writing samples through which students can sharpen their revising skills. Throughout the text, students will analyze and learn from the essays of other student writers.

Peer Editing

Often students share their writing with no one but their instructor. This text is designed for students to share their writing with classmates at each step in the process. They use their classmates as audience, and they develop their critiquing and revising skills by helping other writers. Students learn to view writing as a shared communication rather than a "please the teacher" effort, and they see the effects that their ideas have on readers.

Selected Readings

A selection of essays by professional writers is included at the end of each unit. The readings and subsequent "Questions for Analysis" sections are tied in with the writing emphasis for that unit. These essays serve as models for structural and content analysis, provide a link between the related skills of writing and reading, and offer additional reading experiences that will benefit most students.

Final Editing

Grammar, punctuation, and spelling receive thorough treatment in the final unit of the text. All of the major problem areas—run-ons and fragments, comma usage, subject-verb agreement, pronoun-antecedent agreement, irregular verbs—are covered in detail. Each section contains a number of exercises for students to work through. Ideally, students would refer to editing sections as they proofread and edit their papers throughout the text. Grammar and punctuation study should not be isolated from the editing process students are going through with each writing assignment.

Acknowledgments

The improvements in this fourth edition are the result of many helpful comments from instructors and students. I am especially grateful for the suggestions of Christopher Baker, Lamar University; Jodi Jarvis, Salem State University; Athene Sallee, Forsyth Technical Institute; Caroline Stern, Ferris State University; and Cheryl Wade, McNeese State University. In addition, I am very appreciative of the generosity of authors and publishers who allowed their works to be excerpted. These are listed in the acknowledgments section at the end of the book.

WRITING VOYAGE

SETTING SAIL

Using this writing book can be likened to taking a voyage. No idle passenger, you are in charge of the trip, the directions it takes, and the success of the journey. As you progress through the units, you will develop writing skills to better express yourself and to make your travels more enjoyable. You will also encounter a range of writing experiences to prepare you for future writing ventures.

Already an experienced voyager, you will not sit on dry land listening to the tales of others. Instead you will create your own tales by launching into your writing journey immediately and learning as all writers learn: by doing.

In this unit, you are also introduced to the basic writing process used throughout the book. The process divides the writing experience into a number of steps that lead you to a final destination. By the time you finish the book, you will have personally tailored the process for any writing you may do.

WHY WRITE?

If you are reading this book, you are undoubtedly taking a college writing course. You have probably already done some, or perhaps a good deal of, writing in high school and before, and you may take other writing courses in future semesters.

Throughout your school-related writing experience, however, you may never have asked yourself, or anyone else, why you were having to write. Perhaps your instructors didn't tell you why either. Like most students, you may have just accepted that writing is something that teachers assign and that students dutifully do.

As a college student, you should consider the role writing plays in your education. Since you will be writing for this course and throughout your college years, it would be useful for you to see how developing your skills could benefit you and make your college writing experiences worthwhile.

The purpose of this first activity is twofold: to get you thinking about the importance of writing literacy and to get you writing. Writing is one of those "learn by doing" rather than "learn by reading about" skills. A final purpose is that after reading your paper, other students might discover some good reasons for developing their own writing skills.

ACTIVITY 1.1

With a partner, discuss some possible reasons for writing being a part of the educational curriculum. Why should students develop their writing skills to the extent possible? Consider both short-range and long-range reasons for developing writing literacy, and make a list of all the ideas you come up with. Go beyond the ideas that may come easily to you and generate some reasons that few people may have thought of.

When you have finished, write a short paper in answer to the frequently asked student question, "Why do I have to take a college writing course?" Your purpose is to provide students with some good reasons for taking such a course and some incentive for wanting to do well. Use the ideas that you and your partner generated any way you wish. When you finish, be prepared to share your paper with classmates.

PREWRITING

When you write, what do you do before you actually put pen to paper (or fingers to computer)? Do you sit and scratch your head for a while?

Do you jot down some ideas? Do you have a ritual of sitting in the same chair at the same desk at the same time of day with a favorite writing pad and pen? Do you like to take a walk and think before beginning?

Everything that writers do to help them get started is a part of their "prewriting" process. This process varies greatly from writer to writer, and what works well for one person doesn't necessarily work well for another. Some writers prefer planning a paper in some detail before beginning, while others work best from a general idea or two floating around in their heads.

The purpose of each "prewriting" section is to provide you with different options that writers successfully use to help them get started. For example, the first "partner" activity you did was the prewriting work for your first writing assignment. By generating a list of ideas, you came up with some potential material to use in your paper.

As you work with different prewriting strategies, you will undoubtedly find that some work better for you than others. You may also find that different strategies work best for different types or lengths of writing. You may even take something from one strategy and something from another to devise your own approach.

The purpose of the prewriting activities is to help you find ways to get started that will lead to productive writing. By trying different options, you will hopefully discover what works best for you. It is a trial-and-error process, but one that is worth the experimentation.

THINKING AND QUESTIONING

Sometimes students who sit and ponder when given a writing assignment feel something is wrong with them. "Why can't I just start writing like other people?" they think. "I must have writer's block."

Sitting and pondering is an important part of the writing process for many writers. Thinking about what to write and how best to say it may be as important as anything you do for a paper. As one student said, "Once I know what I'm going to write about and the approach I want to take, the writing comes fairly easily. The hardest part is coming up with a topic and deciding what to do with it."

SELECTING A TOPIC

Deciding what to write about is a task shared by all writers. For some students, it is one of the most difficult parts of writing. Topic selection is a part of the prewriting process that often requires a good deal of thinking.

Thinking about writing often takes the form of asking questions. Writers use the following types of questions to help them decide on a topic.

1. What topics interest me enough to write about?
2. What do I know enough about?
3. What could I write that would interest others?
4. What purpose would I have in writing about a particular topic?

The purpose of this activity is to help provide you with a process for coming up with writing topics by asking and answering questions. If the process helps you select a topic for this writing assignment, you may find it useful in the future.

ACTIVITY *1.2*

Select a topic to write on from among your favorite interests, hobbies, or pastimes. Select a topic that would give classmates, your reading audience for your next paper, some insight into what interests you. Consider a number of possible topics, using the questions presented for topic selection.

SAMPLE STUDENT TOPIC SELECTION PROCESS

Let's see, what interests me or what hobbies do I have? I like to sew, and I've done a lot of it. I also liked raising farm animals for 4-H in high school. I like country music a lot. Raising seeing-eye dogs through 4-H was a good experience.

What do I know enough about to write on? I couldn't write a lot about country music because I just like listening to it. I enjoy sewing, but would I enjoy writing about it? I'm not sure. I know a lot about raising animals. I could write about that for sure.

What might interest my readers? Guys in class wouldn't be interested in my sewing, I don't think. I think the most interesting thing to people might be how I raised guide dogs for the blind. That's something not a lot of people do, and it was a great experience.

What topic would reveal something of me to my readers? I really love animals and I am good with them, and I think writing about raising seeing-eye dogs would bring that out. I also like to help other people, and that could also show through this topic.

. . . .

PLANNING THE FIRST DRAFT

Now that you have selected a topic, think about it awhile before writing your first draft. You may be used to moving straight into your writing once you have a topic, and that's not necessarily bad. However, you may also find that thinking about the topic for a while before writing has some merit. This is part of your prewriting trial-and-error process to help discover what works best for you.

The following general questions may help you decide what you want to say about your topic:

1. How do I feel (or what is my opinion) about the topic, and how can I best express it?

2. What important things do I want to include?

3. What would readers want to know about the topic, or what do I want them to know?

4. What's my purpose for writing, and how can I accomplish it?

The purpose of this activity is to help prepare you to write your first draft as productively as possible. If you have asked and answered a few questions, you will have some ideas about what to include in your first draft.

ACTIVITY *1.3*

Spend some time thinking about your topic by asking and answering the questions just provided. You may either make mental notes or write them down, depending on your preference.

STUDENT SAMPLE RESPONSE   *(raising seeing-eye dogs)*

How do I feel about the topic? I really enjoyed the experience, and I'll make that clear in my writing. I'll present different reasons I enjoyed it so much.

What important things do I want to include? I want to include something about the training I was responsible for. I also want to talk about my attachment to each of the dogs and how it is hard to return them. I want to include meeting the blind people who became the dogs' partners.

What would readers want to know? They may be curious how I got started in the program. They may want to know the kinds of dogs I trained and how long it takes. They may wonder if I still train guide dogs.

What's my purpose, and how can I accomplish it? I want readers to get a good idea of what the experience was like, to see how much I enjoy working with animals, and to see that I enjoy helping people. I hope that comes across in different parts of my paper.

■ ■ ■ ■ ■ ■ ■ ■ ■ ■ ■ ■

FIRST DRAFTS

Now that you've selected your topic and given it some thought, the next step is to write the first draft of your paper. The following suggestions will help you write your first draft without great difficulty:

1. Don't worry about making mistakes. You can take care of any problems that come up later in the writing process.

2. As you write, make use of the things that you thought about during prewriting, but don't limit yourself. You may want to include new ideas, and you may decide not to include all of your prewriting ideas.

3. Feel free to change what you write. If you don't like something, cross it out and write something else. If you think of something to add somewhere, draw an arrow and stick it in the margin. Remember, this is just your first draft, and it doesn't matter how it looks.

ACTIVITY 1.4

Write your first draft on the topic you selected. Don't worry about paragraphing at this point.

STUDENT SAMPLE FIRST DRAFT

RAISING SEEING-EYE DOGS

I've really enjoyed raising seeing-eye dogs for my 4-H project the past five years. 4-H is a high school agricultural club I belonged to, and since I've always had dogs for pets, I decided to participate in the guide dog program. My job was to raise a dog from a pup to a year and a half of age, when he would be turned over to the Hampshire Guide Dog Clinic for special guide dog training.

I raised three dogs over the five years, two labrador retrievers and one German shepherd. I got each of them from the Hampshire Guide Dog Clinic, where they had been bred for their occupation. My job was relatively simple, since I had been around dogs all my life. I was to "potty train" them, teach them to respond to a few basic commands like "come here" and "sit," feed them nourishing food, keep them clean and groomed, and treat them kindly yet firmly. They didn't want the dogs returned spoiled or lacking discipline.

I enjoyed each of the dogs, but the hard part was not growing too attached to them. My second lab named Jethro was a particularly lovable dog, and I would have loved to have kept him forever. Having to give him up after a year and a half was like losing one of the family, and I bade him a tearful farewell when I returned him to the clinic.

Meeting the blind people who the dogs would be paired with was a great experience. All three of them were really nice people, and they were so excited to be getting their guide dogs. After the dogs went through their clinic training, I was able to see them working with their new masters, and it was wonderful to see how well each dog was doing. If I ever doubted that raising guide dogs was worth it, those doubts were erased when I saw the great service they provided for the blind.

I don't raise guide dogs any longer although I could have remained in the program after graduating from high school. Going to college, I just don't have the time it takes to spend with the dogs. Beyond that, I was tired of going through the emotional part of becoming fond of the dogs and then giving them up. Today I've got a great dog of my own, a full-blooded collie, and we plan to grow old together.

I know that raising the guide dogs was influential in my deciding to major in preveterinary medicine. I'm also happy to say that the three dogs I raised are all doing great as guide dogs, and I'm glad to have made a small contribution to help out some people who really deserved it. I'll never forget the experience.

- - - - - - - - - - - -

REVISIONS

Now that you have completed your first draft, you can go back and take a good look at it. Think of your first draft as a roughly hewn sculpture. It has the basic shape and size of your finished figure, but it still requires the finely chiseled finish to be complete.

As you read over your draft, consider the following questions:

1. Is there anything I could add that would be of interest to readers, or that would make something clearer?

2. Is there anything I should delete that isn't really important or that gets off the topic?

3. Is there anything that seems out of place and that would make more sense if I moved it elsewhere?

4. Are there any sentences that aren't as clearly or smoothly worded as I would like?

5. Have I accomplished about what I wanted to in the paper? What might I do better?

6. Think of three or four questions that your classmates might ask and consider answering them in the next draft.

7. Is my paper long enough to divide into a few paragraphs, with new paragraphs beginning when I move to different parts of my topic?

ACTIVITY *1.5*

With a partner, evaluate the student draft on pages 6–7 by applying the suggested revision questions and responding to each one. For question 7, analyze how the draft is divided into paragraphs and what each paragraph contains.

When you finish, read over your own draft and apply the revision questions, deciding on the types of changes you may want to make in your next draft. Then exchange drafts with a classmate and write four or five questions that the draft raises that he or she might answer in the next draft.

Finally, rewrite your draft, including all the revisions that you think would improve your paper.

■ ■ ■ ■ ■ ■ ■ ■ ■ ■ ■

ACTIVITY *1.6*

Write a comparison of your first and second drafts. What kinds of changes did you make in the second draft, and how do you feel they improved your paper?

Next, write a second paragraph evaluating how well you feel the process of selecting and thinking about your topic, writing a first draft, evaluating the draft, and writing a second draft went for you. What, if anything, seemed particularly beneficial, and what might you do differently another time?

■ ■ ■ ■ ■ ■ ■ ■ ■ ■ ■

PARAGRAPHING

During the revision activity for your last writing assignment, you analyzed the paragraphing of a student draft in the book. Next, you paragraphed your own draft following the simple guidelines presented. The attention given to paragraphing, however, was purposely minor to keep the emphasis for your first paper on its content.

As you work through this book, you will learn more about paragraphing in each unit as you write different kinds of papers. While the writing emphasis will remain on content—what you have to say to readers—you will also develop the paragraphing skills to help showcase your content.

Students' paragraph-writing experiences vary widely. Some of you may already be quite sophisticated in your paragraphing skills. Others may have a basic understanding of paragraphing but little experience. Still others may have a vague recollection of writing in paragraphs in elementary or high school. As your instructors become more familiar with your writing skills, they will know how much time you need to spend working on paragraphing.

ACTIVITY 1.7

Why do we write in paragraphs? With a partner, review the three paragraphs that begin this section as well as other groups of paragraphs in other parts of the text. Then discuss the reasons for dividing sentences into different paragraphs. What does paragraphing accomplish?

On your own, write a paragraph explaining to a classmate the reasons that writers (such as yourselves) divide their writing into paragraphs. Then exchange paragraphs with a classmate or two.

. . . .

Paragraphing is not an exact science. Different writers may paragraph the same paper in different ways. However, there are some general rules that apply to writing:

1. Writers often change paragraphs when they move to something new in a paper: a different point, a different event, a new step, a new example, a different aspect of their topic.

2. The sentences within a particular paragraph are related. Some paragraphs will have a *topic sentence* that expresses the main idea of the paragraph while others will not.

    For example, the first paragraph in this section, "How to Paragraph," begins with the topic sentence, "Paragraphing is not an exact science"; the last paragraph preceding Activity 1.7 begins with the topic sentence, "Students' paragraph-writing experiences vary widely." However, the first paragraph in the "Paragraphing" section has no topic sentence although its sentences are related to one subject: how you paragraphed your last writing assignment.

3. Paragraph length varies greatly, but in general, most writers avoid extremely long paragraphs (like a typewritten page or more) or series of short paragraphs (like a couple of sentences each). Readers can get bogged down reading long paragraphs or confused when continually stopping and starting for short paragraphs.

ACTIVITY **1.8**

Following the paragraphing suggestions just presented, divide each of the following papers into paragraphs by marking the beginning of each new paragraph.

CRUISING MONEY

At least one Friday every couple of weeks, my friends and I pile into a car and cruise Mooney Boulevard in Vicksburg. Mooney is a wide four-lane street with malls, restaurants, and parking lots on each side along the three-mile cruising strip. When I tell my mom I'm going cruising, she always looks at me like I'm crazy. She'll say, "How can you spend the night driving up and down a street? Why don't you go to a movie or something?" Well, we do go to movies some weekends, and we also go to Zak's, a teenage nightclub. But on a lot of Friday nights, cruising is my favorite activity. The biggest kick in cruising is checking out all the new guys. At school you're stuck with the same faces every day, but when you're cruising, you never know who's going to drive up next to you. Guys from all over the area come to cruise Mooney. It's fun to see a load of good-looking guys heading the other direction and try to figure out a way to catch them. We'll flip a U-turn just about anyplace to go after a car of "hunks." Most of the time we just check the guys out, but sometimes we'll pull over and talk to them or split up and ride in each other's cars. Nothing much ever happens, but it's fun riding around and talking with guys I've never met. And you never know. Maybe the next car that pulls up beside me will have Mr. Right in it. Anything's possible when you're cruising. Another fun part of cruising is being with the gang. Patti, Marty, Charlotte, Vicki, and I have been pals since our freshman year in high school. We call ourselves the "Stubbs," and when we go cruising, we are very crazy. We turn the radio up full blast and sing our hearts out. We puff on cigarettes like real degenerates. We'll hang halfway out of the car to talk to guys, and we'll race them off the line when the light changes. And we laugh at anything and everything. Cruising brings out the craziness in us, and we have a blast together. Then there's the practical side of cruising. It's pretty cheap entertainment. We split the gas five ways each time we go, and that's about a dollar apiece. Then we stop at Mearle's Drive-in on the way home and buy milk shakes and fries, which is another dollar or two. That's a pretty cheap night compared to going to the movies or a concert. Even when we're short on money, we can always pool enough cash to head for Mooney's. Tomorrow night the Stubbs will head for Mooney's Boulevard in Marty's 1978 Monte Carlo. We may find some great-looking guys, or we may strike out. But either way we'll have a lot of fun because we enjoy cruising and being together. And we'll still have plenty of money left for next weekend. So even though we're in college now, we're not too old to enjoy cruising. Luckily, a lot of college guys like it too.

APARTMENT HUNTING

Two weeks before school started, I started hunting for an apartment along with my future roommate. Actually, I ended up doing most of the looking because she was still working at an ice house. I went into Monroe at least five times looking for a two bedroom apartment to rent, and I usually came home discouraged. Luckily, I found a pretty nice place to rent three days before school began. But shopping for an apartment with a limited budget is hard work. There are a lot of great apartments in Monroe, but they are all too expensive. I found a number of newer two-bedroom, two-bathroom apartments near the college with good-sized living rooms and kitchens, plenty of cupboard and closet space, and a swimming pool or Jacuzzi on the grounds. I'd ask the landlord the rental price, and it would always be somewhere from $375 to $450 a month. Since the maximum we could pay was $325 a month, the apartments were out of our range. It was depressing going through these nice apartments we couldn't afford. Then there's the problem of finding a good location. Obviously, the apartments nearer the college are the best located, but they are also the most expensive. Often when I'd find a decent-sounding apartment in the paper for $300, it would end up being halfway across town from the college or in some run-down neighborhood. The farther an apartment complex is away from the college, the less chance there is that it will have college students in it. We didn't want to end up in a complex with a bunch of older people or young married couples. I drove all over Monroe more than once tracking down a good-sounding deal, and usually the apartment ended up being beside a railroad track or a good twenty minutes from the campus. Then there's the problem of size. The larger apartments are naturally the more expensive ones. Many of the nicer apartments in our price range felt like doll houses: tiny rooms and low ceilings. We had quite a bit of old furniture to move into an apartment, and we both slept on queen-sized beds. We needed adequate closet space for a semester's worth of clothes. We also planned on doing all of our own cooking, so we wanted a good-sized kitchen. Many of the apartments that sounded really nice turned out to be too small to consider. But as time began running out, I figured we'd probably end up taking a small apartment and stuffing everything into it that we could. Luckily, all of the effort finally paid off. After looking at at least twenty-five different apartments and rejecting all of them, I found an apartment complex that was being remodeled. It was an old complex that didn't look too hot from the outside, but inside, the remodeled apartments were like new. The apartments were good-sized and rented for $310 a month, and they were only ten minutes from the college. I put down a deposit immediately, and my search was over. What I thought would be an easy task had turned into two weeks of driving around, making phone calls, scanning newspapers, and finding a lot of places I didn't like or couldn't afford. Finding an apartment is hard work when you can't spend much money, and you need to plan on spending a lot of time looking.

■ ■ ■ ■ ■ ■ ■ ■ ■ ■ ■ ■

ACTIVITY *1.9*

Read and analyze each of the following single paragraphs. If a paragraph contains a topic sentence—one sentence that expresses the main idea of

the paragraph—underline it. If a paragraph has some weaknesses, decide what you would do to improve it.

1. Nothing bothers Herman more than being cold. In the winter, he sleeps with six blankets over him. When he goes to a football game, he wears thermal underwear, numerous sweaters, a ski parka, gloves, five pairs of socks, and army boots. He sets his apartment thermostat at eighty degrees, and he keeps the car heater on until June. You can always recognize Herman by the red knit cap he wears pulled down over his ears.

2. Pagawa County has its share of bad roads, including Cutter Turnpike and Route 39. Tuttle County also has its notorious Highway 6 along the Harmon River. But the worst stretch of road in the state is Highway 402 in Burrow County between Crescent and DePaw. Better known as "blood alley," 402 is a windy four-lane road through fifteen miles of pine-covered hills. There is no divider separating the east- and west-bound lanes, so cars zip by within a few feet of each other. The grades are deceptively steep, and there is no guard rail separating the outside lanes from the canyons below. It is also pitch dark at night except for the glaring headlights leaping out from the curves. Add constant winds of fifteen to thirty miles an hour and the highest motorist use in the county, and you can understand how "blood alley" got its name.

3. Rats eat through the walls above the baseboards. Cockroaches infest the cupboards. Flies are thick everywhere. There is no hot water for bathing and no coolers to bring relief from the heat. The smells from the garbage and the broken sewer line are nauseating. Most windows are broken or boarded up. These apartments should be condemned by the health department.

4. Alicia could never resist a good time. If there was a party anywhere in town, she'd find it. If anyone in the dorms wanted to go eat pizza, she would drop her history book in a second. With Alicia, it was pizza on Monday, a movie on Wednesday, and partying from Thursday to Saturday. She invented the seven-day weekend, and it was a miracle she stayed in school as long as she did.

5. If you're looking for an easy sociology class, take McDermott. If you're looking for a lot of laughs, take Horton. But if you want to learn something, take Phillips. He covers twice the material of the other two, and he makes sure you read it by giving regular quizzes and asking for written chapter summaries. If you don't get at least a C on a test, you have to keep taking it until you do, and the only way to get a C is to read, study, and take good lecture notes. Phillips doesn't let you leave his class without learning a lot of sociology, and it took me two semesters to find that out.

▪ ▪ ▪ ▪ ▪ ▪ ▪ ▪ ▪ ▪ ▪ ▪ ▪

As you can see from each paragraph in the preceding practice, the topic sentence expresses a *definite opinion* or *attitude* about the topic for the paragraph. A strong topic sentence gives direction to a paragraph and gives the writer something definite to support.

ACTIVITY *1.10*

Write your own single paragraph about any *one* aspect of college life: classes (or a particular class), students (or a particular student), expenses, dormitory living, cafeteria food, social life, teachers (or a particular teacher), counseling, financial aid, the bookstore, the library, campus parking, campus atmosphere, and so on. Write the paragraph for your classmates so that they understand how you feel about this particular aspect of college. Keep in mind the general length guidelines for paragraphing.

Begin with a *topic sentence* that expresses the main idea of your paragraph, and follow the general rules presented for effective paragraphing.

STUDENT SAMPLE PARAGRAPH

DORM ROOM

My dorm room is a depressing place to live. It's a tiny nine-by-nine-foot square without any windows. It feels like a jail cell. The walls are a faded yellow color that belongs in a hospital, and there are long cracks running across the walls and ceiling. The floor is usually littered with dirty shirts and underwear, and there are beer cans stacked in pyramids on the sink and table. The smell from the clothes mixed with the stale beer is sickening. The room is always noisy at night with the stereo blaring, and every sound from the adjoining rooms comes through the thin walls. I'm moving out at semester break.

■　■　■　■　■　■　■　■　■　■　■

SENTENCE REVISION

A big part of draft revision for most writers is improving their sentence wording. When you write down an idea for the first time, it doesn't always come out as smoothly and clearly as you would like. Sentence writing is often a two-step process: first getting your thought down on paper, and then reworking the sentence until it sounds right.

An important part of the revision process is to check each first draft sentence to see whether it says exactly what you want. Each sentence should be as clear to the reader as you can make it. The purpose of sentence revision is to make sure you have the words that you want in the most effective order for expressing yourself. The result will be smoother, stronger sentences.

WORDING PROBLEMS

Here are some common wording problems to be aware of as you revise your sentences.

1. *Wordiness:* using more words than are necessary to express an idea.

   EXAMPLE   I am late for school because of the fact that my car wouldn't start.

   REVISED   I am late for school because my car wouldn't start.

   EXAMPLE   The reason why I did well on my test was because I studied hard for my test.

   REVISED   I did well on my test because I studied hard.

2. *Inflated language:* using unnecessarily complicated language rather than simple, direct wording.

   EXAMPLE   The prevalence of moisture in the form of ground-level clouds made maneuvering the automobile difficult.

   REVISED   It was difficult to drive in the fog.

   EXAMPLE   I relish clothing of an uncomplicated nature.

   REVISED   I like simple clothes.

3. *Awkward phrasing:* using words and phrases that don't fit together smoothly and logically.

   EXAMPLE   Lunch you could have in the cafeteria hours between eleven and two o'clock.

   REVISED   The cafeteria is open for lunch between eleven and two o'clock.

   EXAMPLE   Although we went to the swap meet, but we didn't buy anything.

   REVISED   Although we went to the swap meet, we didn't buy anything.

4. *Poor word choice:* not using the best word to express a thought.

   EXAMPLE   We were excited about doing things in the track meet.

   REVISED   We were excited about participating in the track meet.

   EXAMPLE   Jonathan had learned all his children to use a computer.

   REVISED   Jonathan had taught all his children to use a computer.

ACTIVITY 1.11

The following first draft sentences need revising. The sentences have problems with wordiness, awkward phrasing, and poor word choices. Revise and rewrite each sentence to make it smoother and clearer.

EXAMPLES

WORDY	My goal is to lose six pounds of my body weight.
REVISED	My goal is to lose six pounds.
WORDY, AWKWARD	On the left side of the ring has my name on it in initials.
REVISED	On the left side of the ring are my initials.
POOR WORD CHOICE	Our Lady of Sorrows Parish is localized in the town of Fremont.
REVISED	Our Lady of Sorrows Parish is located in Fremont.

1. It was a Wednesday afternoon, and I noticed in my computer class a number of foreign students.
2. Being an only child is a very lonely moment in your life.
3. John's friends envy him due to the fact of the attention he receives, the possessions he possesses, and the privileges he is privileged to have.
4. The day was a total learning process of inestimable value to myself.
5. You will get a lot of responsibility for college.
6. The tables are round and square and setting on a carpet that is indoor and outdoor.
7. The pier has three microscopes planted on it, so you can see across the bay with those microscopes.
8. Working outdoors makes welding a difficult place to work.
9. The feasts on, before, or around Christmas day can be very fulfilling.
10. My room is a fifteen-by-twenty-foot square, and it is white in color on the walls and ceiling.

SENTENCE VARIETY

Another consideration for revising sentences in your draft is sentence *variety*. If you fall into the habit of writing sentences that all look and sound alike, your papers may sound monotonous to a reader despite your interesting ideas. To keep your reader's interest and express the varied thoughts and relationships in your mind, use a variety of sentence forms.

Here is an example of a paragraph that lacks sentence variety.

EXAMPLE

Thelma is my sister. She is twenty-six years old. She has red hair. It is long. It goes down to her tailbone. Sometimes she braids it. Sometimes she wears it up. She does this for formal occasions. She likes her hair long. The problem is washing it. It takes hours to dry. She has to get up at 5:00 to wash it. She does that to get to work by 8:00. Her hair is beautiful. It's a nuisance.

This passage is obviously too full of short, similar sentences. The reader stops and starts so often that the details are disconnected. The paragraph reads like something a child might write. With some sentence variety, however, the paragraph could be effective. Here is a revised version.

EXAMPLE

My sister Thelma is twenty-six years old. She has long red hair that goes down to her tailbone. Sometimes she braids it, and sometimes she wears it up for formal occasions. Although she likes her hair long, it is a problem. It takes hours to dry, so she has to get up at 5:00 to wash it to get to work by 8:00. Her hair is beautiful, but it is a nuisance.

The paragraph now has sentence variety, and it reads more smoothly and interestingly. Some sentences have been combined by eliminating words, and others have been joined with such words as *and, although, but,* and *that.* The paragraph now has a mixture of sentence forms that move the reader smoothly through the writer's thoughts.

Combining Sentences

The best way to get rid of patches of short, monotonous sentences in a draft is to combine pairs or groups of sentences to form more informative and interesting ones. Here are ways to combine short sentences:

1. Eliminate unnecessary words that are duplicated in the sentences.
2. Move descriptive words in front of the word they describe.
3. Join similar sentence parts with an *and, or,* or *but.*

Here are examples of groups of short sentences that have been combined in the revised versions following the methods just described.

EXAMPLES

DRAFT   Joanie is a student. She is a very good one.

REVISED   Joanie is a very good student.

DRAFT   Fernando bought a shirt. It was red. It was long sleeved.

REVISED   Fernando bought a red, long-sleeved shirt.

DRAFT   I bought a car. It was an Impala. It was a 1973. It was sharp.

REVISED   I bought a sharp 1973 Impala.

DRAFT   The book might be in the library. It might be in the bookstore.

REVISED   The book might be in the library or in the bookstore.

DRAFT   Joe was weary after the test. He was concerned. He was quiet.

REVISED   Joe was weary, concerned, and quiet after the test.

DRAFT   Alan went to the barbecue. Felicia went with him.

REVISED   Alan and Felicia went to the barbecue together.

ACTIVITY *1.12*

Each pair or group of short sentences below can be combined to form one improved sentence. Combine the sentences into single sentences by eliminating and moving words around and by joining similar words or groups of words with *and, or,* or *but*.

EXAMPLE   Gwen went to school. Maria went to school. They went with Bob.

REVISED   Gwen and Maria went to school with Bob.

1. The frog leaped onto the log. He plopped into the water. He disappeared.

2. Harry was tired. He was thirsty. He wasn't hungry.

3. Ellie got a B on her term paper. She got the same grade on her algebra test. She flunked her pop quiz in German.

4. Your X rays could be in the drawer. They could be on the shelf. They could be almost anywhere in the house.

5. The kitten was fat. It was fluffy. It was playing with a grasshopper. The grasshopper was badly injured.

6. Marge finally got a letter. It was from her parole officer. She was relieved.

7. The week was long. It was boring. It was almost over. Julian was very happy.

8. Susan's clothes were plain. They were cheap. They were also stylish. They were also in good taste.

9. The car spun toward the wall. It crashed. It burst into flames. The driver wasn't injured. He was lucky.

10. That puppy is very cute. It is black and white. It has droopy ears. It is in the pet store window. It isn't for sale.

. . . .

A second way to combine shorter sentences is to join two complete sentences with *coordinate conjunctions* to form *compound sentences*. These are the most commonly used coordinate conjunctions:

and   or   but   so   yet   for

The following are examples of two first draft sentences joined by coordinate conjunctions to form single compound sentences. Notice that different conjunctions show different relationships between the two sentences they join. The conjunctions are underlined.

EXAMPLE   The Rolling Stones were popular in the 1960s. They are still popular today.

REVISED   The Rolling Stones were popular in the 1960s, <u>and</u> they are still popular today. (And *joins the information together.*)

EXAMPLE   Divorce statistics are rising. Couples are marrying in record numbers.

REVISED   Divorce statistics are rising, <u>but</u> couples are marrying in record numbers. (But *shows a contrast; something happened* despite *something else.*)

EXAMPLE   Rita may go to a movie tonight. She may stay home and read a mystery novel.

REVISED   Rita may go to a movie tonight <u>or</u> she may stay home and read a mystery novel. (Or *shows a choice; alternatives are available.*)

EXAMPLE   James makes his own shirts. He enjoys sewing.

REVISED   James makes his own shirts, <u>for</u> he enjoys sewing. (For *means* because; *something occurs because of something else.*)

EXAMPLE   Working and going to school is difficult. Many students do both.

REVISED   Working and going to school is difficult, <u>yet</u> many students do both. (Yet *is similar to* but; *it shows a contrast.*)

EXAMPLE   The air is moist and cold. We'd better bundle up for the parade.

REVISED   The air is moist and cold, <u>so</u> we'd better bundle up for the parade. (So *is like* therefore; *one thing leads to another.*)

As you can see, different conjunctions serve different purposes. Being able to use a variety of conjunctions at appropriate times makes your writing more effective.

ACTIVITY *1.13*

Combine the following pairs of shorter sentences with *conjunctions* to form compound sentences. Use the conjunction that best joins each sentence pair: *and, or, but, so, yet, for.* Put a *comma* before the conjunction.

EXAMPLE   The weather is miserable today. It should be better tomorrow.

REVISED   The weather is miserable today, but it should be better tomorrow.

1. Jogging is a popular exercise. Some doctors don't recommend it.

2. You can take typing this semester. You can take it next semester.

3. Ms. Avery is an unpopular teacher. She lectures too fast.

4. Jodie didn't like the foreign movie. It was praised by the critics.

5. The smells from the cafeteria were wonderful. The food was disappointing.

6. Rain collected in jars on the back porch. We used the water to test for acid rain.

7. Freddie may be at the Pizza Palace. He may be at the roller derby with Lucinda.

8. Lupe joined the swim team. She wanted the exercise and the units.

9. Sam tried to return the defective smoke alarm. The store was closed.

10. Alicia couldn't study for the essay test. She got a good night's sleep instead.

■ ■ ■ ■ ■ ■ ■ ■ ■ ■ ■

A third way to combine sentences is to join two complete sentences with words called *subordinate conjunctions* to form *complex sentences.* Subordinate conjunctions may be placed between the two sentences or at the beginning of the first sentence. The following subordinate conjunctions are most commonly used in complex sentences.

after	if	whenever
although	since	where
as	unless	whereas
because	until	wherever
before	when	while

The following examples show two first draft sentences joined by subordinate conjunctions to form complex sentences. Notice the different relationships that the subordinate conjunctions show and their use at the beginning or in the middle of the complex sentence. The subordinate conjunctions are underlined.

EXAMPLE   You are going to be late for biology class. You should contact your teacher.

REVISED   Since you are going to be late for biology class, you should contact your teacher.

EXAMPLE   Fred's friends took him home. They went out for pizza.

REVISED   After Fred's friends took him home, they went out for pizza.

EXAMPLE   I'm cleaning up your mess. You are watching television!

REVISED   I'm cleaning up your mess while you are watching television!

EXAMPLE   You have worked very hard. You have gained everyone's respect.

REVISED   Because you have worked very hard, you have gained everyone's respect.

EXAMPLE   George wants to pass the geography test. He will have to identify six mountain ranges.

REVISED   If George wants to pass the geography test, he will have to identify six mountain ranges.

EXAMPLE   Joanna refuses to exercise. She would like to be in shape.

REVISED   Joanna refuses to exercise although she would like to be in shape.

As you can see, subordinate conjunctions can show different relationships: time *(when, as, after, while)*, cause and effect *(since, because, if, unless)*, place *(where, wherever)*, or contrast *(although, even though, whereas)*. You may use them at the beginning or in the middle of a complex sentence depending on what you want to emphasize. Using complex sentences adds variety to your writing and helps you express a wide range of relationships between ideas.

ACTIVITY 1.14

Join the following pairs of shorter sentences with appropriate subordinate conjunctions (from page 19) to form *complex sentences*. You will begin some sentences with subordinate conjunctions and use others between sentences. *When you begin a sentence with a subordinate conjunction, put a comma between the two sentences you are combining.* (Some sentence pairs won't go together well until they are combined with a subordinate conjunction.)

EXAMPLE   The party was over. Ruby drove around until dawn.

REVISED   After the party was over, Ruby drove around until dawn.

EXAMPLE   The dog limped along the road. It had a thorn in its paw.

REVISED   The dog limped along the road because it had a thorn in its paw.

1. You leave for school tomorrow. Please pick me up at the corner.
2. Jim dropped his gymnastics class. He had a time conflict.
3. The economy improves greatly. The unemployment rate will climb.
4. Gina spent a lot of time reading romances. She still did well in school.
5. You believe everything Harley says. You are very naive.
6. I told you before. I'll be glad to water your ferns this weekend.
7. Ms. Howard is a fascinating teacher. She uses slides, movies, and field trips in her anthropology class.
8. The electricity is off in the apartments. Everyone is buying candles.

9. The shower door was broken. Manuel moved into the dormitory.

10. You've had experience with electrical work. Don't try to change that outlet.

. . . .

ACTIVITY *1.15*

Now practice writing your own compound and complex sentences using the coordinate and subordinate conjunctions provided. Write sentences that classmates might enjoy reading.

EXAMPLE   and
                       Sonia fed the chickens, and then she had a rotten egg fight with
                       Billy.

1. and	7. although
2. but	8. because
3. or	9. if
4. so	10. unless
5. yet	11. while
6. for	12. whereas

Share your sentences with classmates, and check each other's use of coordinate and subordinate conjunctions.

. . . .

ACTIVITY *1.16*

Write a short paper about an activity or hobby that you would like to get involved in if you had the time or money. Write for your classmates to provide them another insight into your interests.

When you finish your first draft, read it carefully with two concerns in mind: improving sentence wording and sentence variety. Are there any first draft sentences that are overly wordy, awkward sounding, or weakly worded? Are there sentences that could be combined to form effective compound or complex sentences? Write a second draft including all of your revisions for improving your sentences. Then share your paper with classmates.

STUDENT FIRST DRAFT   *(What sentence revisions might the writer consider for her next draft?)*

SCUBA DIVING

Some day I think that I'd like to learn to scuba dive. My boyfriend scuba dives. He really loves it. He says that it's like a different world underwater. It's beautiful with all of the colorful coral and rocks and fish.

It's also adventurous. You never know what you're going to see. It could be an eel or sea turtle or giant clam or manta ray or jellyfish. Then there's always the threat of a lurking shark to keep you on your toes. It really sounds exciting to me.

The trouble is I'm not a great swimmer. I also don't have the $250 right now for scuba lessons. Worse yet, I live in Iowa. My boyfriend lives in California and is going to school back here. How often am I going to get a chance to scuba dive in Iowa?

■ ■ ■ ■ ■ ■ ■ ■ ■ ■ ■ ■ ■

WRITING REVIEW

For your final paper of this unit, write on *one thing* that has a particularly high priority in your life: family, religion, education, getting rich, being physically fit, getting married, becoming an accountant or physical therapist, traveling the world, and so on. Write this paper for your classmates so that they can get to know you better by discovering what is important to you.

For prewriting, follow the thinking-and-questioning process presented on pages 3 and 5 to help you select a topic and then generate some ideas for your first draft. Next, write the first draft of your paper.

When you finish your first draft, meet with a partner and evaluate the following student first draft, applying the revision questions on page 7. Then evaluate your own first draft and make plans for writing a second draft. If you'd like another opinion, exchange drafts with a classmate and come up with four or five questions about your partner's draft to share with him or her.

Finally, write the second draft of your paper, keeping in mind what you have learned about paragraphing and sentence revision. Continue the evaluating/drafting process until you are satisfied with your final draft, which for some people may mean writing two drafts and for others writing three or more. There is no "magic" number of drafts that equal a finished paper. You are finished when, in your judgment, your paper is ready for its reading audience.

STUDENT SAMPLE PREWRITING

TOPIC SELECTION

Boy, the first thing that comes into my head is my family when I think of priorities. I know education is important to me, but I take that part for granted—it's something I've got to do. Getting married or making money, or getting a great job are all out there somewhere, but they aren't priorities for me yet. So I return to my family—the one constant in my life. That's definitely what I'm going to write about.

PREWRITING THOUGHTS ON MY TOPIC

My mom and dad are really important to me. I want that to come across clearly. They've done a lot for me, and I'll provide examples of that. I also want to bring out how we enjoy being together and still do things together. Plenty of examples. Then I'd like to talk about the ways that I count or rely on them, knowing they're always there for me. I'll be revealing that I'm still pretty dependent on them for being in college, but that's the way it is and I want to be honest. I don't want the paper to sound too sappy but I want my feelings to come through.

STUDENT FIRST DRAFT

MY FAMILY

When I think back through good memories of my life, most of them are in some way associated with my family. Family is the one constant that has always been a part of me, my rock against the storms of life. I can't imagine life without my mom and dad, and I hope they're around for a long, long time.

The one thing my folks always had for me, as well as for my brother, was time. I was on a swim team from the time I was ten years old through high school, and I don't ever remember them missing one of my meets. They were always there rooting me on, congratulating me when I did well and consoling me when I did poorly. It was the same with all my activities: volleyball, basketball, school plays, back-to-school nights, you name it. I never had to worry about my folks not showing up or not caring about what I was doing. I could count on them.

I've also done my share of leaning on their shoulders over the years. I never felt there was anything I couldn't tell my mom and dad, and I'm the kind who has to get it all out when I have a problem. Over the years they've heard it all: the time in junior high when one boy was constantly bugging me, the time in high school when I got caught drinking, the time I wrecked their Volkswagen Rabbit, rough times with my former boyfriend, and on and on. They always listened to me, helped me any way they could, gave me good advice when I needed it, and always showed they cared. Even getting through my freshman year of college away from home with a "roommate from hell" was something I couldn't have survived without many, many long-distance calls home and some timely visits from the folks.

We've had our share of fun too. The swim meets were weekend minivacations where we traveled all over the state and spent lots of good times together. We loved going to movies and eating out as a family, and we still do when I get home on breaks. We also have fun just sitting around the house watching TV and eating popcorn. My parents are fun-loving people, and I still have as much with them as I do with my friends, well almost as much.

The great thing about family, at least about mine, is I know nothing is going to change. Whether I'm twenty, thirty, or forty, I'll have two very special people who care for me and want the best for me. Friends may come and go, good times and bad times lie ahead, and there are lots of uncertainties in this world. Through all of this it's really great to know that family is forever, the one constant in my life. I hope I'm someday able to pass on the same sense of security and love to my own children.

READINGS

The readings at the end of each unit parallel the student writing topics for that unit. You may use the readings to get ideas for your own writing as well as for your enjoyment and analysis.

CROSS-COUNTRY SKIING

by Paul Kaser

1   When I was a freshman in college, some friendly upperclassmen introduced me to the joys downhill (sometimes called Alpine) skiing. They gave me no lessons. "Don't need them," they assured me. "Lessons are for wimps. Just get on the skis and go. You'll stop at the bottom." They took me to the top of the "pro" slope and let me go.

2   They were wrong about my not needing lessons, but they were right about my stopping at the bottom. While one of my skis headed off independently toward the parking lot, I gracefully crumpled myself and remaining ski around a light pole. This was just after I had bowled through a line of real skiers waiting for the ski lift, then through a semicircle of novices sensibly practicing their snowplow stops.

3   But did this early minor catastrophe stop me from pursuing the excellent thrills of downhill skiing ever again? Absolutely. I picked myself up, dusted myself off, and limped with dignity to the lodge bar where I sulked, sopped up cheap brandy, and swore off the deadly sport of downhill forever.

4   It was not till a decade or so later that I returned to skis, but not to those death-dealing downhill monsters. This time, I took up cross-country (sometimes called Nordic) skiing.

5   The very name "cross-country" was more comforting to me than "downhill." After all,

isn't it better to go more or less horizontally as in Nordic skiing than to hurl yourself graveward at a 45 degree angle until a tree, light pole, or boulder stops you?

6   As a cross-country skier, I may occasionally descend for a few short yards, but that is my choice, not my obsession. I find an unassuming hill, introduce myself politely, clamber up its backside, and then drift down at a modest speed, coming to a civilized halt at its bottom—not *on* mine. There is none of that supersonic ascent into white hell that downhillers require of themselves.

7   Alpine skiers like to brag about "challenging nature" and "pushing the envelope," which seems to mean seeking the highest, most lethal slope and plunging down it toward their chiropractor.

8   We cross-country skiers understand that nature is to be appeased, not challenged, since we know that nature, when competed against, can be a very nasty mother who thinks nothing of littering her snowy flanks with the fractured femurs and shattered egos of envelope-pushing downhillers.

9   Cross-country skiers, by contrast, slide around quietly on clean snow, to linger now and then in order to compliment nature on a well-sculpted frozen waterfall or smoothly quilted snow-meadow, then slide inoffensively back to the station wagon.

10   Although some Nordic skiers like to exhaust themselves in more rigorous treks, most set more humble goals, like travelling a carefully plotted loop that gets them back to their

~~tation wagon before they have to answer a~~ "call of nature." Nordic-type skiers, at least those of my ilk, never seek to push any envelope. We know downhillers who pushed their envelope right into traction.

11   Nordic skiing is also much cheaper. This is because cross-country skiers don't flock in swarms of expensively equipped and feathered show-offs.

12   Thus, the cross-country skier need not spend his children's college tuition money or sell his birthright in order to buy his skis and poles. Cross-country equipment costs about a third of what downhill equipment costs.

13   Because manufacturers of Alpine ski equipment continually "improve" their gear (moon-zombie boots, elegant French skis, soon-to-be-snapped poles), the downhiller has to keep remortgaging his house to keep up with the crowd.

14   And that's just the hardware. When it comes to clothes, the conscientious downhiller is required to make weekly trips to the bank, then to the ski boutique to deck himself out in the latest rainbow-splash Spandex glamour outfit. Not to do so would be to risk being ridiculed as a snow-nerd by the more fashionable peacocks of the slopes.

15   Cross-country types, on the other hand, practice their sport in any old outfit they please. I have seen them whisking along in old Levis and sweat shirts, even shorts and T-shirts on bright, windless days. Let the downhillers dress to impress. Cross-country types don't give a designer label how scruffy they look. If it's comfortable, they wear it.

16   Finally, cross-country skiers don't have to pay for lift tickets or entry fees because all they need to do is drive along till they see a fairly level stretch and get out and ski without lining up to ask the permission or pay the fees of some voracious corporation.

17   To sum up, cross-country (or Nordic) skiing is quieter, safer, and less expensive than is its first cousin downhill (or Alpine). It can

also provide steady and efficient exercise and is a great family sport.

18   I like to think that many cross-country enthusiasts had their truth-in-skiing revelation in much the same manner as did I—while tallying up my downhill bruises and contemplating my flattened wallet.

19   I wonder if anyone ever found my other downhill ski?

Questions for Analysis

1.   Why do you think Kaser chose to contrast downhill skiing to his favored cross-country skiing rather than devoting the entire essay to his hobby?

2.   If a person's hobby tells you something about him or her, how might you contrast downhill to cross-country skiing enthusiasts?

3.   What is the general *tone* of the essay (serious? humorous? sarcastic? indifferent?)? Why do you think Kaser chose this particular tone for the essay?

4.   After reading the essay, do you agree with Kaser's viewpoint on the advantages of cross-country skiing? Why or why not?

5.   Analyze the organization of the essay—Kaser's strategy for presenting his information on cross-country and downhill skiing. How effective is the organization? Why?

6.   What did you learn or find of particular interest in the essay? What, if anything, could you relate to your life?

7.   Locate "descriptive" passages you found particularly vivid or interesting. Analyze their appeal.

Vocabulary

novice (2), sopped (3), femurs (8), trek (10), ilk (10), voracious (16)

WRITING MUSIC

by Megan Bell

1   I write music. Actually I compose melodies on the piano and write the first few notes on paper to keep the tunes straight. It's hard to believe that I've been composing for twenty years, having little to show for it.

2   I didn't start writing down the melodies until a couple years ago. Before then, I didn't feel the music was worth the trouble. I'm still not sure it is, but I think it's getting a little better. Unfortunately, even my earliest melodies are as hard to get out of my head as nursery rhymes. I can still remember the first dreadful song I wrote two decades ago. To annoy me, my grown children sometimes hum the melody and have a good laugh. They're stuck with it too.

3   I've never considered my composing a serious hobby, perhaps because I've stopped numerous times, sometimes for months. But I've always gone back to the piano sooner or later and started working on new combinations of notes. No one makes me go back (my family could do without the noise), and I don't do it out of a sense of duty, so I must enjoy something about it.

4   Composing is hard work for me. I start by trying out a relatively random series of notes, using different chords for different effects. I seldom like how my beginnings sound, so I experiment, sometimes for hours, until I come up with some notes and chords that I think sound original together. From this meager start I build a melody with a refrain, which requires much trial and error and replaying parts of the song literally hundreds of times ad nauseum (yes, my children would vouch for that). Seldom do large segments of a melody come to me in a spasm of inspiration. The process is typically slow and laborious as I eke out a few notes at a time, never knowing for certain where I'm heading.

5   Is my music any good? I don't really know. I know it was very mediocre for many years.

Then I started experimenting with different keys and minor chords—moving all over the black keys—and the music started sounding more interesting and complex. From day one my daughter hasn't gotten much out of my music, but my son thinks I've been on to something the last couple years. That's encouraging because I've heard little good about my music, but then again I've never needed approval. I just keep going back to my old untuned piano with the warped keys, never knowing for sure the quality of hash I'm serving up.

6   What keeps me composing? Like thousands of hack writers who dream of writing the great American novel, I guess I'm a hack composer who dreams of writing the great American pop song, something that would put me up there with McCartney, Simon, Wonder, Mitchell, Taylor, John, and King: my composing hall of famers. I listen to songs like "Yesterday" or "The Boxer" and think, "Those melodies are so simple yet so beautiful. Couldn't I by happy accident crank out something like that?" Of course, when I think of the thousands of songs that are recorded, the thousands of songwriters who never get a song recorded, and the handful of truly great melodies written in the last thirty years, I know my chances of creating something terrific rival my winning the state lottery. Besides, as you can tell from my list of composers, I'm musically stuck in a 60's–70's time warp, my favorite songs wafting nostalgically from earlier decades. That probably dates my own melodies, interesting at the most to a few aging flower children.

7   Mainly, I suspect, I compose for myself. If I had ever seriously considered doing something with music, I would have collaborated with a lyricist and put songs on tape by now. I've threatened to do so many times, but I never do. Maybe I don't want to find out how ordinary my melodies are. If I did, I might quit composing. Maybe I'm afraid to make even a little public this small hobby that few people know about. Maybe I'm waiting—and waiting—to

write that one golden melody that will be the culmination of twenty years' effort. Trouble is, writing a good song isn't the culmination of anything. In my opinion, McCartney hasn't written a melody to rival "Yesterday" in thirty years. Who would have guessed.

8 My daily reasons for going to the piano are most mundane: something to do, an escape from problems, a reason not to do something I should be doing (like my monthly bills), a substitute for something I shouldn't be doing (like raiding the fridge). But beyond that, composing is a creative activity I seem to need, like other people need their writing, pottery, crocheting or gardening. It fulfills something in me to put together a series of notes and chords that may have never mixed in quite the same way. Good, bad, or mediocre, it's my creation, and once I found I could compose, I tired of playing other people's music. I just wanted to play my own.

9 Composing melodies has also been a satisfying constant in my life. Through college, job changes and marital ups and downs, successes here and failures there, through my twenties, thirties, and into my forties, I've been composing songs. A couple things strike me about that: one, that I'm much the same person today as the one who sat at the piano two decades ago; and two, that life is awfully short. If I measure time through my song writing, the years become compressed, as if I wrote my first melody not that long ago. Perhaps if I had more to show for those thousands of hours at the piano, the years wouldn't melt together. However, I have no musical milestones to separate them—no first album in '73, no Grammy in '83, no platinum record in '88. Just twenty years of melodies swimming around in my head, perhaps qualifying me as an idiot savant.

10 I have no idea what my musical future holds. If anyone had told me twenty years ago that I'd still be composing today, I would have been amazed. If anyone told me I'd still be composing twenty years from now, I'd be

dumbfounded. You see, I've run dry many times when I felt I didn't have another song in me. Then I'd start fooling around on the piano and discover another small direction to take—some new combination of chords or a different rhythm pattern—and I'd have a rough beginning for a couple more months of composing. I'd mine that vein until it was dry and then hope to discover a new source. Well, there's only so much gold (or fool's gold) in them thar hills, and the mining is getting tougher all the time. Eventually I'll run dry for good, but I don't know whether it will be tomorrow, a year or a decade from now.

11 I may be closer to the end than I want to believe. I played a recent melody for my daughter the other day and she said, "That sounds really weird. What are you trying to do?" Well, actually, I was writing melodies where the dominant note in the chord was almost always one half step above the melody note it went with. To my ear it sounded pretty neat; to my daughter's, pure cacophony. Not a good sign.

12 Years of experimenting in any art form takes one closer and closer to the edge. The great ones make a transcending leap and elevate their art to new heights. The hacks, like myself, merely fall off the edge into the slough of artistic absurdity, creating masterpieces of drivel. I'm feeling closer and closer to the edge, and since I have no interest in retracing my musical steps like some aging "golden oldies" singer, I may just take the plunge, going in my mind where no sane composer has gone. After all, I'm not hurting anyone, as long as I keep the door closed and the music in my head.

Questions for Analysis

1. Why do you think Bell chose to write about her music composing? What purpose may she have had?

2. What do you think has kept her at her hobby for so many years? What might move her to ever stop composing?

3. Bell calls her composing a "satisfying constant in my life." What, if anything, has been a "constant" in your life that gives you satisfaction? How does it affect you?

4. Do you think Bell will ever try to get her music recorded? Why or why not?

5. How does Bell organize her essay? Identify in order four or five different areas that she covers. Does the organization work well for readers? Why?

6. How does Bell paragraph her essay? What does a new paragraph beginning indicate to readers?

7. What did you learn from the essay or find particularly interesting? What, if anything, can you relate to your own life?

Vocabulary

refrain (4), ad nauseum (4), laborious (4), wafting (6), culmination (7), mundane (8), cacophony (11), transcending (12)

LOAFING MADE EASY

by Sam Negri

1   The fabled season of the sun is upon us and it is once again time to hook our thumbs in our suspenders and talk about America's most treasured art form, loafing.

2   The purest form of loafing is practiced in Arizona, where summertime temperatures will often exceed 110 degrees. If we regard the Arizona loafer as a natural resource, as I've been doing for the last eight years, we will see that the art form has applications that go far beyond the business of surviving in hot weather.

3   When I came to Arizona, I was a mediocre loafer, displaying a definite need for a degree of mental reconditioning. I'd moved here from Connecticut, where people relax by putting aside their copy of Gray's "Anatomy" and picking up a novel by Dostoevsky. In Arizona, this is referred to as insanity.

4   Here is a better method:

5   To begin with, shut the damper on your fireplace, if you have one, and turn on your air-conditioner, if you have one. Otherwise, hang a wet sheet in the window and pray for a breeze.

6   Now you are ready to memorize a handful of important and useful phrases. Try these: "I don't know"; "I don't care"; "no"; and the old standby, "well . . ."

7   These phrases are extremely valuable when your jaws are sagging like deflated bicycle tubes and your mind has turned to wax.

8   For example, it is 106 degrees in the shade and your son comes racing in the house, shouting, "Hey, you seen those long-handled pliers anywhere?" With a minimum of effort you are free to say, "no."

9   His anger may mount and he'll insist: "But you were using them yesterday! Where'd you leave 'em?"

10   If you haven't passed out from the strain of this conversation, you can then reply, "I don't know."

11   "But I need those pliers to fix my skateboard," he will cry. Then you break out the ultimate weapon in the loafer's lexicon. Without any inflection whatsoever, you declare, "Well. . ."

12   You can now get back to some serious loafing, which means that you will try to prove that Benjamin Franklin was correct when he observed: "It is hard for an empty sack to stand upright." In short, empty your mind. Learn to ask questions like these: "Mail come yet?" and "Anything doin'?" The responses to these questions usually involve one word, and often they aren't debilitating.

13   There are a few additional rules to keep in mind for successful loafing.

14   First, never loaf near a pool or a lake because you might be tempted to go for a swim. Swimming frequently leaves a body feeling refreshed and may lead to a desire to do something.

15   Second, under no circumstances should you allow anyone to coax you into a camping trip in the mountains. Mountains tend to be lush, green and cool, and next thing you know you'll be wanting to split logs for a fire, go for a hike, or pump up your Coleman stove. Resist. "Patience is a necessary ingredient of genius," said Disraeli. If you want to be a fine loafer you have to make enemies.

16   Of course, it is impossible to get by in life if you don't do something, even in the summer. Household jobs are the easiest for a loafer to contend with, if he is selective and deliberate.

17   One satisfying and undemanding job involves a ball of twine. Find a ball of twine that a cat has unraveled so badly that you can't find the end. Get scissors and slowly cut it into small pieces, scrunch it into a smaller ball, and throw it away. Now look at all the extra space you have in your junk drawer.

18   Another relatively simple and useful job for summertime loafing centers on light bulbs. Limp through your house or apartment, removing the light bulbs from every lamp. Coat the very bottom of each bulb with petroleum jelly and put it back in the lampsocket. This will clean some of the crud off the contact point and solve the problems with flickering lightbulbs. For variety you can take the bulb that was in a living-room lamp and put it in a bedroom lamp. It helps to sigh and gaze wistfully at the base of the lightbulb as you are performing this function.

19   Last, if you have a dog, sit in your most comfortable chair and stare at your dog's eyes for five or ten minutes. Every so often, mutter something incomprehensible. Your dog is certain to understand, and your family will not come near you for the rest of the afternoon.

Questions for Analysis

1. Does Negri's essay extol or poke fun at the "art" of loafing? Support your position through specific essay references.

2. Why does Negri depict Arizona as a haven for loafers and Connecticut as a place to keep busy? Might the comparison go beyond weather?

3. What does Negri mean, "If you want to be a fine loafer you have to make enemies?"

4. Judging from the essay, what are the greatest hindrances to successful loafing? What point, if any, may Negri be making?

5. Why do you think Negri wrote an essay on loafing? What reading audience may he have been writing for?

Vocabulary

mediocre (3), damper (5), lexicon (11), debilitating (12), coax (15), lush (15)

INNER VOYAGES

One of the most valuable writing trips you will take is the "inner voyage" toward self-discovery. When you write and reflect on significant experiences in your life, you discover how those experiences helped shape who you are and why you think and feel as you do.

Most of your writing for this unit focuses on personal experiences that have remained vivid in your memory. You will be recalling some of these experiences for yourself, as well as for your classmates, and you will also be analyzing them to determine the impact they had (or still have) on your life.

Sharing experiences through narrative writing can be enjoyable and rewarding for both writer and readers. You learn to re-create your experiences in writing to make them real and vivid for your readers. You also reflect on the significance of your experiences, and pass on what you learn about yourself, others, and life in general to your readers.

PREWRITING

In writing from personal experience, you are retrieving from memory recollections of a particular time, place, and event. Since you may be recalling experiences that have lain dormant in your mind for many years, you may have to do some serious reflection before the details of a particular incident become clear enough to write about.

REFLECTION

Before beginning to write a personal experience paper, many writers simply reflect on a memorable experience. Here are some things you may want to mull over about a potential topic before going further:

1. What actually happened? Try to visualize an experience as accurately as you can remember it: where it took place, who specifically was involved, what occurred, and what was said. Run the experience through your mind like a moving picture.

2. What did you think and how did you feel? Try to recall your thoughts and feelings at the time of the experience. What different things were going through your mind as the experience unfolded? How did you feel at different times of the experience?

3. What were the results of the experience? How did it turn out for you and for others involved? How did it affect your life?

4. Why is the experience so memorable? What significance does it have? Did you learn anything about yourself, other people, or life in general? What did you gain or lose from the experience?

ACTIVITY 2.1

Select an experience from your childhood to write about. Reflect on different experiences that you recall by answering the questions just presented, and select an experience that (1) you recall in some detail, (2) had an effect on you, and (3) your classmates might be interested in or might learn something from.

STUDENT SAMPLE REFLECTION

There's the incident in first grade where the dad of a girl I liked died and I got in trouble for making noise at her house a few days later. The memory is pretty fuzzy though. Then there was my first "fight" when I was in second grade. It really wasn't much of a fight, just a little wrestling match, but I remember I didn't enjoy it. Not sure I'd have much to write about. I don't even remember how it started.

Then there was the problem I had with a long-time friend in eighth grade, but I'd rather go back further in my childhood. There was the time in first grade when I buried a neighbor kid's gun in a field and we never found it again. I remember that pretty well, including how mad the kid got and how scared I was. There were other neighbor kids around to see what was going on, and I remember my mom getting involved. Then I moved to another town and, of all things, this kid moves in right behind me. What a co-incidence, like my big mistake had followed me to another town. I think I'd like to write about the gun experience because I remember it well, I remember the kid well, and I remember how I felt about my mom helping me. The experience bothered me for some time. It might be interesting to at least some of my classmates.

■ ■ ■ ■ ■ ■ ■ ■ ■ ■ ■

FREE WRITING

Another prewriting strategy that helps writers generate ideas is called "free writing." It is particularly useful for narrative papers because writing freely about an experience often helps "unlock" pieces of memory as you begin putting together different parts of the experience.

Here are some suggestions for writing freely on the personal experience you have selected:

1. Your emphasis in free writing is on content: putting down everything you recall about an experience without concern for paragraphing or mechanics.

2. Begin your free writing with your first recollections of the experience and continue wherever your memory takes you. Often as you write about an experience, you will recall details and connections that were previously buried in your mind. You may be surprised at the things you remember.

3. Write for at least ten to fifteen minutes, and with little hesitation. Remember, this is a *pre*writing activity; its purpose is to help you get on paper as much as you can recall of the experience.

4. After you have written freely, you should know whether you have selected a topic you want to write about. You may find in writing the draft that you don't remember as much as you thought you would or that there really wasn't much to the experience: perhaps some initial pain or fright, but nothing to develop in an essay.

ACTIVITY 2.2

Write freely for ten to fifteen minutes on the personal experience you have chosen to write about. Begin with whatever comes to your mind first, and continue wherever your memory leads you. The purpose of the free writing is to see how much you can recall about the experience before writing your first draft.

SAMPLE STUDENT FREE WRITING

I was only in kindergarten when this happened. There was a big vacant lot beside my house where the neighborhood boys including myself would play cowboys. I think there were only four or five of us, and I remember there were some old rabbit hutches and some eucalyptus trees in the front of the lot. The youngest kid, named Brian, had a new gun, and it was pretty neat. I was jealous of him as I remember, and I asked him if I could see it. The next thing I remember is burying it somewhere in the dirt in a corner of the lot when he wasn't looking. I figured I could always find it, but when I went back to dig it up, I couldn't. I remember panicking and going home. Then he comes to my house and my mom goes out and we dig for the gun, but no luck. I felt lousy, and I think Mom bought him a new gun later. Then we moved and believe it or not, that kid moved in right behind us some months later. I didn't like him and he didn't like me and I don't remember that ever changing. He was younger than me, and I think I let him push me around back at the lot. I remember being embarrassed.

■ ■ ■ ■ ■ ■ ■ ■ ■ ■ ■ ■ ■

FIRST DRAFTS
■ ■

When you write your narrative paper, you are telling readers a story. Whether the story is fictional, or in your case true, there are certain storytelling elements to consider as you write your drafts:

1. *Setting:* Setting provides the "where" and "when" of your story. Effectively told stories usually provide a visual landscape so that readers can picture the experience.

2. *Characters:* The characters in your story are the people who are a part of the experience: yourself, other main participants, and perhaps some minor characters who, from your perspective, added something to the experience.

3. *Plot:* The plot is what happens to the characters. It includes the incidents within the experience, leading up to and including the main incident that the story builds to—its climax.

4. *Resolution:* The resolution concludes the story, telling readers what happened as a result of the experience, and what, if anything, the narrator (yourself) or others learned from it.

ACTIVITY 2.3

Read the following student draft, and with a partner, identify the story elements just presented: the setting, the characters, the plot, and the resolution. Be prepared to share your findings with the class.

THE LOST GUN

On Saturdays, the neighborhood gang gathered at the vacant lot to play cowboys. The open space was great for range wars, and the eucalyptus trees were used for hideouts. There were even some old rabbit hutches for locking up prisoners. As we gathered with our assortment of guns and holsters, Brian swaggered in with the biggest, shiniest six-shooter I'd ever seen. It had a ten-inch barrel and an ivory handle. It made my gun look like a peashooter. It wasn't fair that the youngest, brattiest kid in the gang had the best gun.

Before we started, I asked Brian to let me see the gun. He reluctantly handed it over, and I told him I wanted to borrow it for a while. Since I was the big leader of the gang, he couldn't refuse. As soon as we broke up for cowboys and Brian was out of view behind the trees, I ran to a far corner of the lot and buried the gun in the soft dirt. I wanted to give Brian a scare.

Before long, the bad guys were rounded up, and Brian was demanding his gun back. I let him squirm awhile, then laughed and said I'd hidden it. He didn't laugh and demanded I find it. We all trudged across the lot to the corner, and I dug where I thought I'd buried it. No gun. I dug some more, and then I dug deeper and faster. Still no gun. Brian started yelling, "Find my gun!" and I started getting sick. I knew it was there somewhere, but the whole corner was looking the same to me. Everyone stood around and watched as their big leader desperately pawed at the ground. No one helped. Brian finally screamed, "My dad's gonna get you, you bastard!" My eyes started burning, and I knew I was going to cry if I stayed around. I took off running across the lot with Brian yelling, "You bastard! My dad will get you!"

That afternoon, I lay down with my mom for a nap, but I couldn't sleep. I felt terrible about what I had done, and I was frightened about what would happen to me. I hadn't told Mom a thing, but when I heard Brian calling outside the window, I confessed everything to her. She calmly listened to me, then went out to the garage and got the shovel. We met Brian outside and the three of us returned to the lot.

By now it was very hot outside, and my mom dug in the heat for an hour. She turned up most of the dirt in that corner, but the gun was never found. I stood and watched her helplessly, and I felt worse and worse as she worked and sweated because of me. I'd never felt more worthless.

My parents bought Brian a new gun, so he was satisfied. But I wasn't the big shot of the gang any more. Little Brian had pushed me around that day, and the gang didn't forget. I was just one of the boys, and that was where I belonged. I wasn't particularly brave, and I still needed Mom to bail me out of trouble. We moved to another town the next year, and of all coincidences, Brian moved into the house behind the alley. His moving there reminded me I wasn't the big shot I had pretended to be. That one incident with the gun kept us from ever becoming friends although we were neighbors for five years.

. . . .

ACTIVITY *2.4*

Write the first draft of your personal experience paper, using the material you generated in your free writing any way you wish. Your reading audience will be your classmates, and your purpose is to tell your story as clearly and interestingly as you can, and to reveal to readers how the experience affected you, and what, if anything, you learned from it.

Paragraphing a personal experience paper is not too difficult. As a general rule, you change paragraphs as you move to something new in your story: a different time, a different place, or a different incident within the experience. (You may want to look at the paragraphing of the student sample draft on page 35 before writing your own.) Don't be overly concerned about paragraphing on your first draft.

. . . .

REVISIONS

First drafts of narrative papers often have similar revision needs. Sometimes writers spend so much time building up to the main incident that they don't give it enough attention. At other times they may omit their thoughts and feelings at points where a reader is anxious to know how they're reacting. A common first-draft weakness is for the experience to occur in a ''vaccuum,'' with no established sense of time or place. Finally, first drafts often end rather abruptly, leaving readers wondering what the point of the paper was.

The following questions should help you evaluate your first draft and consider the types of revisions you may want to make in your next draft:

1. Have I provided enough setting details so that readers can visualize where and when the experience occurred? What might I add to help readers ''see'' both what is happening and where it occurs?

2. Have I included all of the people who are a part of the experience, and do I present enough about them (how they look, what they are like) for readers to visualize them and understand their role?

3. Have I included my thoughts and feelings at critical times in the experience, where readers might wonder how I reacted to what was happening?

4. Have I focused clearly on the heart of the experience: the main incident? Have I spent so much time leading up to it that I didn't give it enough attention?

5. Have I left readers (my classmates) with some sense of why the experience was meaningful to me? Will they understand why I wrote about this particular experience? Will they have a sense of conclusion when they finish reading?

6. Have I paragraphed the essay so that readers can move easily from one part of the experience to the next, and have I avoided extremely long paragraphs or strings of short paragraphs? (If you are having any problems with paragraphing your draft, refer to Activity 2.6 before revising your draft.)

7. Are there sentences that I can make clearer or smoother by eliminating unnecessary words, changing any awkward phrasing, or replacing questionable word choices with more appropriate ones?

8. Putting myself in the place of my readers, what are four or five questions that the draft might raise that I should answer in the next draft?

9. Does the draft capture the experience as I remember it? Will readers understand why it was so frightening, embarrassing, thrilling, sad, or humorous for me?

ACTIVITY *2.5*

Read the following student draft, and with a classmate, evaluate it by applying the questions for revision. Make a list of things the writer does well along with suggestions for revision.

Next evaluate your own draft similarly, making revision plans for your next draft. For a second opinion, exchange drafts with a classmate and write down four or five questions about your classmate's draft that you want to share.

When you are ready, write the second draft of your paper. You may continue evaluating and rewriting drafts until you are satisfied with the final product; that may occur after two drafts or after three or more. There is no magic number of rewrites that satisfies every writer.

THE SPELLING BEE

I went to a small country school from the first through sixth grade. I was a pretty good student, but one thing I could really do was spell. In grades four and five, I went a year and a half without missing a word on weekly spelling tests based on our workbook lists, and I was usually the last one left standing in classroom "spell downs."

In the sixth grade, our state had a statewide spelling competition beginning with small regional contests and ending months later with the final competitors competing for the state championship. Our teacher, a tall, dark-haired woman who was married to a tax collector, announced the contest and explained how a person got from step one to the state championship. I figured if I ever was going to enter a contest, this would be it. I even imagined myself having some success.

Things started out well. I won my room spelling bee when Billy Dayton, my main competitor, misspelled a word and I spelled it correctly. That also made me the school representative because we only had one sixth grade class. I moved on to the district contest, which had the winners of the six schools in our small district, and I won again. I received a winner's certificate, and the superintendent of the district said something that made me feel so proud that I had an emotional reaction, and the audience responded.

My confidence was high until I walked into the Laurel Community Center for the area competition. The building was bigger than our whole school, and there were over a hundred people in the audience, including ten of my relatives who, along with Mom and Dad, had come to cheer me on. Then I saw my competitors, and the way they looked and acted and the places they were from made me scared. I quietly made my way to the chair with my number on it and sat staring at my feet, my confidence replaced by anxiety.

Finally, the spelling bee began, and one by one, the students walked up to the microphone, were given a word, spelled it, and returned to their seats. If a word was spelled incorrectly, a small bell was rung, but it hadn't rung yet. The bell had made a high tinkling sound, not unlike the sound you hear in an ear test. I was number eighteen out of twenty, and I was in agony waiting my turn. When the moderator called my name, I walked to the microphone. Then I looked out into the audience and saw all my relatives beaming at me. Then I heard the moderator say, "Mary Sue, spell 'chauffeur.'" I knew what the word meant, but I had never seen it in print. I had no visual image of the word, so I started spelling it out like it sounded: "s-h-o-f-e-r." I heard a sympathetic groan from the audience, then the little bell sounding my doom. I walked back to my chair, and the next contestant spelled chauffeur correctly.

I sat for almost an hour in humiliation, the first person to go down and the only person out in the first round. The only perverse pleasure I got was watching others miss and join me in misery. I listened to kids spell wondrous words that I couldn't have pronounced, much less spelled, and I realized this was a whole new world. I didn't belong here with these smart kids; I belonged back at Tucker Elementary with my slow-witted friends.

When the contest was finally over, my relatives were kind, and my dad said something that made me feel better and made me cry at the same time. It was a long ride home, and all I could think of was how dumb I was and how smart everyone else was. Even when I did well at school in the next weeks, I'd think, "Big deal. You're the smartest of the dummies." It wasn't until I moved up to the big high school in the tenth grade that I began to realize that it really wasn't that the city kids were any smarter. By twelfth grade I didn't feel inferior to many students, and I had gotten over the old feelings. But to this day if someone wants to bring me off my high horse, all they have to do is say, "Spell 'chauffeur,' Mary Sue."

▪ ▪ ▪ ▪ ▪ ▪ ▪ ▪ ▪ ▪ ▪

PARAGRAPHING

Paragraphing a paper basically requires common sense. Most readers don't enjoy wading through extremely long paragraphs because they can lose important points buried in the middle or get bogged down. They don't particularly enjoy reading strings of short paragraphs either because they lose the continuity of the writer's thoughts by having to stop and start so frequently. Readers can also get confused by paragraphs that jump randomly from idea to idea because from past reading experience, they expect sentences within a paragraph to be related.

If you remember these three common-sense points—don't run your paragraphs on too long, don't string short paragraphs together, and make sure the sentences in a paragraph are related—you will avoid most paragraphing problems that trouble readers.

ACTIVITY 2.6

Paragraph the following student papers by marking the beginning of each new paragraph. Change paragraphs as the writer moves to something new within the experience, and avoid overly long paragraphs or strings of short ones (a couple of sentences each).

HUMILIATION

I remember first grade was going along well. I was having fun in school. I liked my teacher, I got to play the wood block in the percussion band, and I even had a girlfriend. Then a string of events happened that ruined the year for me. My girlfriend's name was Karen, a quiet, dark-haired girl with a shy smile. After school, we'd go over to her house and sit on top of the slanted shingle roof, enjoying the sun, the view, and just being together. We'd sit there day after day, sometimes holding hands, and I was very happy. Then Karen was absent from school for a while, and the teacher, Mrs. Bray, told us Karen's father had been killed in an electrical accident. I remember being shocked by the news. I'd never heard of anyone's father being killed; it wasn't something that happened. I wondered how Karen was doing, but I was afraid to go and see her. Then one day the entire class walked together to Karen's garage to pick up some old hobby horses and props Karen's mother was lending our class for a play. We were all in the dusty old garage collecting the wooden stick horses and everyone was pretty quiet. Then I blurted out something loudly, I don't remember why. I liked to be the center of attention, but why I picked that time to say something stupid is beyond me. When I did, Mrs. Bray really jumped me. "Shut up, Ben!" she hissed angrily. And I didn't open my mouth the rest of the day. Walking back to school, I felt awful. Mrs. Bray had never scolded me before, and I now had done something so terrible that she told me to shut up. On top of that, I had been acting stupid at Karen's house only a week after her father died. That made me a doubly evil person, and even though Karen hadn't been in the garage with us, I knew she'd find out. I felt miserable. I never saw Karen again. She stayed home from school for a long time, and then apparently she and her mother moved away. I walked by her house a couple of times before she moved, but I never had the courage to stop. I really never recovered that year from the incident. Things weren't right again between me and Mrs. Bray; I always felt I'd failed her. We moved that summer, and since I never saw Karen again, I assumed she thought the worst of me, and I'd never believe otherwise. Thinking back on that year, I still feel sad some fifteen years later. It's an awful feeling to do something you feel is terrible and never be able to make amends. I just wish I could have seen Karen one last time and said, "I'm sorry."

PIANO RECITAL

I'd always enjoyed playing the piano until my first recital in the fifth grade. I didn't mind playing for my teacher, Mrs. Scott, and I didn't mind playing for my family. But playing for a roomful of strangers and piano students was more than I could handle. We all gathered in Mrs. Scott's living room. There were about twenty folding chairs in rows across the room with sofas lining the walls. All the chairs and sofas were filled with parents and other students, and it felt as though a hundred people were packed in the hot room. Since I was the fifth student on the program to play, I sat stiffly and listened to the others. I wasn't too nervous at first, but as my time came closer, I got tense. The students before me were playing like angels, and the audience applauded for each one. I knew I wasn't as good as the others, and the more I listened, the more I wanted to escape. Finally, my turn came. Mrs. Scott introduced me and told the audience I would be playing "Country Gardens," a song I'd practiced a hundred times. I put my hands to the piano, and before I knew it, they were playing "Country Gardens." I didn't feel in control, and I was moving through the song mindlessly. I started to panic. My hands kept playing but I was blanking out. Finally, I stopped playing. I couldn't play another note. I sat paralyzed at the piano having no idea what to do next. Finally, I felt Mrs. Scott's arm on my shoulder. She asked me quietly if I'd like to start the song again. I told her I didn't. She tried to encourage me by saying how beautifully I played it. The audience started applauding for me. I didn't move a finger to the keyboard. I don't know how long I sat there, but Mrs. Scott finally took me back to my seat. The next student went to the piano, and the recital continued. I sat in a daze. I don't remember much of the rest of the afternoon. There was punch, and everyone tried to console me. I just wanted to go home. I knew this was my last recital. I did take lessons a couple more weeks, and then I quit. The recital had done me in. I still remember sitting at the piano like a zombie. That was the first experience I remember choking with the pressure on, and all my life I've tried to avoid situations where the pressure was more than I could handle.

SEEING GRANDPA

A week after my grandfather died, my mother told me she saw him standing in our back-yard. She said he had returned to speak to her and that he would be back again. Mother believed in dead relatives returning to visit loved ones before they finally rested, and she said he might visit me too. It scared me to think about it. Three nights later I awoke and saw Grandpa standing at the foot of my bed. There was no doubt that it was Grandpa: the tall, thin body, the tousled white hair, the big, watery eyes. He stood there and stared at me with those big, sad eyes, but he never spoke. It somehow seemed natural for him to be standing there, and he was such a kind, gentle man that I wasn't the least frightened. We just looked at each other for the longest time, and then he turned slowly and walked out my bedroom door. I crawled out of bed and followed him. He walked out the back door, and by the time I peeked out the back window, he was gone. It was the last time I ever saw my grandfather. I slept with my mother the rest of the night, and the next morning I told her about Grandpa. She wasn't at all surprised or concerned. She said he was probably contented now and wouldn't return. We talked about the incident as though it was the most natural thing in the world. No matter how absurd it sounds, it seems like the right thing for my grandfather to have come back one last time. It made me feel good, and it must have helped him. Since the incident, I have had more respect for some of my mother's beliefs that I once thought were nonsense. There are some things that happen that logic can't explain. Grandfather's return was one of them.

■ ■ ■ ■ ■ ■ ■ ■ ■ ■ ■ ■ ■

TRANSITIONAL WORDING IN PARAGRAPHS

Another important consideration for effective paragraphing is to tie your ideas together with appropriate *transitional wording*, so that a reader may read smoothly through your paragraph and understand the relationship of your ideas. Transitional words or phrases make a paragraph more easily readable.

The following paragraph contains no transitional wording. As you read it, notice that the ideas don't flow together smoothly.

I've had a real problem with my car leaking oil on the driveway lately. There's a pool of oil two-thirds of the way up on both sides of the driveway. There's a pool of oil inside the garage where I park the car. I clean the oil up. The next day it's back again. I took the car to a garage to have the oil changed and the leak stopped. The problem was more difficult than I suspected. The rear main bearing seal was leaking, but to replace it, the engine would have to be pulled. I couldn't afford that, so I had to wait and save up some money. I put three oil pans on the spots where the car leaks oil when it's parked. I can't think of any other solution for now.

Now here is the same paragraph with some transitional wording added to tie the ideas together. The transitional wording is underlined.

I've had a lot of trouble with my car leaking oil lately. <u>First</u>, there's a pool of oil two-thirds of the way up on both sides of the driveway. There's <u>another</u> pool in the garage where I park the car. <u>After</u> I clean up the oil, it's back again the next day. <u>Finally</u>, I took the car to the garage to have the oil changed and the leak stopped. <u>However</u>, the problem was more difficult than I expected. The rear main bearing seal was leaking, but to replace it, the engine would have to be pulled. I couldn't afford that, so I had to wait and save up some money. <u>In the meantime</u>, I put oil pans on the three spots where the car leaks oil when it's parked. I can't think of any other solution for now.

The following transitional words and phrases will be useful for most writing you do:

1. **Transitions that show movement in time, place, or sequence:** *first, second, next, then, after, before, while, now, in the meantime, finally, last.*

2. **Transitions that connect supporting points, ideas, or examples:** *first, second, also, another, in addition, additionally, furthermore, moreover.*

3. **Transitions that show relationships between thoughts:** *however, therefore, nevertheless, thus, despite, in spite of, on the contrary, on the other hand, for example, for instance, consequently.*

Transitions such as *however, therefore, furthermore,* and *nevertheless* are often preceded by a *semicolon* (;). The semicolon indicates the beginning of a new sentence closely related to the sentence preceding it. When you use a semicolon to separate two sentences, you do *not* capitalize the first letter of the second sentence.

EXAMPLES   I need to go Christmas shopping; however, I don't know when I will find time.

Louise is living at home this semester; therefore, she'll save the cost of renting an apartment.

Alicia got an A on her English final; furthermore, she passed biology after two previous attempts.

Felix bowled a score of 23 his first game; nevertheless, he had a good time.

ACTIVITY 2.7

Fill in the following paragraphs with *transitional words* from the list above. Fill each blank with the word or phrase that makes the most appropriate connection between steps.

EXAMPLE   <u>Before</u> buying a new typewriter, shop around for a used one.

Then look for reasonably priced typing paper.

Buying a used car is a complicated business. _____ , decide the make and year of car you're interested in. _____ look through the newspaper to see what's available. You will find the largest number of cars in the ads for used car lots. _____ , you may find your best buy under the private owner ads since these cars aren't marked up for profits as much as lot cars are. _____ , pick out a few cars that look interesting and spend a day looking at them. Take along pen and paper so you can take notes on each car and make comparisons.

_____ you look at a car, check the odometer for mileage, and confirm that the reading is accurate. The fewer miles on the car, the longer life it will have. _____ check the tires for wear and the body for dents or indications of body work done for accident repair. If the body looks good, the miles are reasonably low, and the tires are safe, take the car for a test drive. _____ , test the brakes. _____ see how the car handles. Does it veer to the right or left when you release the wheel? Does it vibrate as you increase speed? Does the engine make any suspicious noises? Are there bothersome rattles inside the car? Does everything work: lights, radio, windshield wipers, heater, turn signals? Any combination of negative signs could indicate serious problems for the future. _____ , some problems are easily curable, and if you like the car except for a problem or two, don't completely write it off.

_____ you finish with one car, check out the other cars similarly. _____ compare all the cars to see which one you prefer. You may not like any of them; _____ , you should wait for new cars to surface in the paper and try again instead of settling for a car you don't want. If there is a car you are interested in, take one last step. Take the car to a professional mechanic to give it a thorough inspection. For about $30, he can check it over carefully and test drive it to give you an expert's viewpoint. _____ you have done all you can to ensure you're getting a good car. _____ all your precautions, you may still have some trouble, but you've gone a long way toward buying a reliable used car.

▪ ▪ ▪ ▪ ▪ ▪ ▪ ▪ ▪ ▪ ▪ ▪

ACTIVITY 2.8

Write a short paper for classmates explaining some kind of game or activity you remember playing as a child. Make use of *transitions* to help you tie your thoughts together clearly for readers.

STUDENT FIRST DRAFT PARAGRAPH   (*transitions underlined*)

One of the fun games I remember playing as a child was a card game called "Frustration." My brothers and I got to play it with the adult relatives, and that was exciting. The object of the game is to take the exact number of card tricks that you "bid." First, ten cards are dealt to each player. Then you organize your hand by suits, highest to lowest card. You decide how many tricks you think you can take based on the number of high (or low) cards you have. <u>For example</u>, if you have some aces and kings, you might bid 3 or 4. <u>However</u>, if you have nothing higher than a 9 or 10, you might bid 0.

Once everyone is ready to bid, you "knock" three times on the table and then show your bid by the number of fingers you stick out. You must take the exact number of tricks you bid or you get 0 points. If you make your bid, you get 10 points if you bid 0 and one additional point each for bidding 1, 2, 3, etc.

After playing a ten-card hand, you next deal nine cards and go all the way down to one and up to ten again. <u>By the way</u>, there is also one suit that is drawn as "trump" for each hand, and a trump card can take any other suit's card. It's a fun game for all ages.

■ ■ ■ ■ ■ ■ ■ ■ ■ ■ ■ ■

SENTENCE REVISION

Revising first draft sentences to make them smoother, cleaner, and stronger is a task shared by all writers. In this section, you learn to replace vague language with more "concrete" wording, and you review basic revision considerations introduced in Unit 1.

CONCRETE LANGUAGE

Another sentence revision consideration is replacing vague, general language with more specific, *concrete* wording. Here are some suggestions for using concrete language in your writing:

1. Use the most specific term possible to refer to a particular thing. For example, you might use *German shepherd* instead of *dog*, *TWA 747* instead of *airplane*, *six-lane freeway* instead of *road*, *Buddhist temple* instead of *church*, and *lemon chiffon pie* instead of *dessert*.

2. Use vivid, descriptive verbs to make your sentences lively and interesting. For example, you might write, "The boxer *staggered* across the ring and then *crumpled* to the canvas" instead of "The boxer *moved unsteadily* across the ring and then *fell down on the canvas*."

3. Make your writing as visual as possible. Use language that allows the reader to see and feel what you are expressing. For example, compare "The huge man careened down the slope and crashed into a startled skier, knocking her head-first into a snow bank" to "The man raced down the slope and hit another skier, knocking her into the snow."

4. In an attempt to be descriptive, avoid overusing modifying words that, when clumped together, weaken the effect. For example, compare "The tall, large, heavily muscled, strong woman easily

and effortlessly lifted her short, skinny, lightly muscled, weak husband above her large, angular head'' to ''The huge woman effortlessly lifted her scrawny husband over her head.''

Here are some examples of vaguely worded first draft sentences followed by more descriptive revisions:

VAGUE	The tree in my yard is very colorful.
BETTER	The pear tree behind the house is covered with pink blossoms.
VAGUE	Liquid comes out of my dog's mouth at certain times.
BETTER	Slobber dribbles down my bulldog Murphy's mouth when he gets excited.
VAGUE	The girl moved across the ice in a nice fashion.
BETTER	The eight-year-old in pigtails glided smoothly across the ice.
VAGUE	The weather is terrible this morning.
BETTER	It's five degrees below zero with a wind of thirty miles an hour.
VAGUE	Bothered by a leg problem, the football player moved differently.
BETTER	Hobbled by a swollen ankle, the halfback ran at half speed.
VAGUE	That old person just left with my glasses.
BETTER	That blue-haired old lady just made off with my sunglasses.

ACTIVITY 2.9

Revise the following vaguely worded sentences by replacing general terms with specific ones and weak verbs with vivid ones, and by adding appropriate modifiers. Your revised sentences will be more concrete and visual than the originals.

EXAMPLE	We left to go downtown and take care of some business.
REVISED	My best friend and I left school at noon to order our class rings from the jewelry store downtown.

1. There is a funny smell coming from one part of the garage.

———————————————————————————————

2. Melissa has a very strange hairdo.

———————————————————————————————

3. That man is strong for his age.

———————————————————————————————

4. The horses left from the starting gate and moved down the track.

———————————————————————————————

5. The moon is beautiful tonight.

_____

6. The nervous, excited young teenage girl waited anxiously and expectantly for her evening's date to finally and unquestionably arrive.

_____

7. The boxer put his right glove in the other boxer's face and then did it again with the other hand.

_____

8. After a long hike, the boy didn't feel great at all.

_____

9. Your relative is quite small for his age.

_____

10. The bird went up to the top of the tree and sat on a piece of it.

_____

■ ■ ■ ■ ■ ■ ■ ■ ■ ■ ■

WORDING PROBLEM REVIEW

Here is a review of some basic problems to consider as you revise your sentences.

1. *Wordiness:* **using more words than necessary to express a thought.**

   EXAMPLE   The hailstones that had collected on the lawn in front of the house gave the appearance of snow to anyone who saw them on the lawn.

   REVISED   The hailstones on the front lawn of the house looked like snow.

2. *Inflated language:* **using more complicated language than necessary to express a thought.**

   EXAMPLE   The amount of hair atop the head of Uncle Oswald appears to be diminishing in thickness, thus revealing some previously hidden scalp.

   REVISED   Uncle Oswald is losing his hair.

3. *Awkward phrasing:* **using words and phrases that don't fit together smoothly or logically.**

   EXAMPLE   Because we've lived in weather where the temperature is cold all our lives, so we are used to dressing the proper way.

   REVISED   Because we've lived with cold weather all our lives, we're used to dressing warmly.

4. *Poor word choice:* using an incorrect or questionable word to help express a thought.

EXAMPLE   Your speech on positive thinking transpired all of us.

REVISED   Your speech on positive thinking inspired all of us.

■ ■ ■ ■ ■ ■ ■ ■ ■ ■ ■ ■

ACTIVITY *2.10*

The following first draft sentences need revising because they have problems with wordiness, awkward phrasing, and poor word choices. Revise and rewrite each sentence to make it smoother and clearer.

EXAMPLE   John had a bald spot that parted his hair in the middle that was black. *(wordy, awkward, poor word choice)*

REVISED   John had a bald spot in the middle of his black hair.

1. The first thing is to let the oil settle down on the oil pan and let the oil cool down right there.
2. In football you don't have to have that good of an endurance to play it.
3. We went to a good show, and we saw it last weekend together.
4. Even though I am his cousin, but he doesn't let me borrow his notes.
5. From all of the dish washing, your hands are pruning and aging with rapidity.
6. It's hot outside tonight with very few breezes.
7. The doctor told my dad I was on time to stop the infection from spreading.
8. By looking at their patio from north to south, it is 12 feet by 12 feet.
9. The accident almost cost me to lose my life.
10. I was curious to see what a group of cat's behaviors were together, so I followed that group of cats.

■ ■ ■ ■ ■ ■ ■ ■ ■ ■ ■ ■

SENTENCE VARIETY: COMBINING SENTENCES

As you learned in Unit 1, another important consideration in revision is sentence variety. You don't want all of your sentences to look and sound alike. Sentence variety makes your writing more interesting to read, and it allows you to express different ideas and relationships most effectively.

In Unit 1, you learned that combining sentences is the best way to eliminate pairs or patches of short, similar sentences in your writing. Here is a review of the three combining methods you used.

1. Combine sentences by eliminating repeated words, by placing modifiers before the words they describe, and by grouping similar words or phrases and joining them with *and, or,* or *but.*

   EXAMPLE   Tridol soap is new. It is improved. It works well in hot water. It also works well in cold water.

   REVISED   New, improved Tridol soap works well in hot or cold water.

2. Combine sentences by joining them with a *coordinate conjunction* (*and, or, but, so, for, yet*) to form a *compound sentence.*

   EXAMPLE   Alicia is going to visit her sister. She will have to leave work early.

   REVISED   Alicia is going to visit her sister, <u>so</u> she will have to leave work early.

3. Combine sentences by joining them with a *subordinate conjunction* (*when, as, before, because, unless, although, since,* and so on) to form a *complex sentence.*

   EXAMPLE   The beach is very narrow. The storm waves washed most of the sand away.

   REVISED   The beach is very narrow <u>because</u> the storm waves washed most of the sand away.

   EXAMPLE   You may think you'd like loafing your entire life. You would probably go crazy doing nothing.

   REVISED   <u>Although</u> you may think you'd like loafing your entire life, you would probably go crazy doing nothing.

ACTIVITY *2.11*

Combine the following pairs and groups of sentences using these combining methods: (1) eliminating repeated words, moving modifiers in front of words they describe, and grouping similar words or phrases and joining them with *and, or,* or *but*; (2) joining two complete sentences with a coordinate conjunction (*and, or, for, but, yet, so*) to form a compound sentence; or (3) joining two complete sentences with a subordinate conjunction (*before, as, because, when, while, unless, although, since, if, whenever,* and so on) to form a complex sentence. (Note: Remember, you can put a subordinate conjunction at the beginning or in the middle of your sentence.)

EXAMPLE   Ed sent a letter to his fiancée. It was a mushy one.

REVISED   Ed sent a mushy letter to his fiancée.

EXAMPLE   Maria likes nuts in her chocolate-chip cookies. Henry prefers raisins in his.

REVISED   Maria likes nuts in her chocolate-chip cookies, <u>but</u> Henry prefers raisins in his.

EXAMPLE   I'm not going to the ball game Friday. I wish I were going.

REVISED   I'm not going to the ball game Friday <u>although</u> I wish I were going.

1. Elvira is a good speller. Michael is also a good speller. Sam has trouble with spelling.

2. Sally has a sister. She has red hair. She is twenty-six years old. She is younger than Sally.

3. The dog couldn't jump the fence. She couldn't squeeze through it. She dug a hole under it.

4. We could study tonight. We could go dancing at the Ajax Casino. It's still early.

5. Noreen has flat feet. She is badly nearsighted. That didn't keep her off the basket-ball team. She loves the game.

6. Myrtle talks slowly. She thinks very fast. She also writes very fast.

7. The grease melted in the skillet. It started to bubble. It splattered on the stove. It burned my arm.

8. Horacio is silly. He is also overweight. He is a flirt. Girls like him.

9. You jog early in the morning. Be sure to warm up well. You could pull a muscle.

10. Put the periodicals on the rack. Return the encyclopedia to the shelf. You've found what you needed.

11. George made a mistake. He spread on the shark repellent too thinly. It didn't work well.

12. You need a doctor badly. Call one. Use my cordless phone. It's in the kitchen.

13. I've got a new yo-yo. It is red. I've also got a new Hula-Hoop. It is also red. I'll take them to the fifties party.

14. Marta finally found the salamander. It was small and frightened. It was in her drawer. She put it in the pond. It was in her backyard.

15. Marcia was stumped by square roots. Her teacher tutored her after class. It didn't help much. She failed the next test.

16. Used cars can be a disaster. Don't buy the first one you look at. You could get a real loser.

17. Darrin started jogging after school. He wanted to lose ten pounds. He jogged for a week. He quit. He saw no results.

18. Attendance at the noon rallies had been poor. The remaining rallies were canceled. No one seemed to care. No one even noticed.

ACTIVITY *2.12*

Rewrite the following passage. Combine sentences by adding joining words, moving words and phrases around, and eliminating unnecessary words. Try to combine the sixteen sample sentences into a few well-crafted ones.

EXAMPLE   Nona moved into her apartment today. She paid her rent a week ago. She was living alone. She was looking for a roommate to share expenses.

REVISED   Nona moved into her apartment today, <u>but</u> she paid her rent a week ago. <u>Although</u> she was living alone, she was looking for a roommate to share expenses.

Corrine collects records from the fifties and sixties. She has over one thousand 45 rpm discs. Her brother is a disc jockey. She buys duplicate records from his station cheaply. She enjoys the music of the eighties. She prefers the sound of early rock 'n' roll. She has every record Buddy Holly ever recorded. He was her favorite singer. She'll invite her friends over. They'll listen to old songs for hours. She's heard them hundreds of times. She never gets tired of them. She never considers her collection complete. She'll spend the weekend looking for records by Bo Diddley and Danny and the Juniors.

■ ■ ■ ■ ■ ■ ■ ■ ■ ■ ■

ACTIVITY *2.13*

Fill in subordinate conjunctions to complete the following complex sentences. Notice that subordinate conjunctions can either begin a complex sentence or come in the middle. Refer to the list of subordinate conjunctions on page 48 if you need help.

EXAMPLE   *Although* the trip was tiring, it was worth it.

Each section of the botanical garden is different. You begin in a tropical rain forest with thick foliage and humid heat. _____ you know it, you're climbing from the forest onto a dry plain. _____ you look, there are scrub pines, sagebrush, yuccas, and cactus. _____ you walk another fifty feet, you drop into a valley. _____ the temperature was just ninety degrees, it's dropped to sixty-five. There is lush grass growing by a stream and knots of maple and birch trees along the bank. _____ you happen to lose your way, your next steps ascend a mountain path. The air is even cooler _____ the plants have changed to redwoods, pines, manzanita, mountain fern, and dogwood. The air smells sweet _____ the dogwood is in bloom. The entire walk is wonderful _____ you reach the last section. You walk down from the mountains into a smog-infested atmosphere. The plant life is dead or ashen looking _____ the

smog has poisoned the air. This section reminds you what will happen to all plant
life _____ we don't prevent it. _____ the gardens are beautiful,
they leave you with a sobering message.

. . . .

ACTIVITY **2.14**

**Write a paragraph (or short paper) for your classmates on an experience
from your childhood when you made an adult very angry: a parent,
neighbor, boss, teacher, and so on. Relate how the situation was resolved
and how you felt about it.**

**When you complete your first draft, check your sentences to see how
you could improve your wording and sentence variety. Replace vaguely
worded phrases with more concrete ones, smooth out awkward sentences, shorten wordy sentences, and combine weaker sentences to form
compound and complex sentences.**

When you finish your second draft, share it with your classmates.

STUDENT FIRST DRAFT   *(How might some of the sentences in this draft be
improved?)*

I don't remember my dad spanking me very often. When he did, it was usually for something I said rather than something I did. I had a quick temper and smart mouth. They got
me in trouble sometimes. Once when I was fairly young, Dad had said he would get
me my favorite ice cream at the store. I couldn't wait until he got home so that I could
chow down on my favorite ice cream. He got home from the store. I rushed into the
kitchen. However, he had forgotten to get the ice cream. "You're a liar!" I shouted without thinking. "You're a big fat liar and I hate you!" Today I can't believe I actually said
that. He couldn't believe it then. He grabbed me and took me out back so fast my feet
never touched ground. Then he walloped me pretty good. I was really mad and cried for
a while. Then true to my nature, I was over it just as fast. I hadn't meant a word I'd said
to my dad. I knew I deserved what I got. Later that night he brought me some ice cream.
I guess he felt guilty for spanking me so hard, but he really shouldn't have felt guilty for
spanking me. He was too nice. He had a brat for a son. I ate all the ice cream.

. . . .

WRITING REVIEW
. . . .

**For your final paper of this unit, write to your classmates about one
person from your childhood who had a strong effect, positive or negative,
on your life: a parent or grandparent, brother or sister, friend or enemy,**

teacher, boss, priest, and so on. Write so that your classmates both get to know this person and your relationship with him or her. The purpose of your paper is for readers to understand how one person in your childhood (and perhaps continuing into the present) helped to shape your life in some important way(s).

For prewriting, first take your time thinking about different people in your childhood who were in some way important to you. Then select someone you would like to write about. Once you have decided, either do a free writing on the person for ten minutes or so or ask and answer questions as you did in Unit 1 to generate ideas for your paper.

When you finish your prewriting, write the first draft of your paper. Then consider the following questions for revision:

1. Have I described the person so that readers can visualize him or her in the way that I intended?

2. Have I presented plenty of examples throughout the paper to *show* readers what this person was (or still is) like?

3. Have I clearly revealed the relationship I have with this person? Have I provided examples that show readers this relationship? Will they clearly understand why I feel as I do?

4. Have I shown what effect this person has had on my life? How and where have I done this?

5. When reading my paper, will readers have a sense of moving from opening to middle to conclusion? How have I engaged their interest in the opening? What have I left them with in the conclusion?

6. Is my paper effectively paragraphed? Have I changed paragraphs as I moved to different points or ideas? Do I have any overly long paragraphs that need dividing or groups of short paragraphs that need combining? Are the sentences within each paragraph related?

7. How can I improve the wording of individual sentences to make them as smooth, clear, and structurally effective as possible? Can I replace any vague wording with more concrete language? Can I add a transition here or there to tie sentences or paragraphs together?

8. Reading the paper through the eyes of my classmates, what four or five questions might arise that I can answer in the next draft?

Read and evaluate your draft by applying the questions for revision. Then exchange drafts with a classmate and come up with four or five questions to share about his or her paper. When you are ready, write your second draft, continuing the evaluating/drafting process until you are satisfied.

STUDENT SAMPLE TOPIC SELECTION

Only one person comes strongly to mind when I think about childhood influences: my mom. She's the one. There's no one else I'd really want to write about. Dad's a nice guy, but Mom really raised us. This was an easy topic for me to choose.

STUDENT SAMPLE PREWRITING THOUGHTS

What do I want people to know about my mom? What a good person she is, how good a job she did of raising me, how she has helped other people, how she was both mom and dad in many ways. I'll include all that and provide examples.

What do I want people to know about our relationship? That it was good but that we are different people. That I've got a long way to go to be as good a person as my mom. That I kind of hold her up there as my model. Also that she probably doesn't know I feel this way because I've never told her.

What effect has she had on my life? Whatever good qualities I have, and there aren't that many, I feel I owe to Mom in some way. Whenever I have to make hard decisions or am tempted to do bad things, Mom's always there somewhere in my mind. I don't always do the right thing, but because of her at least I don't feel good about it later.

SAMPLE FIRST DRAFT

MOM

After having lived with my mother for over nineteen years, I'm an expert on her good and bad points. The trouble is, there's hardly anything to put down on the bad side, which makes her unusual for our family. I guess if there's anything bad to say about Mom it's that she's too good, which makes the rest of us suffer by comparison.

Mother's always been a hard worker. She raised four kids almost single-handedly, because my dad was on the road a lot as a trucker. She did all the cooking, cleaning, and washing for us, and when she wasn't doing housework, she was sewing us clothes or making jam. I can't ever remember her just sitting down doing nothing. Even watching television, she'd always be knitting a sweater or darning socks.

Mom is also very religious. She taught Sunday school for over ten years, and she made sure my two brothers, my sister, and I went to church every Sunday. She also lived her religion, tithing generously to the church, donating what she could to poorer families, and never speaking badly about other people. Religion never appealed to me the way Mom wanted it to, and she still prays for me today in hopes I'll get "right with the Lord," as she says.

One thing Mom has always done is stick up for all of us in the family. Growing up, my youngest brother Ned had his share of problems in school, and Mom was down at that elementary school seeing the principal or some teacher almost every week, making sure Ned was getting a fair shake. When Dad's union went out on a truckers' strike over wages, Mom spent as much time on the picket line as any trucker. And when I was having a bad time in junior high with some girls who picked on me, Mom had the nerve to go to every one of those girls' parents and talk to them. Mom always said that as long as a family sticks together, they can get through anything, and she has proved that to be true.

Most importantly, Mom preached to all of us to believe in ourselves and what we could do. She'd tell me, "Rhonda, there's nothing you can't do if you just set your mind to it. And don't be afraid to make mistakes. That's how you learn." Growing up with that kind of support, I always had confidence in myself, sometimes more than was justified. But if it wasn't for Mom's encouragement, I know I wouldn't be in college today. I hope I can do half as much for my own kids someday.

READINGS

WE'RE POOR

by Floyd Dell

1   That fall, before it was discovered that the soles of both my shoes were worn clear through, I still went to Sunday school. And one time the Sunday-school superintendent made a speech to all the classes. He said that these were hard times, and that many poor children weren't getting enough to eat. It was the first that I had heard about it. He asked everybody to bring some food for the poor children next Sunday. I felt very sorry for the poor children.

2   Also, little envelopes were distributed to all the classes. Each little boy and girl was to bring money for the poor, next Sunday. The pretty Sunday-school teacher explained that we were to write our names, or have our parents write them, up in the left-hand corner of the little envelopes. . . . I told my mother all about it when I came home. And my mother gave me, the next Sunday, a small bag of potatoes to carry to Sunday school. I supposed the poor children's mothers would make potato soup out of them. . . . Potato soup was good. My father, who was quite a joker, would always say, as if he were surprised, "Ah! I see we have some nourishing potato soup today!" It was so good that we had it every day. My father was at home all day long and every day, now; and I liked

that, even if he was grumpy as he sat reading Grant's *Memoirs*. I had my parents all to myself, too; the others were away. My oldest brother was in Quincy, and memory does not reveal where the others were: perhaps with relatives in the country.

3   Taking my small bag of potatoes to Sunday school, I looked around for the poor children; I was disappointed not to see them. I had heard about poor children in stories. But I was told just to put my contribution with the others on the big table in the side room.

4   I had brought with me the little yellow envelope, with some money in it for the poor children. My mother had put the money in it and sealed it up. She wouldn't tell me how much money she had put in it, but it felt like several dimes. Only she wouldn't let me write my name on the envelope. I had learned to write my name, and I was proud of being able to do it. But my mother said firmly, no, I must not write my name on the envelope; she didn't tell me why. On the way to Sunday school I had pressed the envelope against the coins until I could tell what they were; they weren't dimes but pennies.

5   When I handed in my envelope, my Sunday-school teacher noticed that my name wasn't on it, and she gave me a pencil; I could write my own name, she said. So I did. But I

was confused because my mother had said not to; and when I came home, I confessed what I had done. She looked distressed. "I told you not to!" she said. But she didn't explain why. . . .

6   I didn't go back to school that fall. My mother said it was because I was sick. I did have a cold the week that school opened; I had been playing in the gutters and had got my feet wet, because there were holes in my shoes. My father cut insoles out of cardboard, and I wore those in my shoes. As long as I had to stay in the house anyway, they were all right.

7   I stayed cooped up in the house, without any companionship. We didn't take a Sunday paper any more, but the Barry *Adage* came every week in the mails; and though I did not read small print, I could see the Santa Clauses and holly wreaths in the advertisements.

8   There was a calendar in the kitchen. The red days were Sundays and holidays; and that red 25 was Christmas. (It was on a Monday, and the two red figures would come right together in 1893; but this represents research in the World Almanac, not memory.) I knew when Sunday was, because I could look out of the window and see the neighbor's children, all dressed up, going to Sunday school. I knew just when Christmas was going to be.

9   But there was something queer! My father and mother didn't say a word about Christmas. And once, when I spoke of it, there was a strange, embarrassed silence; so I didn't say anything more about it. But I wondered, and was troubled. Why didn't they say anything about it? Was what I had said I wanted (memory refuses to supply that detail) too expensive?

10   I wasn't arrogant and talkative now. I was silent and frightened. What was the matter? Why didn't my father and mother say anything about Christmas? As the day approached, my chest grew tighter with anxiety.

11   Now it was the day before Christmas. I couldn't be mistaken. But not a word about it from my father and mother. I waited in painful bewilderment all day. I had supper with them, and was allowed to sit up for an hour. I was waiting for them to say something. "It's time for you to go to bed," my mother said gently. I had to say something.

12   "This is Christmas Eve, isn't it?" I asked, as if I didn't know.

13   My father and mother looked at one another. Then my mother looked away. Her face was pale and stony. My father cleared his throat, and his face took on a joking look. He pretended he hadn't known it was Christmas Eve, because he hadn't been reading the papers. He said he would go downtown and find out.

14   My mother got up and walked out of the room. I didn't want my father to have to keep on being funny about it, so I got up and went to bed. I went by myself without having a light. I undressed in the dark and crawled into bed.

15   I was numb. As if I had been hit by something. It was hard to breathe. I ached all through. I was stunned—with finding out the truth.

16   My body knew before my mind quite did. In a minute, when I could think, my mind would know. And as the pain in my body ebbed, the pain in my mind began. I knew. I couldn't put it into words yet. But I knew why I had taken only a little bag of potatoes to Sunday school that fall. I knew why there had been only pennies in my little yellow envelope. I knew why I hadn't gone to school that fall—why I hadn't any new shoes—why we had been living on potato soup all winter. All these things, and others, many others, fitted themselves together in my mind, and meant something.

17   Then the words came into my mind and I whispered them into the darkness:

"We're poor!"

18   That was it. I was one of those poor children I had been sorry for, when I heard about them in Sunday school. My mother hadn't told me. My father was out of work, and

we hadn't any money. That was why there wasn't going to be any Christmas at our house.

19   Then I remembered something that made me squirm with shame—a boast. (Memory will not yield this up. Had I said to some Nice little boy, "I'm going to be President of the United States"? Or to a Nice little girl: "I'll marry you when I grow up"? It was some boast as horribly shameful to remember.)

20   "We're poor." There in bed in the dark, I whispered it over and over to myself. I was making myself get used to it. (Or—just torturing myself, as one presses the tongue against a sore tooth? No, memory says not like that—but to keep myself from ever being such a fool again: suffering now, to keep this awful thing from ever happening again. Memory is clear on that; it was more like pulling the tooth, to get it over with—never mind the pain, this will be the end!)

21   It wasn't so bad, now that I knew. I just hadn't known! I had thought all sorts of foolish things: that I was going to Ann Arbor—going to be a lawyer—going to make speeches in the Square, going to be President. Now I knew better.

22   I had wanted (something) for Christmas. I didn't want it, now. I didn't want anything.

Questions for Analysis

1. What are the two main incidents that form the narrative? How does the first incident lead to the second one?

2. What is Dell's childhood perspective of his living situation? Find places in the narrative where he reveals this perspective.

3. Why does Dell choose the following details for his narrative: potato soup, the money envelope, his shoes?

4. What moment does the entire narrative build toward? How does Dell build tension in the narrative leading up to this moment?

What impact did Dell's sudden realization have on his life? What examples does he use to reveal this impact?

Why do you think Dell chose to write about this experience? What did he want to share with his audience? How did you react to the essay?

Vocabulary

arrogant (10), bewilderment (11), ebbed (16)

SCIENCE

by David R. C. Good

1   This morning at breakfast my ten-year-old daughter said that mockingbirds make one hundred seventeen different sounds. She was working in her science book, doing her last-minute homework. "One hundred seventeen?" I asked. It seemed impossible at first; then the more I thought about it, the more I listened to the chatter-boxes (I could hear them right there from the sink), the more I began to believe it was true. I've always thought they were amazing birds.

2   "So what else does it say about them?" I asked.

3   "About what?"

4   "About mockingbirds and how many sounds they make."

5   "No, Dad," she said. "While I was lying in bed this morning, I counted them." She said what she was studying was intestines, large and small, and did I know that my small ones would unravel to equal my height.

6   I didn't know that.

7   Science has always baffled me. I took Earth Science, a general science class, when I was sixteen. Earth Science was the science required for those of us who weren't going to go

anywhere. Most of my friends were going to go to Berkeley or UCLA to work in plastics and electricity, so they took chemistry and physics. As for the rest of us, those in Earth Science, I guess we were going to be working in dirt. Anyway, my complete memory of Earth Science is the day I had the class under my control. It was early in the spring semester and one of those rare moments in my life. I mean I could not make a bad joke. *No duds.* Of course the teacher didn't see it that way. You see he made the mistake of laughing at first. I don't remember his name, but I do remember he was young and inexperienced enough.

8 Anyway, we were studying astronomy, and things had gotten so bad that he finally had to stop the class to straighten me out. He threatened me with a trip to the dean or worse, and I could sense the guy was serious. I really never meant him any harm, and I knew when to quit. So I said I would and I meant it. Then he did the inexperienced thing and tried to draw me back into the discussion by asking in a most serious tone of voice a question related to his astronomy lesson.

9 "Now, David," he said. "What do we call the path a satellite follows around a planet when the path swings out wider at one end than the other?" He had me there, of course. I knew it was one of those questions to which he had just given the answer, an easy one, I guessed, but of course I hadn't been paying attention. I had been laying down one-liners. I had been preoccupied, and now the whole class was waiting, large gulps of laughter wallowing deep in their throats. They knew I was faced with the choice—give the simple answer and save my hide, or give the smart-assed one and see the dean.

10 "I can't say for sure," I said most seriously. The teacher was eyeing me for any sign of indiscretion, ready to cut me off at the first sign of a joke, "but I do remember you said it went around, not in a circle, but in the shape of *a frog's butt.*" The moment was there, then.

It was that perfect one, that moment of absolute stunned silence, that moment when everybody in the room knew the right answer, and I had led them all right up to it, so close that it took them that special moment to realize what I'd said. Then the laughter began, and I walked out of the room to spend the rest of that day and every fifth period for the rest of the year in the dean's office. There I got to know the dean's secretary by name and within a week I was handling special deliveries of emergency passes, passes to counselors, and passes for athletes to be released early for away games.

11 As for science, I was given credit (for staying away?) and allowed to pass to the next grade. Of course I was glad at the time. However, in the years since, there have been times when I've wondered what I missed out on while running summons for the dean: elliptical orbits, the length of intestines, the number of songs a mockingbird can sing.

Questions for Analysis

1. How does the opening of the essay tie in with the school experience the author relates? Why do you think he opened the essay as he did?

2. What things do we learn about the author from his behavior in Earth Science class? Why was he such a "wiseguy"?

3. Students have two audiences to consider: the teacher and the class. How do the two audiences create a conflict for Good?

4. Relate a school experience where you were more interested in the class's reaction than the teacher's. What was the result?

5. Reflecting on his experience in the last paragraph, what regrets does Good have? How does the concluding paragraph relate to the opening?

6. What, if anything, do you regret about some aspect of your high school experience?

7. Why do you think the author wrote about this particular experience? What audience may he have had in mind?

THE WOMAN WARRIOR

by Maxine Hong Kingston

1   My American life has been such a disappointment.

2   "I got straight A's, Mama."

3   "Let me tell you a true story about a girl who saved her village."

4   I could not figure out what was my village. And it was important that I do something big and fine, or else my parents would sell me when we made our way back to China. In China there were solutions for what to do with little girls who ate up food and threw tantrums. You can't eat straight A's.

5   When one of my parents or the emigrant villagers said, "Feeding girls is feeding cowbirds," I would thrash on the floor and scream so hard I couldn't talk. I couldn't stop.

6   "What's the matter with her?"

7   "I don't know. Bad, I guess. You know how girls are. 'There's no profit in raising girls. Better to raise geese than girls.'"

8   "I would hit her if she were mine. But then there's no use wasting all that discipline on a girl. 'When you raise girls, you're raising children for strangers.'"

9   "Stop that crying!" my mother would yell. "I'm going to hit you if you don't stop. Bad girl! Stop!" I'm going to remember never to hit or to scold my children for crying, I thought, because then they will only cry more.

10   "I'm not a bad girl," I would scream. "I'm not a bad girl. I'm not a bad girl." I might as well have said, "I'm not a girl."

11   "When you were little, all you had to say was 'I'm not a bad girl,' and you could make yourself cry," my mother says, talking-story about my childhood.

12   I minded that the emigrant villagers shook their heads at my sister and me. "One girl—and another girl," they said, and made our parents ashamed to take us out together. The good part about my brothers being born was that people stopped saying, "All girls," but I learned new grievances. "Did you roll an egg on my face like that when I was born?" "Did you have a full-month party for me?" "Did you turn on all the lights?" "Did you send my picture to Grandmother?" "Why not? Because I'm a girl? Is that why not?" "Why didn't you teach me English?" "You like having me beaten up at school, don't you?"

13   "She is very mean, isn't she?" the emigrant villagers would say.

14   "Come, children. Hurry. Hurry. Who wants to go out with Great-Uncle?" On Saturday mornings my great-uncle, the ex-river pirate, did the shopping. "Get your coats, whoever's coming."

15   "I'm coming. I'm coming. Wait for me."

16   When he heard girls' voices, he turned on us and roared, "No girls!" and left my sisters and me hanging our coats back up, not looking at one another. The boys came back with candy and new toys. When they walked through Chinatown, the people must have said, "a boy—and another boy—and another boy!" At my great-uncle's funeral I secretly tested out feeling glad that he was dead—the six-foot bearish masculinity of him.

17   I went away to college—Berkeley in the sixties—and I studied, and I marched to change the world, but I did not turn into a boy. I would have liked to bring myself back as a boy for my parents to welcome with chickens and pigs. That was for my brother, who returned alive from Vietnam.

18   If I went to Vietnam, I would not come back; females desert families. It was said, "There is an outward tendency in females," which meant that I was getting straight A's for

the good of my future husband's family, not my
own. I did not plan ever to have a husband. I
would show my mother and father and the
nosey emigrant villagers that girls have no outward tendency. I stopped getting straight A's.

Questions for Analysis

1. What particular incidences in the narra-
    tor's life make up the essay? How are
    they related?

2. When Maxine told her mother she got
    straight A's, why did her mother say,
    "Let me tell you a true story about a girl
    who saved her village"?

3. Why were girls treated differently than
    boys in Chinese families? What effect did
    this have on Maxine?

4. Why did Maxine decide not to ever have
    a husband? Why did she stop getting
    straight A's?

5. Why do you think the author wrote
    about her life as a Chinese girl? How
    do you think her childhood affected her?

6. Are girls treated differently than boys
    within your ethnic group? In what ways,
    if at all?

7. What was your reaction to the essay?
    What, if anything, did you learn?

Vocabulary

emigrant (5)

CLEAR DIRECTION

Successful voyages usually involve knowing where you are going and how you plan to get there. Writing voyages are no different. If you know where you want to go with a paper and have some idea of how to get there, you have an excellent start on accomplishing your purpose.

The direction for a piece of writing is provided by its *thesis:* the main idea the writer conveys about his or her topic. When readers ask themselves what the point of a particular article or essay is, they are asking about its thesis. An essay without a thesis is like a voyage without a clear destination; the vessel may drift aimlessly, leaving passengers (or readers) rather perplexed.

The writing emphasis in this unit is on thesis-directed essays. You will find the work you did in Unit 1 on topic sentence paragraphs particularly useful in structuring your papers. Unit 3 also takes you through the same basic writing process as the earlier units, introducing new writing skills and reinforcing previously covered ones. You are also encouraged to make adjustments in the writing process to suit your personal writing needs.

PREWRITING

For most writers, prewriting involves coming up with a topic and deciding what to do with it. It can also include generating ideas for the paper and a plan for presenting them. If this were a neat four-step process, it would answer in order these simple questions:

1. What am I going to write about?
2. What approach do I want to take?
3. What do I want to include in the paper?
4. How can I best organize my thoughts?

While most writers consider variations of these questions during prewriting, they don't necessarily do so in a neat linear fashion. Instead, they may start anywhere within the process and work backward or forward, deal with questions in tandem (like considering topic and approach simultaneously), give some questions (like topic selection) much thought and others (like organization) little or none, or they may not deal with all considerations consciously (like a writer discovering a topic approach while drafting).

For your prewriting activities in this unit, you will learn how to generate a potential thesis statement, and you will come up with ideas for your paper using a prewriting strategy called *brainstorming*. Rather than providing you a rigid ''how to'' guide for writing preparation, the prewriting activities give you options to try and then apply in ways you find useful for your writing.

THESIS STATEMENT

When you hear the term *thesis statement*, you may picture some kind of elevated, formal writing that sounds a bit intimidating. However, if someone asks questions about a paper you've written like, ''So what's your point?'' or ''What are you getting at?'', they are asking thesis-related questions. In reality, ''thesis'' is a simple writing concept that provides direction for all of us, whether we are writing informal letters (''Just writing to let you know what happened at school last week'') or a twenty-page research paper (''This paper will show that the hole in the ozone layer over the North Pole does not pose an environmental threat'').

With the kinds of writing you will be doing in this unit and throughout the text, it is important to decide what you want to do with a topic: the approach or the direction you'd like your essay to take. To help you accomplish this, it is useful to come up with a tentative thesis statement early in the writing process.

The following points will help you understand the thesis concept:

1. A thesis statement expresses the main idea you want to develop in a paper. It usually expresses your *viewpoint* on the topic.

2. Your thesis statement determines the way in which you develop a topic in an essay. You write your essay *in support* of your thesis.

3. Without a thesis, an essay lacks direction. There is no *controlling idea* to tie the paragraphs together and to help the reader understand the writer's intent.

4. There is no "right" or "wrong" thesis statement; it reflects the way a writer views a particular topic. The *effectiveness* of the thesis is usually determined by how well it is supported in the paper.

Here are examples of thesis statements students have used for a variety of topics. Notice that different writers use varied approaches to the same topic.

TOPIC	water beds
THESIS	Water beds are a health hazard to millions of users.
THESIS	Within ten years, water beds will make mattresses obsolete.
THESIS	For a healthy night's sleep, buy a water bed.
TOPIC	daylight saving time
THESIS	I'd like to live on daylight saving time all year around.
THESIS	For a nocturnal person, daylight savings is a disaster.
THESIS	Daylight savings has both advantages and disadvantages.
TOPIC	gun control
THESIS	Gun control laws are a threat to every law-abiding American.
THESIS	Gun control is the only way to reduce violent crime in America.
THESIS	The only effective gun control is the total elimination of handguns.
TOPIC	"The Cosby Show" TV program
THESIS	"The Cosby Show" was the best family comedy of the decade.
THESIS	"The Cosby Show" was a fantasy representation of life for black Americans.
THESIS	"The Cosby Show" was a great showcase for young black actors.

Deciding on a thesis for a particular paper is an important part of the writing process. Not only does the thesis direct your writing, it shapes your readers' perception of how you think or feel about a topic.

Whatever time it takes you to come up with the best thesis for a particular paper is well spent.

When thinking about a thesis for a specific topic, consider the following:

1. *How do you really feel about the topic?* Don't worry about how other people feel or how you think you *should* react or what approach might look best to readers. Your thesis should develop from your honest feelings about the topic.

2. *What is most important or most interesting about a topic?* For example, what is the most important thing that readers should get from a paper you would write on selecting a college major? Or what might interest readers most in a paper you are doing on great white sharks (their threat to humans? their voracious eating habits?)?

3. *What thesis could you do the best job of supporting in a paper?* No matter how strongly you feel about a particular viewpoint on a topic, your paper will run out of gas if you can't support your thesis effectively. For example, although you may feel strongly that there are forms of human life on other planets besides earth, you may find little evidence that would convince readers or help you write an effective paper.

ACTIVITY 3.1

For any five of the following topics, write a thesis statement expressing a definite viewpoint. Select a statement that you believe in and feel you could support in a paper.

EXAMPLE

TOPIC   a particular hobby (writing songs)

THESIS   It takes little talent to write country songs.

1. TOPIC   a particular town (_____)

   THESIS   _____

2. TOPIC   a particular team (_____)

   THESIS   _____

3. TOPIC   a particular TV program (_____)

   THESIS   _____

4. TOPIC   a particular job (_____)

5. TOPIC   a particular holiday (_____)

   THESIS   _____

6. TOPIC   a particular school (_____)

   THESIS   _____

7. TOPIC   a particular type of music (_____)

   THESIS   _____

8. TOPIC   a particular pastime (_____)

   THESIS   _____

9. TOPIC   a particular eating place (_____)

   THESIS   _____

10. TOPIC   a particular book or movie (_____)

   THESIS   _____

■ ■ ■ ■ ■ ■ ■ ■ ■ ■ ■ ■ ■

BRAINSTORMING

Another strategy for generating ideas for writing is called *brainstorming:* writing down any idea about a topic that comes to mind. Brainstorming is similar to free writing in that you associate ideas freely and discard nothing.

Brainstorming a topic is a good way to generate ideas for a paper as well as to get down thoughts and feelings that may help you decide on a thesis. Here are some basic suggestions for brainstorming a particular topic:

1. Write down everything that comes to mind about the topic without distinguishing main points, details, or examples.

2. List more items than you may ever use in a paper; do not discard any idea.

3. After you brainstorm a list of twenty or thirty entries, go over the list and identify main points and supporting details or examples, grouping similar entries together, discarding irrelevant information, and adding new information that you think of.

4. Turn your brainstormed list into a rough outline showing the relationship among the different entries and the order in which you'd like to include them in a paper.

A writer generated the following list of thoughts by brainstorming on the topic of jogging:

exhausting	becomes addictive
hard on the legs	lonely exercise
hard on the heart	hard on marriage
bad weather	expensive
too much time	injuries
bad on the back	overrated as exercise
bad on the feet	don't lose weight
boring	can't ever quit
other exercises better	makes everything sag
too competitive	painful

When she completed her brainstorming, it was clear how she felt about jogging, and she was ready to commit to a tentative thesis statement: *Jogging is an overrated form of exercise.* Next, she went over her list and created some order out of it by putting similar items together in categories:

1. hard on the body (foot, leg, and back injuries and heart problems)

2. not any fun (exhausting, boring, lonely, painful)

3. hard on relationships (too much time, addictive, too competitive)

4. overrated (don't lose weight, don't feel better, doesn't do more for you than walking)

5. better options (walking, tennis, racquetball, bicycling)

In reformatting her original list of brainstormed items, the writer found five main points to develop and a number of details and examples to put under each point.

ACTIVITY 3.2

With a partner, organize the following brainstormed list of entries in this manner:

1. **Put similar entries together, using numbers, letters, or arrows.**

2. **Locate potential main points for an essay, or create main points that are suggested by the brainstormed entries.**

3. **Match supportive entries (examples, details, illustrations) with the main points they support.**

4. **Make an informal outline, organizing the information in the best way for presenting it in an essay.**

TOPIC   apartments I used to live in

THESIS   The Poplar Apartments were an intolerable place to live.

BRAINSTORMED LIST

hot in summer	rats in apartments
flies everywhere	not enough hot water
flooding in winter	holes in walls
no place for kids to play	cold in winter
near-accidents in driveway	broken windows
filthy outside	dangerous wiring
smell from open dumpsters	gas stoves for heating
garbage strewn all over	kids sick in winter
coolers worked poorly	fights at night
faucets leaked	no landlord on premises
toilets backed up	prostitutes
floors in bad shape	drug trafficking
mildewed ceilings	police seldom came around
nothing got fixed	overflowing sewer
overcrowded apartments	loud music
hard to sleep	holes and cracks in linoleum
unsanitary place	thousands of cockroaches
dead animals under building	water heaters in kitchens
all one bedroom	gun shots
lots of nighttime drinking	poor insulation

■ ■ ■ ■ ■ ■ ■ ■ ■ ■ ■ ■

ACTIVITY *3.3*

Select a topic to write on considering the following:

1. **Select any topic that really interests you. (It may be one of the topics you worked on in Activity 3.1.)**

2. **Select a topic that you know something about.**

    Once you decide what you want to write about, consider the following:

1. **What group of people (reading audience) do you want to target? Who might be most interested in your topic?**

2. **What could your tentative thesis be for your paper: the main idea you want to share with readers?**

3. **What is your purpose in writing to this audience? What do you want to accomplish?**

STUDENT SAMPLE TOPIC/AUDIENCE/THESIS

As an architecture major, I'm finding my Building Designs class fascinating this semester. Since I've liked sketching houses and drawing different kinds of floor plans for my dreamhouse, I found the information in class on house designs particularly interesting. I think I'd like to write something about that.

My thesis approach and my topic go hand-in-hand. One thing is clear to me now, and that is that most houses could be designed a lot better to take into account the needs of homeowners. Most houses aren't as functional as they could be. That's what I'd like to write about as my main idea.

The audience I think I'd be writing for are future home owners. That could include my classmates. But I'd also like to have some architects and building contractors read the paper because they're the ones who influence home design. I'll write primarily for the architects and contractors, but I could also share the paper with classmates who may be interested. My writing purpose for the architects and contractors would be to get them to consider more functional designs for family homes.

TOPIC	house design
TENTATIVE THESIS	Most homes aren't designed to meet the needs of families.
AUDIENCE	Architects and building contractors, with classmates as secondary readers
PURPOSE	To have architects and building contractors see the limitations on the homes they're building and to consider more functional designs.

■ ■ ■ ■ ■ ■ ■ ■ ■ ■ ■ ■

ACTIVITY 3.4

Brainstorm a list of twenty to twenty-five ideas related to your topic. Write down anything that comes to mind. Your purpose is to generate some possible material for your paper; in addition, if you haven't already decided on a thesis, brainstorming may help you come up with one.

When you finish, look over your list to see what you might have in the way of main points, supporting details, and examples. If you think it would be helpful, rearrange your items in a rough outline, discarding what you're sure you won't use and adding anything useful you think of.

STUDENT SAMPLE

TOPIC   house design

BRAINSTORMED LIST

useless living rooms	tiny closets
cramped family rooms	little storage space
cramped kitchens	low ceilings

wasted laundry room space	wasted hall space
too many small rooms	wasted entry space
short drawers	cramped patios
bathrooms too big	unreachable shelves
eating/living areas separated	no counter space
bedrooms too big	tiny eating area

OUTLINE   *(ordered by importance, most to least)*

1. useless rooms (living room, laundry room)

2. overly cramped areas (family room, kitchen, closets)

3. inconveniences (separate eating/living areas, no counter space, unreachable shelves, short drawers, limited storage space)

4. wasted space (bedrooms, bathrooms, entry hall, hallways)

. . . .

FIRST DRAFTS

. . . .

Now that you have selected a topic, decided on a tentative thesis statement and writing audience, and brainstormed for ideas, the next step is to write your first draft. Before beginning, consider the following basic suggestions for organizing a "thesis-driven" paper.

Most writing, whether it is essays, letters, articles, or even essay exam answers, is organized roughly into three parts: the *opening* (or introduction), the *middle* (or body), and the *ending* (or conclusion). The length of each section and its content may differ widely from paper to paper and writer to writer, but the writer's intent in each part is fairly constant: (1) to establish contact with readers in the opening and introduce the topic in some way, (2) to say most of what has to be said about the topic in the middle paragraphs, and (3) to wrap up the paper in the ending and give readers a sense of conclusion.

As you write your first draft, consider doing the following:

1. In your opening, which may be a paragraph or two, engage your readers' interest in the topic. You may also present your thesis in the opening, wait to present it at the end, or develop your middle paragraphs to clarify your thesis for your readers. How and when you present your thesis depends on what seems best to you as you write the draft. The important thing is that your readers are clear on what the main point of your paper is.

2. Your middle paragraphs basically make the case for your thesis, explaining why you feel or think the way you do about the topic. For

example, if your thesis were "Today's college automotive program is high tech compared to even ten years ago," your middle paragraphs would convince readers this is true by presenting all the high-tech changes in the program. If your thesis were "The campus police cadets need a lesson in courtesy," your middle paragraphs would provide whatever evidence you had—personal experiences, observations, experiences of other students—to convince readers that the cadets in general behaved discourteously to students.

3. Your ending paragraph(s) wraps up your paper in a suitable manner based on what you've written to that point. If you haven't come out directly with your thesis, do so in your ending. You might sum up the main points of your paper, clarify your writing purpose for readers, or leave them with one last idea to ponder. You probably won't know what to write in your ending until you see how the rest of the paper develops. When readers finish your paper, they should feel a definite sense of conclusion.

ACTIVITY 3.5

Read the student draft "Returning to College" on page 71 and the essay "Black Wasn't Beautiful" on pages 90–92, and then answer these questions:

1. What is the topic of each essay? What is the essay's thesis—its main point? Where is it found?

2. What is accomplished in the opening of each essay? Where does the opening end and the middle paragraphs begin?

3. What is accomplished in the middle paragraphs? When do the writers move from paragraph to paragraph?

4. Where does the ending of each essay begin? What is accomplished in the ending?

ACTIVITY 3.6

Write the first draft of your paper. As you write, consider the following:

1. Keep in mind your thesis to provide a writing focus. Write your draft in support of your thesis.

2. Keep in mind your readers—the people you have decided to write for—and what you want to accomplish.

3. Move from opening to middle paragraphs to ending as you write your draft; have a purpose in mind for each section.

4. **Use your brainstorming ideas any way you wish, and feel free to change your thesis if you discover a better (more honest, more interesting, more easily supportable) approach for your paper.**

TOPIC   returning to college

AUDIENCE   people who are returning (or thinking of returning) to college after some years

RETURNING TO COLLEGE

After twenty years of mothering and being a housewife, I returned to college to finish up my degree and then go after a teaching credential. I hadn't been in college since 1966, nor had I set foot on a college campus. Now I was returning to the same college I'd left at the end of my sophomore year twenty years ago. I figured that there would be a lot of changes in college in the past twenty years, and I was preparing to enter a strange and alien world. Now that I'm over five weeks into the first semester, what really strikes me as strange is how little anything has changed.

Sure, there have been a few changes. There are more foreign students on campus than in the 1960s, and there are more people my age and older returning to school. Some buildings have been added (a new library wing, two new dorms, a new administration building), plus two new parking lots and a baseball stadium. And walking has replaced bicycles as the main mode of transport around campus. But other than that, I could be back in the sixties as easily as being on campus in the eighties.

First, the students have changed very little. A minority of students in my classes work really hard and are grade oriented, and a majority do what they must to slide by, just like in the sixties. There are still the cliquish fraternity and sorority types, the down-to-earth, friendly students, the oversized athletes, and the bookish loners.

Students still hang out in the same places: downstairs in the student union, in the study sections of the library, in the upstairs cafeteria, or on warm days, in the square between the cafeteria and bookstore. They even dress similarly to the sixties: guys in T-shirts, Levi's, and tennis shoes, and girls in culottes, stretch pants, Bermuda shorts, and short straight skirts. Most of the students seem nonpolitical and bent mainly on enjoying themselves, similar to the campus attitude during the early sixties.

But it's not just the students who are similar to their sixties counterparts. Teachers and teaching methods haven't changed much either.

For example, I have a biology lecture section in the main science lecture hall. When I enrolled for the course, the instructor was just listed as "staff," so I was shocked when Dr. Darmby strode up to his lectern and began lecturing nonstop, lickety-split for a full fifty minutes. This was the same Darmby I'd had twenty years ago, and neither he nor his teaching method had changed much. I was surprised to find that a number of the faculty were still teaching twenty years later, and it appeared that those who had stayed had hired clones of themselves to replace the retirees. The faculty was depressingly similar to the none-too-energetic group I'd remembered.

Earlier in the semester, I'd gone upstairs to eat in the cafeteria, and I even sat at the old table where our "gang" sat twenty years ago. I selected chicken-fried steak, potatoes, a green salad, and milk, not really thinking about what the food had been like before. Well, the chicken-fried steak was full of gristle, the potatoes were watery, the salad had wilted, and the milk was barely cool. I ended up leaving three-fourths of everything on my plate and kicking myself for not remembering how bad the food had been in the sixties. Another déjà vu experience.

With so much unchanged at Tabor College in twenty years, my adjustment to college life has been rather easy. In some ways I'm rather disappointed. I guess I was somehow hoping that everything would be elevated with time: brighter, more involved students, challenging, enthusiastic instructors, an electric political atmosphere, and even gristle-free chicken-fried steak. But things seem just about the same, except of course for me, who's now looking at life through forty-year-old eyes instead of twenty-year-old. And maybe that's the problem. As a twenty-year-old, I remember thinking college life was pretty wonderful and exciting, and I'm sure it feels the same for most of the first-time students here. Maybe all of the old excitement of being a college student is still here, but I'm too old to catch it.

■ ■ ■ ■ ■ ■ ■ ■ ■ ■ ■ ■ ■ ■

REVISIONS

Now that you have written your first draft, you have a good start on your paper. In fact, if you are like some writers, you may have "more" than just a first draft. As you were writing, you may have made some other changes in your draft—rewording a sentence you didn't like, moving another sentence to a better location, or catching and correcting a spelling or run-on error. Although this text doesn't encourage you to revise as you write a first draft, some writers do it naturally. If you are one of those, you may already be well into your second draft.

As you read your draft, consider the following revision questions:

1. Do I have an interesting opening? Will it engage my readers' interest? Does it clearly introduce the topic and present the thesis for the paper (if you so intended)? What can I do to make the opening clearer or more interesting?

2. Do my middle paragraphs clearly present all the reasons that I view the topic as I do? Have I provided good examples and details to support and clarify my reasons? Have I convinced readers of the truth (or accuracy or good sense) of my thesis by providing them all the necessary evidence they may need? What can I add or change to strengthen the support for my thesis in the middle paragraphs? (If you are having problems developing your middle paragraphs, see the following section on "Paragraph Development.")

3. Do I have a strong ending for my paper? Does it leave my readers with a good understanding of my purpose in writing to them? What could I do with my ending to make it more interesting or purposeful?

4. Have I paragraphed my paper effectively? Do I change paragraphs as I move from opening to middle to ending, and do I change paragraphs as I move to different points in my paper? Do I have any overly long paragraphs that need dividing or groups of short paragraphs that need combining or developing further? Have I used *transitions* to tie my ideas together within each paragraph?

5. Have I presented my ideas in the most effective order? Would anything (a sentence, a part of a paragraph, a whole paragraph) make better sense if I moved it to a different location?

6. What can I do to improve the wording of my sentences? Are there any sentences that seem to run on too long or that sound awkward? Does any particular wording sound stilted? Are there any sentences that don't make sense?

7. Read the draft one last time from the viewpoint of your readers. What four or five questions might the draft raise that you could answer in your next draft?

ACTIVITY 3.7

With a partner, read and evaluate the following student first draft, applying the revision questions. Then evaluate your own draft similarly, noting any changes you may make for the next draft. Also exchange papers with a classmate and note four or five questions that you want to ask the writer. When you are ready, write the second draft of your paper, and continue the drafting and evaluation process until you are satisfied with the final draft.

DOWN WITH JOGGING

For a while, my neighborhood was taken over by an army of joggers. They were there all the time: early morning, noon, and evenings. There were little old ladies in gray sweats, sleek couples in matching White Stag sweats and Adidas shoes, pot-bellied, middle-aged men with red faces, and even my friend Alex, who'd never exercised more than his beer-hoisting elbow. "Come on!" Alex urged me as he jogged by my house every evening. "You'll feel great."

Well, I had nothing against feeling great, and I figured if Alex could jog every day, anyone could. So I took up jogging seriously and gave it a good two months of my life, and not a day more. Based on my experience, jogging is the most overrated form of exercise around, and judging from the number of defectors from our neighborhood jogging army, I'm not alone in my opinion.

First of all, jogging is very hard on the body. Your legs and feet take a real pounding running around a track or down a paved road for two or three miles. I developed shin splints in my lower legs and stone bruises in my heels that are still tender. Some of my old lower-back problems that had been dormant for years also started flaring up. Then I read about a nationally famous jogger who died of a heart attack while jogging, and I had something else to worry about. I'm sure everyone doesn't develop the foot, leg, and back problems I did, and jogging doesn't kill hundreds of people, but if you have any physical weaknesses, jogging will surely bring them out, as they did with me.

Secondly, I got no enjoyment out of jogging, and few people stick with an exercise they don't enjoy. Jogging is boring. Putting one foot in front of the other for forty-five minutes isn't my idea of fun. Jogging is also a lonely pastime. Some joggers say, "I love being out there with just my thoughts." Well, my thoughts began to bore me, and most of them were on how much my legs hurt. If I can't exercise and socialize at the same time, I'm not interested.

And how could I enjoy something that brought me pain? What's fun about burning eyes, aching lungs, rubbery legs, and heavy arms? And that wasn't just the first week; it was practically every day for two months. I never got past the pain level, and pain isn't fun.

Jogging can have other negative spin-offs, too. It can be very bad on relationships. Husbands and wives start out as friendly jogging mates until hubby runs away from wife in a macho surge and thereafter only runs grudgingly at a "woman's" pace. Then there's the time involvement. Joggers run once or twice a day, thirty minutes to an hour at a time, along with the jogathons that take up the weekends. You've heard of golfing widows? Try jogging widows.

A friend of mine named Mildred started out as a three-time-a-week jogger three years ago. Harmless exercise. Today, she jogs thirty miles a week, runs in jogathons twice a month, subscribes to Jogger's Weekly, spends thousands a year on equipment and travel, and, not coincidentally, is no longer married.

But forget everything I've said. What about the great benefits of jogging, the ones that allow you to live longer, lighter, and happier than any nonjogger?

From my perspective, jogging is really overrated in those areas. I ran for two months and didn't lose a pound. The calories burn off very slowly when jogging, and the appetite, in my case, increased. I got my heart and respiratory system in better shape, but what a torturous way to do it. So many other exercises, including walking, accomplish almost the same results painlessly, so why jog? And the happier part? Jogging did not make me feel better, period. I didn't have more energy, I didn't look forward to the next day any more, I didn't spring up wide awake each morning. Jogging made me tired, sore, and irritable. And I can be all of those things without jogging.

I don't jog any more, and I don't think I ever will. I'm walking two miles three times a week at a brisk pace, and that feels good. I also play tennis and racquetball occasionally, and I bicycle to work when the weather is good. I'm getting exercise, and I'm enjoying it at the same time. I could never say the same for jogging, and I've found a lot better way to stay in shape. Anyone care to buy a pair of slightly worn size-six jogging shoes?

■   ■   ■   ■   ■   ■   ■   ■   ■   ■   ■

PARAGRAPH DEVELOPMENT

As a writer, how do you get from the beginning to the end of a paragraph? Fortunately, putting together the sentences for a paragraph is a relatively natural thing to do. Since we tend to think in associated thoughts rather than jump randomly from one idea to another, we also tend to develop paragraphs by connecting related ideas.

Writers develop their paragraphs and papers in the following ways:

1. *Through examples:* Writers provide examples to support their points.

   Maria had a lot of bad luck this semester. First, two of the classes she needed for her major were canceled. Then she lost out on her financial aid for the semester because she could only enroll in three classes. Then three days before finals she caught a bad case of the flu and was hospitalized for a week. She had to make special arrangements to take her finals during Christmas vacation, and therefore missed out on a family trip to Mazatlán. *(Four examples of Maria's bad luck.)*

2. *Through description:* Writers provide description to help readers visualize the material.

   The wrecked car was grotesque looking. The entire front end had been twisted around like a snake looking back at its tail. The front seat area looked as if it had been put in a giant vice and squeezed, and the seat itself had moved to the backseat. There was no glass in the front and side windows, and the tires were flattened. Luckily, no one was in the parked car when a runaway semi hit it on the shoulder of a steep mountain downgrade. *(Writer describes the "grotesque-looking" car.)*

3. *Through explanation:* Writers clarify their thoughts by explaining them.

   Harold is the "Pigpen" of the auto shop. Like Pigpen in the Charlie Brown cartoon, Harold naturally attracts dirt. After working on a car, he'll have grease and oil on face, his arms and hands, and all over his clothes. The lab instructor has quit checking out work overalls to Harold because he gets them dirty beyond cleaning. Harold's becoming a good mechanic, but he wears his work home with him. *(Writer explains how Harold is like Pigpen in the cartoon strip.)*

4. *Through providing reasons:* Writers tell their readers *why* they think as they do.

   You shouldn't practice hitting golf balls off the artificial turf at some driving ranges. With the proper golf swing, the club head drives down through the ball and into the grass, leaving a hole in the grass called a divot. With artificial turf set on concrete, you cannot drive the club head down through the ball, so you must resort to a shallower swing. Then when you get on grass, you tend to top the ball or hit it "thin" rather than driving through it. Hitting off artificial turf can mess up your golf swing and hurt your game. *(Writer provides reasons for not practicing on artificial turf.)*

5. ***Through supporting general statements:*** **Writers try to clarify general statements that would leave readers with a question.**

Hilda has been acting strange lately. *(What has she been doing?)*

Malcolm didn't enjoy the rap concert last night. *(Why not?)*

My dog has to have an operation. *(What's wrong with him?)*

Samantha has a way of making anyone smile. *(How does she do it?)*

The water polo team played its best game of the year. *(How did they do?)*

After three years of college, Luann is still unsure of herself. *(What's the problem?)*

My sister is always there for me. *(What does she do?)*

The "Fuzz Buster" is a great device for truckers. *(How does it work?)*

ACTIVITY 3.8

Choose two of the following topic sentences, and develop paragraphs using one or more of the methods just presented.

1. My classes this semester are _____ .

2. _____ is a great looking _____ .

3. I'm really looking forward to _____ .

4. My biggest problem right now is _____ .

5. Eating at _____ is _____ .

6. I never get tired of _____ .

■ ■ ■ ■ ■ ■ ■ ■ ■ ■ ■ ■ ■

ACTIVITY 3.9

Revise one or two of the following paragraphs by adding your own sentences to support each general statement that would probably raise a question with readers.

Michael is an excellent typist. He can already type faster than most professional secretaries. Besides that, he is extremely accurate. On timed tests, for every one-hundred words he types, he makes an average of only two errors. Perhaps best of all, he has a way of making his boss's letters sound better on paper than when she dictates them. Finally, Michael has his own unique typing style.

The campus is really nice looking. First there's the lovely fountain in the middle of central plaza. Then there's the beautiful landscaping everywhere. All of the buildings have the same Spanish-style architecture with rough-textured tan exteriors, red-tiled roofs, and dark-brown trim. Finally, there's the great natural setting that most colleges don't have.

Grandma Malone is full of energy for her age. She still loves to dance. In addition, she gives lectures at the college once a week. She also works outside in her yard almost every day. Finally, she always finds time for a special group of people.

. . . .

SENTENCE REVISION

In the last two units, you worked on improving first draft sentences by eliminating problems with wordiness, awkward phrasing, poor word choice, and vague language. Another problem that may creep into first draft sentences is nonparallel structures, which are covered in this section. In addition, you will continue working on a variety of sentence structures, including sentences with *relative clauses*.

PARALLEL CONSTRUCTION

One sentence problem that leads to awkward and confusing wording involves *parallel construction*. It is not uncommon for a writer to join two or more groups of words together in a sentence. For the sentence to be clearest, these groups of words need to be very similar, or *parallel*, in structure. Here is an example of a sentence with parallel construction. The groups of words joined together are underlined.

EXAMPLE   Last night we <u>ate outside</u>, <u>sat by the river</u>, and <u>listened to the frogs</u>.

The underlined groups of words are parallel because they follow the same structure: past tense verb followed by modifying words. Now read the same sentence with some problems with parallelism.

EXAMPLE   Last night we <u>ate outside</u>, <u>by the river sat</u>, and <u>listening to the frogs</u>.

This sentence is very awkward. In the second group of words, the order of the past tense verb and the modifying words is changed, and in the last group, the verb has the wrong ending. The resulting sentence would bother any reader.

Here are other examples of sentences with parallelism problems followed by revised corrected versions.

EXAMPLE   Joleen is <u>tall</u>, <u>slender</u>, and <u>brown hair</u>. (Brown hair *isn't parallel with* tall *and* slender.)

REVISED   Joleen is tall and slender and has brown hair.

EXAMPLE	I leaped across the creek, landed on the bank, and back in the water did slip. *(Back in the water did slip is not parallel with the first two parts.)*
REVISED	I leaped across the creek, landed on the bank, and slipped back into the water.
EXAMPLE	Swimming, jogging, and a tennis game are good forms of exercise. *(A tennis game is not parallel with swimming and jogging.)*
REVISED	Swimming, jogging, and tennis are good forms of exercise.
EXAMPLE	The MG is metallic blue, has four speeds, and racy. *(Racy isn't parallel with the other parts.)*
REVISED	The MG is metallic blue, has four speeds, and is racy.

ACTIVITY 3.10

The following sentences have problems with *parallel construction*. Rewrite each sentence and improve the wording by correcting the nonparallel part of the sentence.

EXAMPLE	John looked out the window, scanned in all directions, and no one.
REVISED	John looked out the window, scanned in all directions, and saw no one.

1. I enjoy skating, reading, to swim, and the sport of hockey.
2. Claude is short, stout, intelligent, brown eyes, and generosity.
3. We walked through the field, finding hundreds of acorns, and bring them home in baskets.
4. You may check out the periodical or in the library you may read it.
5. Doing dishes, cleaning her room, homework, to baby-sit her brother, and the flossing of her teeth were chores Eileen avoided.
6. Mildred walked into the class, does one-hundred push-ups, and out the door.
7. You can chew gum in Kaser's class, but gum chewing in Bowie's class you can't do, and no gum in Borafka's class.
8. Not only is college harder than high school but also greater is the cost and more is the difficulty.
9. The news about the earthquake was terrible, the reports being shockingly graphic, the death count is tragically high, and more bodies being uncovered still.
10. Georgia is willing to organize activities for her sorority but no more tutoring pledges for their finals, and not willing to chair the pledge meetings.

ACTIVITY 3.11

The following paragraph contains sentences that need revising. Rewrite these first draft sentences to make them smoother and clearer. Look for wordiness, awkward phrasing, poor word choices, misplaced modifiers, and problems with parallelism.

EXAMPLE   The girl is exploding her gum in pigtails.

REVISED   The girl in pigtails is popping her gum.

Hanna thought the fair sucked. She belongs to the Future Farmers of America, and a steer she had to be judged. The steer didn't place in the top ten, and no award money. When she brought it to the tent to be auctioned off, it breaks loose and running around the livestock area. She finally gathered it in and took it back to the auction. There were only two men of the cowboy type left to bid on the animal, so the steer went for a lower amount of money than if there had been more men of the cowboy type to bid. The steer it was sold for $350, but Hanna was just glad to be of it rid. She took the $350, bought a piglet, raised it to a sow of full growth, bringing it to the fair the next year, and wins grand prize.

Compare your revisions with a classmate. Be prepared to share them with the class.

■ ■ ■ ■ ■ ■ ■ ■ ■ ■ ■ ■

ACTIVITY 3.12

The following first draft sentences need revising. The sentences have problems with wordiness, awkward phrasing, poor word choices, and misplaced modifiers. Revise and rewrite the sentences to make them smoother and clearer.

EXAMPLE   When I work this summer at a job, I'm going to save my money for a car that is used.

REVISED   When I work this summer, I'm going to save my money for a used car.

1. One person I'll always remember and never forget is a girl named Cloretta.

2. It takes a special person who can deal with the many problems faced daily by an automotive mechanic to be one.

3. I have been learning my boys, two of them, to swim, but they haven't learned yet.

4. My best friend I ever had was not a person that I even liked to begin with.

5. The trees are easy to see if you go through the sidewalk.

6. The tree is full of golden leaves, and there are some leaves that are about to fall and about to announce that fall is almost upon us.

7. When buying a used car, the first thing you do is to find a lot of used cars to look at.

8. The game of golf can be conducted with the whole family in assemblage.

9. She is the type of person whom you can tell secrets to and not worry about spreading of those secrets.

10. In the profession of boxing, the price of successfulness is often physical damage that could last a lifetime or even less.

11. The taillights and turn signals are together, red being the taillights and yellow the turn signals, the taillight above the turn signal.

12. The Volkswagen was a vast growth in Germany in the 1940s.

13. The next step is for you to go over every one of your sentences and try to find different ways that you can improve each one to make better sentences.

14. It was with immense difficulty that we affirmatively located the establishment selling foods of a fried nature.

15. Lonette couldn't find a way that was best for her to study for the biology test that covered over four chapters and over 100 pages of material.

▪ ▪ ▪ ▪ ▪ ▪ ▪ ▪ ▪ ▪ ▪ ▪

COMPLEX SENTENCES WITH RELATIVE CLAUSES

Another useful type of complex sentence involves clauses beginning with the relative pronouns *who, whom, whose, which,* and *that*. *Relative pronouns* differ from regular pronouns (*he, she, we, they,* and so on) in their function. A relative pronoun directly follows the word it replaces and introduces a modifying clause, while a regular pronoun replaces a word so that it isn't unnecessarily repeated in a sentence. In the following examples of complex sentences, the relative clauses are underlined:

EXAMPLES   The man who borrowed your lawnmower moved to Alaska.

Here on the table are the books that you left at my house.

The math problem that Joan had trouble with is puzzling everyone.

The men who own the fruit stand are selling some beautiful nectarines.

That blue Mazda is the car that I'd like to own someday.

Ralph picked the watermelon that was the largest and ripest.

The woman whose money you found lives in Paris.

Hanna's umbrella, which she bought for $30, has a hole in it.

The students who did well on the geology final all studied together.

As you can see, the underlined clauses beginning with *who, which, that,* and *whose* describe or identify the word directly before them. Here is how the relative pronouns are used.

WHO	used with *people*	(The child who ate the gooseberries got sick.)
WHOM	used with *people**	(The plumber whom you sent to my house was expensive.)
WHOSE	used with *people*	(The girl whose book was lost is in the library.)
THAT	used with *people*	(The family that lives next door moved.)
	used with *things*	(The magazine that you subscribe to is terrific.)
WHICH	used with *things*	(The "L" Street route, which is lined with trees, is very direct.)

ACTIVITY *3.13*

Complete the following complex sentences with your own words. Underline the relative clause in each sentence.

EXAMPLE   The man who lives behind us _____ *mows his lawn at night.* _____

1. The alligator that _____

2. She was the actress who _____

3. The only students who _____

4. Your new toaster, which _____

5. That new teacher whom you _____

6. The rock group that _____

7. I like a hamburger that _____

8. Please return my stamp collection, which _____

9. The kind of dog that _____

10. The movie star whose _____

11. I really prefer a doctor who _____

To punctuate relative clauses correctly, follow these basic rules:

1.   Never use commas with relative clauses beginning with *that*:

The students who sit in back of the room are very talkative.

I'd like to see the watermelon that weighs over fifty pounds.

---

* *Whom* is used instead of *who* when *followed* by the *subject* of the clause. The man whom *you* introduced is famous. The speaker whom *we* met was very arrogant. The teacher whom *the students* admire is Ms. Alvarado. When *who* is used, it is the *subject* of the clause: The man *who* bought our car was from Italy. The girl *who* took your seat doesn't intend to move.

2. **If a *who* or *which* clause is needed to identify clearly the word it modifies, don't set it off with commas.**

The men <u>who work for my aunt</u> live in Trenton. (Who work for my aunt *identifies the men.*)

The directions <u>which you gave us</u> were easy to follow. (Which you gave us *identifies the directions.*)

I'd like to meet the woman <u>who painted that strange picture.</u> (Who painted that strange picture *identifies the woman.*)

3. **If the word modified by a *who* or *which* clause is clearly named or identified, the clause is set off by commas.**

Mary Garcia, <u>who owns the dress shop on "G" Street</u>, is my neighbor. (Mary Garcia *clearly names the person.*)

The Golden Gate Bridge, <u>which spans San Francisco Bay</u>, is painted annually. (Golden Gate Bridge *clearly names the bridge.*)

The new fish market on Oliver Avenue, <u>which opened its doors last Friday</u>, specializes in shellfish. (New fish market on Oliver Avenue *clearly identifies the market.*)

Matt Golden, <u>who drives a milk truck</u>, married Emma Blue, <u>who lives on his route.</u> (Matt Golden *and* Emma Blue *clearly name the people.*)

■ ■ ■ ■ ■ ■ ■ ■ ■ ■ ■   ■

ACTIVITY 3.14

Put commas in the following sentences that need them. Mark C in front of any sentence that doesn't need a comma. Remember, only use commas with *who* and *which* clauses where the modified word is clearly named or identified.

EXAMPLES   __*C*__ The man who sits next to me in biology always smells like fish.

           __*C*__ Randy Pitts, who sits next to me in French, wears cologne.

1. _____ The librarian who wears her hair in a ponytail is an avid reader.

2. _____ Emma Goldberg who wears her hair in braids only reads cookbooks.

3. _____ The fish that you caught in the Eel River were delicious.

4. _____ Cutthroat salmon which are mainly found in Alaskan lakes have beautiful red coloring.

5. _____ I'd like you to meet Farnsworth Wormwood who has set many breath-holding records.

6. _____ All of the girls who performed in last night's musical sang off-key.

7. _____ Millie Jones and Alicia Barron who are stepsisters look like they could be blood sisters.

8. _____ Half of the meatloaf that we were saving for dinner was eaten by our cat.

9. _____ Mom's famous rhubarb pie recipe which she shares with no one was stolen from her recipe box.

10. _____ The ivy that is growing across the back fence is full of aphids.

11. _____ The new branch manager of the Knoxville Bank of America who is also a professional musician has been bald since he was eighteen.

12. _____ Teddy Hargrove who used to baby-sit for the family that lives on the corner of Peach and Alcorn drives a 1986 Buick Seville which was General Motors' best-selling car for the year.

■ ■ ■ ■ ■ ■ ■ ■ ■ ■ ■ ■ ■ ■

COMBINING SENTENCES REVIEW

Here is a quick review of what you have learned about sentence combining:

1. You combine sentences in a draft only when the newly created sentence is an improvement over the sentences you combined.

2. When looking for combining possibilities, check your drafts for patches of short sentences and for sentences that have almost identical structures. If you find yourself describing just one detail or one action in each sentence, you may have some combining possibilities. (Example: Joan is bright. She is studious. She is romantic.)

3. So far, you have learned three ways to combine sentences:
   a. by eliminating repeated words, moving modifiers in front of words they describe, and grouping similar words or phrases and joining them with *and, or,* or *but*
   b. by combining complete sentences with coordinate conjunctions (*and, or, but, so, far, yet*) to form compound sentences
   c. by combining complete sentences with subordinate conjunctions (*when, as, before, although, because, unless, since, where,* and so on) to form complex sentences

ACTIVITY 3.15

Combine the following sentences to form single sentences using the combining methods you have learned.

EXAMPLE   The bed is below the picture. It has a walnut headboard. It is a single bed.

REVISED   The single bed with the walnut headboard is below the picture.

EXAMPLE   Jane got to the museum early. She still had to wait in line for an hour.

REVISED   Jane got to the museum early, but she still had to wait in line for an hour.

EXAMPLE   Sam had a good time at the drag races. He thought they would be boring.

REVISED   Sam had a good time at the drag races, although he thought they would be boring.

1. The gymnast was short. She was slender. She was strong for her size. She was determined.

2. The seats were slashed. They were in the back of the theatre. A gang of girls did it. They did it maliciously.

3. I met a man on the train. He was very friendly. He was very tall. He was going to Memphis. He was from Cleveland.

4. Marge was having trouble breathing. She went to the infirmary. The doctor kept her there overnight. He wanted to observe her.

5. We are planning on taking a ferry to Falcon Island. Our plans for Saturday could change. They could stay the same.

6. Jacques often missed class. It was history. His instructor seldom noticed. Jacques sat in the back of the room. He was very quiet.

7. Marsha was tired of wearing her shirt. It was an old sweat shirt. She bought a new one. It was just like her old one.

8. The large sailboat battled the wind for hours. It was off the coast of North Carolina. It finally capsized. No one was hurt.

9. Gilda was awakened by thunder. She couldn't go back to sleep. She tossed and turned. She did this until morning.

10. Max was a great clown. Holly was a great clown too. Ralph was a lousy clown. Marvin was a lousy clown. They all had fun.

■ ■ ■ ■ ■ ■ ■ ■ ■ ■ ■ ■ ■

ACTIVITY 3.16

Write a paragraph or short paper for your classmates about one thing you like (or dislike) about the neighborhood (or house or apartment or dorm) you live in, including your suggestions for improving the situation.

When you finish your first draft, read each sentence carefully to see if it might be improved. Reword sentences to eliminate wordiness, awkward phrasing, vague language, or nonparallel structures, and combine sentences to improve sentence variety. Are you finding any use of complex sentences with relative (*who, which, whose, that*) clauses? Are you using transitions to write a second draft to share with classmates?

SAMPLE STUDENT PAPER

The thing I like least about the apartments I live in is the topless dumpster sitting in front of the west bank of apartments. First, it creates a bad smell. In the summer when it is full of garbage and used diapers, a putrid odor sweeps across the apartments when the afternoon breeze comes up. Second, it is too small to accommodate a week's supply of trash. The garbage that gets piled up on top falls out, and dogs and the wind scatter it all over the driveway and lawn. By Friday before pickup time, the place is a littered mess.

The worst problem is the flies. The garbage in the open dumpster attracts thousands of flies in warm weather, and they take up residence at the apartments. If you are outside, you constantly have to swat them off your face and body. They also find their way indoors, congregating in the kitchen while you eat and attacking your face while you sleep at night. From May to September, you can always hear flies buzzing somewhere in the apartment.

Obviously, the apartments need a new dumpster, one that is covered to keep the flies away and the stench in, and one that is large enough to hold a week's worth of garbage. It should also be moved to the east side of the apartments so that the breeze will carry the odor away from the buildings. If the owner isn't willing to pay a little more for a decent covered dumpster, I think the health department should be called.

■ ■ ■ ■ ■ ■ ■ ■ ■ ■ ■

WRITING REVIEW

■ ■

For your final writing assignment, you will apply what you have learned to this point, which will help you write an interesting and effective paper.

Select a writing topic that follows these considerations:

1. **It would be of interest to incoming freshman at your college—your writing audience for this paper.**

2. **It interests you.**

3. **You are knowledgeable about it.**

After you have selected a topic, do some type of prewriting to generate ideas: asking and answering questions, free writing, brainstorming, or a combination of things. Also decide on a tentative thesis—the main idea you want to convey to readers. Finally, decide on a purpose for writing to your audience of incoming freshmen. What do you hope to accomplish?

STUDENT SAMPLE THOUGHTS

What could I write that would be of interest to incoming freshmen? I could write on what kind of expenses to plan on, but that doesn't interest me that much. I could warn them about some of the teachers not to take or some good teachers to take. Nah. They can find that out for themselves as I did.

One struggle I had was coming up with a major, and I changed it a couple of times. I've got a definite viewpoint about that—that students shouldn't be rushed into selecting a major before they're ready—because that's what happened to me. I think I'd like to write about selecting a major, and it is an important topic for most incoming freshmen.

My purpose, I guess, would be to convince students not to get railroaded into selecting a major prematurely and to warn them that they might feel pressure to do that.

TOPIC	choosing a major for college
AUDIENCE	incoming freshmen to this college
TENTATIVE THESIS	Selecting a major is important, so take your time and make a wise decision.
PURPOSE	To convince students not to succumb to the pressure of selecting a major before they're ready, and perhaps to give them some advice on how to select a major.
PREWRITING	I think I'll brainstorm some ideas before writing my first draft.

BRAINSTORMED LIST

counselor pressure
parent pressure
student pressure
self-inflicted pressure
not knowing majors
not knowing jobs leading from
    majors
you have time
don't try to please
don't be afraid to change
not knowing what professions entail
worrying about courses

having little knowledge of different
    fields
not knowing what you're good at
still influenced by parents' desires
skeptical of aptitude tests
skeptical of high school counselor's
    advice
talk to professionals in field
talk to teachers
do some research
put everything on hold
let major come to you

When you've done your prewriting work, write the first draft of your paper keeping the following in mind:

1. **Let your thesis help direct your writing. Write your paper in ways that support your main idea.**

2. **Have a sense of opening, middle, and ending as you write. Get your readers' attention in the opening. Why should they read further?**

3. **Keep your audience and what you hope to accomplish with them in mind as you write.**

4. **Use your prewriting in any manner you wish, and feel free to add things you never considered in your prewriting. The drafting process itself helps generate ideas.**

SELECTING A MAJOR

Everyone tells you to get a major in college as soon as possible: counselors, advisors, parents. That way you'll have direction throughout your college career, and you won't waste time taking classes you don't need.

Like a good freshman, I listened to people and selected a major as soon as I got to college: pre-optometry. My girlfriend's father recommended it. I liked the idea of being called "doctor," and I wouldn't have to go to school nearly as long as an MD. Did I have any idea what optometrists really did? Not actually. Choosing a major before I was really ready was a big mistake.

As I progressed through my first two years, I dutifully took every math and chemistry class required and ignored most of the general ed requirements since I wouldn't need them for a BS degree to transfer to the optometry school I wanted to go to. I stuck to my pre-optometry schedule, happy to have a major and the "direction" that many of my friends still lacked.

However, something happened near the end of my sophomore year. I started thinking for myself a little. I began wondering what optometrists really did, and I arranged to meet an optometrist friend and spend a day with him at an eye clinic. I'd never been so bored in my life. The work was very routine, and there appeared to be no challenge or excitement to the job. I began to have real doubts about my major, and I felt guilty about that.

During this same time, I was taking a biology class that had me excited. I was learning a lot about DNA, genetic research, and the career opportunities for doing really meaningful work in medical research. I was getting excited about genetics from the work I was doing in the lab and from talking to researchers rather than from some vague career notion that I'd had as a seventeen-year-old. For the first time, I was ready to declare a major.

So how did a change in major affect me? First, it cost me an extra undergraduate year and an extra year of expense. I have to take two semesters of general ed requirements I'll need to graduate, and then in my fifth year I'll take biology major courses exclusively. I was also made to feel guilty by my dad, who tried to talk me out of changing majors, and my counselor, who told me, "Most students have doubts about their majors from time to time. Hang in there!" Bad advice that I didn't take.

From this experience, I'd say the worst thing a person can do is to declare a major because he or she feels pressured to do it. Many seventeen- and eighteen-year-old college freshmen aren't ready to make this decision, and counselors and parents should accept this. It makes a lot more sense for undecided students to get their general ed requirements out of the way and take that time to find out more about what interests them. Sometimes taking a lot of courses from different disciplines is the best way to "shop" for a possible major.

The one positive thing from the experience is that I did change majors to something I liked rather than stick out my first choice. I feel really good about my schooling and my future for the first time. So if someone does feel stuck in a prematurely selected major, my advice is that it's better to change majors and spend another year in school than to stick with a major you don't feel good about.

In the end, I was the only person who could ultimately decide what I wanted in a major and a career, and I was the only one who had to live with my decision. So don't let anyone pressure you into selecting a major before you're ready, and if you feel at some point like changing majors, don't feel guilty about it. It may be the best decision you ever make.

When you finish your draft, read it over and apply the following questions for revision. If you'd like a second opinion, exchange drafts with a classmate or two, bringing up questions with the writer that their draft raises for you. When you are ready, write your second draft, and continue the evaluating and drafting process until you are satisfied.

1. Does my opening introduce the topic clearly and engage my readers' interest? Is my thesis clear (if you decided to include it in your opening)? Do my readers have an idea of the importance of the topic to them?

2. What reasons have I presented to support my thesis? Have I provided good examples to substantiate these reasons and make the paper interesting? Have I included my own experiences (and/or those of others) so that readers can see where I get my viewpoint?

3. Is my paragraphing effective? Does each paragraph develop a particular idea, point, or example well, and are the sentences all related? Do I use transitions to tie my thoughts together? Do I change paragraphs as I move to new points?

4. Do I have a clear ending? What do I accomplish with my conclusion? What of value have I given my readers?

5. Do I have sentences that aren't as clear, smooth, or strong as I'd like? How could I reword or combine some sentences to improve them?

6. Have I organized my ideas well? Could any sentence or paragraph be more effectively located?

7. As I read the draft through my readers' eyes, what four or five questions might it raise that I could answer in the next draft?

READINGS

VICTIMS OF THE AGE OF PROSPERITY

by Donald Murray

1   The students are back in school but not I. I came to teaching late and I'm leaving early, well, slightly early. First the no-necks return, the football players in cut-off T-shirts and cut-off shorts, walking with rehearsed menace, their arms hung away from their sculptured torsos. How few mirrors they must pass without posing.

2   Then the freshman camp counselors, the campus politicians, the fraternity and sorority insiders, tans by Wianno, uniforms by North Conway. Then the freshmen and the freshwomen, their parents, proud, worried, relieved, looking at their watches and kissing goodbye at the same time.

3   At last the upperclass scholars, the hope of the future, heads unbalanced by huge earrings on only one side; wearing clothes left to rot in Cuban mountains by Castro generations ago; sporting skin heads and rooster heads and swooped skulls and pink hair. They swirl around, speak no language taught in school and are rarely caught carrying a book. It is easy to despair.

4   But I have seen beneath their disguises for years, and I am a bit sad they will not write for me this fall semester, and I will not sit reading and listening as they come, one by one, unable to keep their masks from slipping bit by bit.

5   As they write and reveal themselves to themselves on the page, their secrets will be revealed. Behind the sophistication is innocence—and fear and hope and longing and pain and a thirst for the answers to the questions we have always asked and an idealism that may not be ours but is real to them, embarrassing for them to admit and nothing less than inspiring to observe.

6   They do not appear to be like us, and that can spark fear and anger and worry and even disgust—some would like nothing more than to inspire disgust in someone of our age. We must remember that these college students are the survivors of wars most of us do not know, and these young veterans deserve our understanding, compassion and respect.

7   Many are the victims not of Depression but of a prosperity that brings its own aching hunger. To have a car, a computer, a portable compact disc player and speakers that can crack ledge, to wear the correct sneakers and have been at the right beach does not bring peace—or happiness or security or comfort.

8   They are often surprised to discover that and such a pain may be all right. A little—even a great—discomfort may be just fine in university students. It may spark questions that will bring the answers we need. Certainly, our generation cannot be smug about our values, whatever they are.

9   Our children—or our children's children—have emigrated from a world far different from ours. At an educational meeting to plan for the future of the study of reading, writing and language, the participants were told that 93 percent of the students in elementary school right now come from homes that are radically different from the imaginary environments for which our curriculums are designed. Ninety-three percent!

10   Five students out of 25 or more in the classrooms I visit live with their biological parents, and the teacher knows that some of those marriages will break up next year or the year after. A "normal" home is now abnormal.

11   I personally know of several parents who have left town to live with companions—and left teenagers alone and unsupervised in the house—for years. Many of my students come from a world that seems far different from—and often far harsher than—my Depression, prewar years.

12   My last freshman section was composed of well-educated—and often well-heeled (a historic cliche that comes from a time when you had old shoes resoled if you were lucky)—young people who have survived in a suburban world that seems to deny reality and therefore makes dealing with it all the more difficult. They did not live on the street. They lived in homes that were supposed to look stable and, indeed, have the appearance of happiness, success and belonging.

13   I only know a little of the lives of these freshmen, but in one section alone I had a glimpse behind their premature sophistication. One student had to miss several classes for the latest in a series of difficult operations. Another

gave an anniversary present to her parents as she left for school. They rejected it, telling their daughter their marriage was over—a common freshman trauma. A student leaves for college and the parents take off—some don't even tell their children where they have gone for weeks or months. Other students spent their first semester on the phone playing counselor to parents who were thinking of breaking up.

14   Two students had friends who tried suicide—one made it. Five—that I knew of—had a parent, a sibling, or a close friend institutionalized for drug treatment. A student, whose mother died when he was 15, lived in the homes of friends or slept on the floor where he worked for most of the last two years of high school, although his father was a successful businessman.

15   None of the stories surprised me. I'd heard them all before. Your children, perhaps your grandchildren, are survivors. Most of them are not immigrants, exploited in mills, but will make it as those who came before us made it.

16   This fall I'll smile at some of their get-ups, get angry at their rudeness, worry at examples of stupidity, but I hope I will remember the struggles they have had to get this far. I'll remember—I hope—that they are remarkably like I was at their age—scared, eager, rude, impatient, full of concerns and empty of knowledge, clumsy, idealistic and young, wonderfully young.

Questions for Analysis

1. What is the topic of the essay? What is the essay's thesis? Where is it found?

2. What are the main points of support for the thesis? What evidence is provided for each point?

3. What comparisons does Murray make between today's college students and those of his generation? What is the purpose of the comparisons? Do you agree with him?

4. Analyze the opening and conclusion of the essay. What is accomplished in each? How does each affect you? How do they tie together, if at all?

5. What audience might Murray be writing for? What is his purpose in writing the essay? How well is the purpose accomplished?

6. Compare your own experiences with those of Murray's students. How are they similar or different? Do you agree with the essay's thesis? Why?

BLACK WASN'T BEAUTIFUL

by Mary Mebane

1   In the fall of 1951 during my first week at North Carolina College, a black school in Durham, the chairman's wife, who was indistinguishable from a white woman, stopped me one day in the hall. She wanted to see me, she said.

2   When I went to her office, she greeted me with a big smile. "You know," she said, "you made the highest mark on the verbal part of the examination." She was referring to the examination that the entire freshman class took upon entering the college. In spite of her smile, her eyes and tone of voice were saying, "How could this black-skinned girl score higher on the verbal than some of the students who've had more advantages than she? It must be some sort of fluke." I felt it, but I managed to smile my thanks and back off. For here at North Carolina College, social class and color were the primary criteria used in deciding status. The faculty assumed light-skinned students were more intelligent, and they were always a bit nonplussed when a dark-skinned student did well, especially if she was a girl.

3   I don't know whether African men recently transported to the New World considered themselves handsome or, more important, whether they considered African women beau-

tiful in comparison with native American Indian women or immigrant European women. But one thing I know for sure: by the 20th century, really black skin on a woman was considered ugly in this country. In the 1950s this was particularly true among those who were exposed to college. Black skin was to be disguised at all costs. Since a black face is rather hard to disguise, many women took refuge in ludicrous makeup.

4   I observed all through elementary and high school, in various entertainments, the girls were placed on the stage in order of color. And very black ones didn't get into the front row. If they were past caramel-brown, to the back row they would go. Nobody questioned the justice of this—neither the students nor the teachers.

5   Oddly enough, the lighter-skinned black male did not seem to feel so much prejudice toward the black black woman. It was no accident, I felt, that Mr. Harrison, the eighth-grade teacher, who was reddish-yellow himself, once protested to the science and math teacher about the fact that he always assigned sweeping duties to Doris and Ruby, two black black girls. Mr. Harrison said to them one day in the other teacher's presence, "You must be some bad girls. Every day I come down here you all are sweeping." The science and math teacher got the point and didn't ask them to sweep any more. Uneducated black males, too, sometimes related very well to the black black woman. They had been less indoctrinated by the white society around them.

6   Because of the stigma attached to having dark skin, a black black woman had to do many things to find a place for herself. One possibility was to attach herself to a light-skinned woman, hoping that some of the magic would rub off on her. A second was to make herself sexually available, hoping thereby to attract a mate. Third, she could resign herself to a more chaste life-style—either (for the professional woman) teaching and work in established churches or (for the uneducated woman) domestic work and zealous service in "holy and sanctified" churches.

7   Lucy had chosen the first route. Lucy was short, skinny, short-haired and black black, and thus unacceptable. So she made her choice. She selected Patricia, the lightest-skinned girl in the school, as her friend and followed her around. Patricia and her friends barely tolerated Lucy, but Lucy smiled and doggedly hung on, hoping that those who noticed Patricia might notice her also. Though I felt shame for her behavior, even then I understood.

8   A fourth avenue open to the black black woman is excellence in a career. Since in the South the field most accessible to such women is education, a great many of them prepared to become teachers. But here, too, the black black woman had problems. Grades weren't given to her lightly in school, nor were promotions on the job. She had to pass examinations with flying colors or be left behind. She had to be overqualified for a job because otherwise she didn't stand a chance of getting it—and she was competing only with other blacks.

9   The black woman's training would pay off in the 1970s. With the arrival of integration, the black black woman would find, paradoxically enough, that her skin color in an integrated situation was not the handicap it had been in an all-black situation. But it wasn't until the middle and late 1960s, when the post-1945 generation of black males arrived in college that I noticed any change in the situation at all. *He* wore an Afro and *she* wore an Afro, and sometimes the only way you could tell them apart was when his Afro was taller than hers. Black had become beautiful. It was then that the dread I felt at dealing with the college-educated black male began to ease. Even now, though, when I have occasion to engage in any transaction with a college-educated black man, I gauge his age. If I guess he was born after 1945, I feel confident that the transaction will turn out all right. If he

probably was born before 1945, my stomach tightens, I find myself taking shallow breaths, and I try to state my business and escape as soon as possible.

10   When the grades for the first quarter at North Carolina College came out, I had the highest average in the freshman class. The chairman's wife called me into her office again. We did a replay of the same scene we had played during the first week of the term. She complimented me on my grades. Then she reached into a drawer and pulled out a copy of the freshman English final examination. She asked me to take the exam over again.

11   At first I couldn't believe what she was saying. I had taken the course under another teacher; and it was so incredible to her that I should have made the highest score in the class that she was trying to test me again personally. For a few moments I knew rage so intense that I wanted to take my fists and start punching her. I have seldom hated anyone so deeply. I handed the examination back to her and walked out.

Questions for Analysis

1. What is the topic of the essay? What is the essay's thesis? Where is it located?

2. How is the thesis supported? What are the main points of support? What evidence is provided for each point?

3. What sources does Mebane rely on for her thesis and support? How credible are they?

4. Analyze the opening and conclusion of the essay. What is accomplished in each? What effect(s) do they have on you?

5. What audience might the essay be intended for? What is Mebane's purpose for writing the essay? How well is the purpose accomplished?

6. What discrimination have you experienced because of your race, ethnicity, background, looks, or behavior? How did you deal with it?
    Do you agree with the essay's thesis? Why?

Vocabulary

nonplussed (2), indoctrinated (5), stigma (6), chaste (6), zealous (6), doggedly (7), paradoxically (9)

LONG LIVE HIGH SCHOOL REBELS

by Thomas French

1   Ten years ago I was in high school. It was the most absurd and savage place I have ever been.

2   To listen to the morning announcements, you'd have thought the most pressing crisis in the world was our student body's lack of school spirit. Seniors were grabbing freshmen, dragging them into the bathrooms and dunking their heads in the toilets—a ritual called "flushing." Basketball players were treated like royalty; smart kids were treated like peasants. And the administrators worshiped the word "immature." Inevitably, they pronounced it "imma-tour." Inevitably, they used it to describe us.

3   The principal and his assistants told us to act like adults, but they treated us like children. Stupid children. They told us what we could wear, when we could move, how close we could stand to our girlfriends, how fast we could walk to lunch and what topics were forbidden to write about in our school newspaper.

4   When I went out for the tennis team, I remember, the coach told me to cut my hair. It was down to my shoulders and looked terrible, but I loved it. I asked the coach what was the point. Just do it, he said.

5   If we were taught anything, it was that high school is not about learning but about keeping

quiet. The easiest way to graduate was to do what you were told, all of what you were told, and nothing but what you were told. Most of us did just that. I smiled at the principal, stayed out of trouble, avoided writing articles critical of the administration, asked only a few smart-alecky questions and cut my hair as ordered. I was so embarrassed afterwards that I wore a blue ski cap all day every day for weeks.

6   I admit to some lingering bitterness over the whole affair. I'd still like to know, for one thing, what the length of my hair had to do with my forehand. Maybe that's why, to this day, I almost always root for high school students when they clash intelligently with administrators. High school needs a good dose of dissension. If you've been there in recent years, and I have because I work with student newspapers around Pinellas County, you'd know it needs dissension more than ever.

7   A reminder of this came with the news that one day last month an assistant principal at St. Petersburg High was rummaging through a student's car in a school parking lot. When the assistant principal found three empty wine-cooler bottles and what was suspected to be some spiked eggnog inside the car, the student was suspended for five days.

8   Though the student has argued that the search was an unconstitutional violation of his rights, the incident should not have come as any huge surprise. High school officials around this country have been searching through kids' cars and lockers for some time. One day a couple of years ago, a teacher tells me, officials at Lakewood High allowed police to search for drugs with dogs. At the time, students were gathered at an assembly on God and patriotism.

9   Searches tell students plainly enough what administrators think of them. But in this county, such incidents are only part of a larger tradition of control. Some memorable moments over the years:

•   In 1983, a group of boys at Lakewood High decided it was unfair that they weren't allowed to wear shorts to school but that girls were allowed to wear miniskirts. The rationale for the rule was shorts—but not miniskirts—were too "distracting." To make fun of the rule, the boys began wearing miniskirts to school.

11   Administrators laughed at first, but once the rebellion began attracting publicity, the principal suspended the ringleader. When dozens of students staged further protest in front of the school and refused to go to class, the principal suspended 37 of them, too. Later, although close to 1,400 signatures were gathered on a petition against the rule, the Pinellas County School Board bore down and decided to ban shorts from all middle and high schools. Miniskirts, however, were still allowed.

12   "We need to set a moral standard for our children," explained board member Gerald Castellanos.

•   Last year, William Grey, the principal of St. Petersburg High, suspended a ninth-grader who dyed her hair purple. "I just don't think school is the place for multi-colored heads," Grey said. He did acknowledge that he allowed students to dye their hair green for special events—the school's colors are green and white—but he insisted that was different because it was "promoting school spirit."

•   Earlier this year at Pinellas Park High, two of the school's top students—they're number one and two in their class academically—were criticized by the principal when they wrote articles in the student newspaper pointing out that many of the school's students are sexually active and do not use birth control. I was working with the staff that year, and

I know the two students wrote the articles in an effort to prevent teen-age pregnancies. But the principal called their work irresponsible—he disagreed with their methodology—and told the newspaper staff it should write more "positive" articles.

- This fall, says a teacher at Pinellas Park, the administration cracked down on cafeteria infractions by warning that anyone caught leaving a lunch tray on a table would be suspended.

- Last year, 16-year-old Manny Sferios and a group of other students from public and private high schools put together an underground magazine called *Not For Profit* and distributed several issues to students around the county. The magazine ridiculed apartheid, protested the proliferation of nuclear weapons and tried to prod students into thinking about something more than their next pair of designer jeans.

17 *Not For Profit* also contained a variety of swear words and ridiculed the small-mindedness of many school officials, and when administrators saw it, they began confiscating copies from kids and warning that those caught with the publication risked suspension.

18 Though the officials said their main objection to *Not For Profit* was its language, the magazine's activist stance also came under fire. Gerald Castellanos, the school board member, said he did not believe students were sophisticated enough to put together such a magazine.

19 "I sincerely sense the hand of some very anti-American, anti-free enterprise types in here," he said. "And I don't believe they're students."

20 Castellanos' attitude was not surprising. Too often the people who run our high schools and sit on our school boards are not prepared to accept or deal with students who think for themselves and stand up for themselves. It would mean a loss of some control, increased resistance to petty rules and a slew of hard questions for those officials who'd rather present a "positive image" than openly confront the real problems in our schools.

21 There are plenty of real problems that need confronting. Alcohol. Drugs. Broken families. Teen-age pregnancies. Not to mention what's happening in some of our classrooms.

22 While working on an article published earlier this year, I sat in a couple of classes at St. Petersburg High—the school run by William Grey, the principal who took a stand on purple hair—and what I saw were rows and rows of kids who were bored beyond description. They were trading jokes while the teachers tried to speak. They were literally falling asleep at their desks. One boy who had no interest in the subject matter—it was American history, by the way—was allowed to get up and leave. Another sat in his seat, strumming his finger across his lips, making baby noises.

23 Dealing with apathy as deep as this is challenge enough for anyone. It requires more teachers, more money, inspiration, real change—all of which are hard to come by. Throw that in with the other problems in our high schools, and the task becomes monumental.

24 I'm not saying that administrators aren't trying to cope with that task. I know they are. But frequently they waste time and distance themselves from students by exerting their authority in other ways. Make sure the kids don't wear shorts. See to it they put away their lunch trays. Bring in the dogs every once in a while and let them sniff around the lockers. In the face of everything else, keep the school quiet. It's a way the adults tell themselves they're in charge. It's a way they tell themselves they're making a difference.

25   In the meantime, the ideas that our high schools should promote—freedom of thought and expression, for one—get shoved aside. And the students whom we should be encouraging—the ones who have the brains and spirit to start their own magazine, to protest silly rules, to ask what the color of one's hair has to do with an education—are lectured, suspended and told to get back in line.

26   Kids know it stinks. Once in a while, they find the guts to step forward and say so, even if it means getting in trouble. I think they should do it more often. Because if there's anything I regret about my own days in high school, it's that more of us didn't fight against the absurdity with every ounce of adolescent ingenuity and irreverence we had.

27   We should have commandeered the p.a. system one morning and read aloud from Thoreau's *Civil Disobedience*. We should have boycotted the food in the cafeteria for a solid week. We should have sent a note home to the principal's parents informing them he was suspended until he grew up. We should have boned up on our rights in a law library and published what we found in the school paper. And every time an adult said ''imma-tour,'' we should have pulled kazoos out of our pockets and blown on them to our heart's content.

Questions for Analysis

1.   What is the topic of the essay? What is the essay's thesis? Where is it located?

2.   How is the essay's thesis supported? What are the main points of support, and what evidence is provided for each point?

3.   What sources does French draw on in the essay for his support? How credible are they?

4.   Analyze the opening and conclusion of the essay. What is accomplished in each? What effect(s) do they have on you?

5.   What audience might the essay be intended for? What is French's purpose for writing the essay? How well is the purpose accomplished?

6.   How does your high school experience compare to the experiences provided in the essay? What specific examples can you recall? Do you agree with the essay's thesis? Why?

Vocabulary

inevitably (2), dissension (6), methodology (14), apartheid (16), proliferation (16), monumental (23), irreverence (26)

MAKING
JUDGMENTS

A traveler on a voyage makes judgments along the way that affect
the quality of the trip. As a writer, you also make judgments for
your readers to consider. Evaluating information and making judgments are critical to the writing experience. In this unit you write
papers that require considering alternatives and making decisions
to share with your readers.

A traveler choosing a particular route without knowing of possible
dangers or alternate routes is taking a risk. When you draw a conclusion in your writing, you are also taking a risk if you don't know
your subject well enough to provide sound judgments for your readers. For example, if you decide that your school board made a fair
decision by doubling the cost of tuition, you might regret not knowing that many students had to quit school, that the board had other
options, and that a small pressure group influenced the board. If
you talk a friend into attending your school, you might regret not
having checked on the cost of out-of-state tuition or on the quality of
the school's courses in her dental hygiene major. The more you
know about your topic, the wiser the conclusions you can draw for
your readers.

PREWRITING

All writing requires making decisions. You must decide what to write about, what approach to take, what choice of words to use, what to include and what not to, what to emphasize, and how to begin, continue, and end your writing. All these decisions are based, knowingly or unknowingly, on some *criteria*, or set of standards, that you apply as you write.

WRITING CRITERIA

Your writing criteria help you make thoughtful decisions. For example, when you consider different topics for a paper, you might apply criteria similar to the following ones:

1.   How much do I know about the topic?
2.   How interested am I in the topic?
3.   How interested would readers be in the topic?
4.   Why would I write about it?

As you consider different topics, you would weigh each of them against those standards to help you choose your subject.

ACTIVITY 4.1

For your next paper, you will make a comparison for your readers and then draw a conclusion that would help them make a decision or form a judgment. Select a topic for comparison based on the criteria just presented: your knowledge of the topic, your interest in it, your readers' probable interest, and your purpose for writing. You may compare anything you'd like: cars, teachers, colleges, religions, restaurants, diets, types of exercise, rock groups, cities, living situations, majors, and so on.

STUDENT SAMPLE TOPIC SELECTION

What shall I compare? I know a lot about car stereos, I've owned enough of them, and I could compare two or three different brands that people might consider buying. This might interest readers who own cars and are into music. I've taken three different math

teachers at the college, and they are very different. I could compare them for other students so they would know what to expect when they had them. This might interest
freshmen who have their math ahead of them.

I could compare college to high school because they are very different, but I'm not
sure what my purpose would be. Students can find that out for themselves. I could compare two or three movies that I've seen recently and recommend them to people who
haven't seen them, but that could be pretty hard. The movies were so different. What
about comparing dorms and apartments? I've lived in both places. That doesn't sound
too exciting to write about though.

I keep going back to my first topic: comparing car stereos. That topic interests me,
and I know there are always people who are shopping for car stereo systems.

TOPIC   comparing three brands of car stereo systems

AUDIENCE   anyone interested in getting a car stereo

PURPOSE   help readers decide on the best car stereo buy

■ ■ ■ ■ ■ ■ ■ ■ ■ ■ ■ ■ ■ ■

ACTIVITY *4.2*

As the student did in the previous activity, write down the thoughts that
led you to decide on a topic for comparison: the topics you considered,
the factors that you weighed, and how you finally made your decision.

■ ■ ■ ■ ■ ■ ■ ■ ■ ■ ■ ■ ■ ■

Your next criteria to consider are the ones you will use to judge your
subjects for comparison. What are the most important factors that a
reader should consider in making a choice between or among the subjects
you present? Those factors would form your criteria for comparison.

For example, say that you are comparing two instructors who teach
the same subject. Your criteria for comparing the two instructors might
include the following:

1. knowledge of the subject
2. willingness to help students
3. ability to make class interesting
4. other subjective factors (looks, mannerisms, personality, etc.)

Once you determine what you consider a fair criterion, it is relatively
easy to present the differences and similarities between instructors as you
write your draft.

ACTIVITY *4.3*

With a partner, come up with four to five criteria for judging the quality of each of the following topics:

1. used cars
2. presidential candidates
3. a future spouse
4. different occupations
5. colleges to attend

· · · · · · · · · · ·

ACTIVITY *4.4*

Read the essay "Through the One-Way Mirror" on page 131, and identify the criteria Atwood uses to compare Canada and the United States. Why do you think she uses those particular areas of comparison?

· · · · · · · · · · ·

ACTIVITY *4.5*

Decide on criteria for your topic of comparison. List those factors that you may want to include in your first draft.

STUDENT SAMPLE CRITERIA

TOPIC   comparing three popular brands of car stereo systems

1. quality of sound
2. price
3. features
4. warranty

· · · · · · · · · · ·

CLUSTERING

Now that you have a writing topic and tentative criteria for comparing subjects, the next step is to do some prewriting work to generate potential material for your paper. The prewriting strategy for this section is called *clustering*; that is, diagramming your ideas in a way that shows the relationships between them. Clustering is an "organized" type of brainstorming or an informal type of outlining.

With a clustering diagram, you start with a general idea and then make increasingly specific associations. For example, if you were writing a paper comparing two instructors, part of your clustering diagram might look like this:

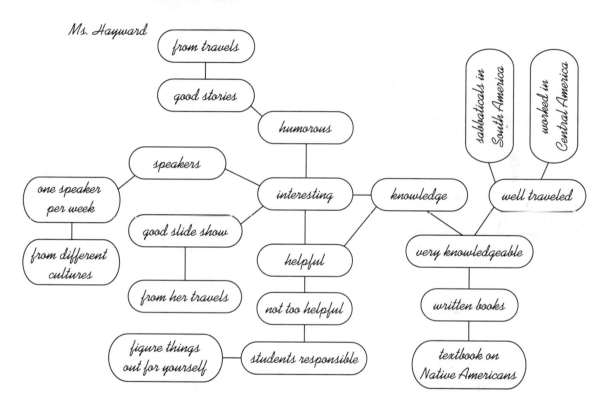

As you can see, from each main idea springs increasingly specific associations that can help provide examples and details for a paper. You would do the same type of diagram for each subject you were comparing.

ACTIVITY 4.6

Do a clustering diagram for the subjects of comparison for your paper. Begin with the four or five important factors that form your criteria for comparison and work outward to more specific associations. Do a diagram for each subject, using the same factors to begin each one.

STUDENT SAMPLE

COMPARING STEREOS--FIRST SUBJECT (ALPINE)

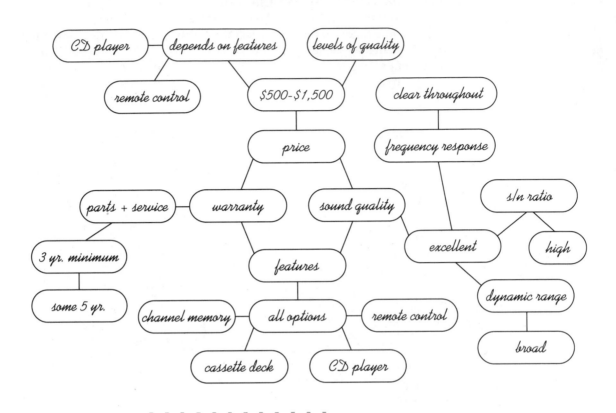

. . . .

FIRST DRAFTS

Now that you have (1) selected a topic for comparison, an audience to write for, and a purpose for writing, (2) developed criteria for making judgments, and (3) done a clustering diagram to generate potential material for your paper, the next step is to write your first draft. This section provides you with suggestions for organizing your draft and for drawing conclusions based on your comparison.

ORGANIZATION

Organizing a comparison paper can be a bit tricky since you are dealing with more than one subject. What would be the best way, for example, to present information on three different brands of car stereo systems that you want to compare in terms of price, quality of sound, volume, features, and strength of warranty?

While there is no "best" way to organize a comparison paper, there are a few options that writers use effectively. Consider the following organizational options for your own paper:

1. **Compare your subjects on one point at a time. For example, if you were comparing community colleges and four-year colleges on four points—cost, relative difficulty, activities, and curriculum—your organization would look like this:**

    1. Cost
          community colleges
          four-year colleges

    2. Relative difficulty
          community colleges
          four-year colleges

    3. Activities
          community colleges
          four-year colleges

    4. Curriculum
          community colleges
          four-year colleges

SAMPLE PARAGRAPH

One advantage of community colleges is their cost. Throughout the country, community college tuition is less expensive than for four-year colleges, ranging from $300 to $600 per year. Most community college students also live at home, saving on the cost of room and board. Four-year colleges, on the other hand, range in tuition from $1500 a year for some state-operated colleges to $15,000–$25,000 a year for private schools. On top of that, most four-year college students live away from home, spending $5,000–$8,000 per year on room and board. It is not surprising that many students choose to spend two years at a community college before transferring to a more expensive four-year school.

2. **Cover one subject on all points of comparison, and then do the same for the next subject:**

    1. Community Colleges
          cost
          relative difficulty
          activities
          curriculum

2. Four-Year Colleges
        cost
        relative difficulty
        activities
        curriculum

SAMPLE PARAGRAPHS

Community colleges are relatively inexpensive. Across the country, annual tuition ranges from $300 to $600. Since there are community colleges either in or within traveling distance of most communities, students can live at home and save room and board money.

On the whole, community colleges are also easier than four-year colleges. Studies show that for the first two years, the GPA's of transfer students from community colleges are on average higher than those of four-year college students. However, those differences disappear in the next two years. Surveys also indicate that community college transfer students find four-year college courses more difficult and time-consuming than community college courses.

(Subsequent paragraphs would cover activities and curriculum for community colleges, and then move on to four-year colleges.)

3. **Comparison papers can also be organized by "advantages" and "disadvantages" of the subjects:**

    1. Community Colleges
            advantages
            disadvantages

    2. Four-Year Colleges
            advantages
            disadvantages

    or

    1. Community Colleges
            advantages

    2. Four-Year Colleges
            advantages

    3. Community Colleges
            disadvantages

    4. Four-Year Colleges
            disadvantages

SAMPLE PARAGRAPHS   *(second option, disadvantages of community colleges)*

On the whole, community colleges are not as difficult as four-year colleges. Studies show that GPA's for community college transfer students drop in their third year while those of four-year college students do not. Surveys also indicate that most community college transfer students find their four-year college courses more difficult and time consuming than community college courses. Therefore, it appears that community colleges may not pre-pare students as well as four-year colleges do, and some community students may find themselves at a disadvantage when they transfer.

Community colleges also don't have the activities that four-year colleges do. Since community colleges are by and large "commuter" schools, with students living at home, participation in campus activities is much lower than at four-year schools with their live-in dormitory populations. Participation in school government and on-campus clubs is lim-ited, and student attendance at football and basketball games often numbers a hundred or fewer. Community college students on the whole miss out on the excitement and social involvement that can be an important part of the college experience.

ACTIVITY *4.7*

Read the essay "Neat People vs. Sloppy People" on page 129, and analyze its organizational plan. How effective is the organization for presenting the comparison?

. . . .

ACTIVITY *4.8*

Think about the different options for organizing your comparison in the first draft, and decide which option you feel would be most effective, given your topic and the purpose of your paper.

STUDENT SAMPLE

A COMPARISON OF CAR STEREO SYSTEMS

I think for me the simplest and most effective way to organize my draft would be to take the subjects one point at a time and compare all three of them. That way readers could see how they measure up on each point side-by-side, which I think would be easiest for readers to follow. Doing advantages and disadvantages seems a little confusing. I don't want to break things into good and bad categories since the differences among systems is more a matter of degree than some things being bad and some good.

. . . .

DRAWING CONCLUSIONS

The most typical purpose for writing a comparison paper is to help readers make a decision or judgment on the topic by influencing their

viewpoint. For example, a paper that compares different brands of car stereo systems or different college systems could help readers decide what to buy or where to enroll. A paper that compares different political candidates or different types of stock market investments could help readers decide how to vote or where to put their money.

In any of those cases, a writer would usually draw a conclusion at the end of the paper for readers to consider. The conclusion, of course, would be based on the information presented in the comparison, so by the time readers get to the conclusion, they should already have a good idea of what to expect.

There are two types of conclusions that writers reach:

1. *Unqualified conclusion:* With an unqualified conclusion, the writer makes a single unconditional recommendation. For example, after comparing two candidates for the office of city mayor, the writer may recommend that everyone vote for incumbent Martha Vaughn. After comparing different fast-food restaurants, the writer may recommend that everyone try Fast Jack's. An unqualified conclusion implies that the position the writer takes is best in all situations and for all readers.

2. *Qualified conclusion:* With a qualified conclusion, the writer takes into account differences among readers or the circumstances of the subjects being compared:

   a. *Differences among readers:* After comparing electric blankets, the writer might recommend that for those who can afford it, the Sunbeam Deluxe blanket is the best blanket on the market. However, for those on a tight budget, the Northern Lights blanket is a good alternative.

      After comparing investment options, the writer might recommend mutual funds for younger couples who will put their money in for fifteen years or more, treasury bills and certificates of deposit for older people who want short-term no-risk investments, and junk bonds for people who can afford to invest money on high-risk, high-return options. The qualified conclusion implies that different options are better for different readers, depending on their life circumstances.

   b. *Circumstances of the subject:* After comparing free trade among countries to government-protected trade, the writer may recommend free-trade agreements, provided the countries agree to maintain environmentally sound manufacturing practices and a standard minimum wage for workers. After comparing gun control to unregulated gun ownership, the writer might favor gun control, providing it is limited to a ban on hand guns and automatic weapons. With this type of qualified conclusion, certain conditions or limitations on a subject are an important part of the writer's recommendation.

ACTIVITY *4.9*

For each of the following topics, decide whether you feel a qualified or an unqualified conclusion would be most appropriate. Then write your own qualified or unqualified conclusion for each comparison and at least one reason to support it.

SAMPLE TOPIC

Should members of US Congress have term limits or should they be able to serve as long as they are reelected?

UNQUALIFIED CONCLUSION

U.S. congressional representatives should not have term limits since there are many effective members who should serve as long as they are doing a good job. If constituents don't like the job a representative is doing, they should not reelect him or her.

SAMPLE TOPIC

Should students be allowed to take more than 18 units per semester or quarter, given 15 units as an average load.

QUALIFIED CONCLUSION

Students should be allowed to take more than 18 units only after they have proven through earlier semesters' results that they can handle it. The 18-unit limit should be applicable to all freshmen with sophomores eligible to apply for more than 18 units based on their freshman grades and units.

1. Should college students be allowed to drop classes during a semester, or should they have to finish any class they enroll in?
2. Where is the best place for a weekend vacation: the mountains or the coast?
3. What is the best form of all-around exercise: swimming or weight-lifting?
4. Should an adult convicted of murder be given the death penalty, life in prison without parole, or life in prison with the possibility of parole?
5. Should a student attend a community college or a four-year college first?

■ ■ ■ ■ ■ ■ ■ ■ ■ ■ ■ ■ ■

ACTIVITY *4.10*

Read the essay "American Space, Chinese Place" on page 133, and determine what conclusion Tuan draws, whether it is qualified or unqualified, and how effective it is.

■ ■ ■ ■ ■ ■ ■ ■ ■ ■ ■

ACTIVITY *4.11*

Based on what you know about the subjects of comparison for your paper, what kind of a conclusion do you think you might draw— unqualified or qualified? If you think your conclusion may be qualified, how might you qualify it?

STUDENT SAMPLE

My conclusion will definitely be qualified. What people buy depends on what they can afford and how important a car stereo is to them. I'll give different suggestions for people in different circumstances.

■ ■ ■ ■ ■ ■ ■ ■ ■ ■ ■

ACTIVITY *4.12*

Now write the first draft of your comparison paper, keeping in mind the following:

1. In your opening, think about creating interest among your readers as well as introducing your topic. Why should they be reading this paper?

2. Follow some type of organization as you compare your subjects.

3. Use your prewriting material—the criteria you developed and your clustering diagram—in any manner you wish.

4. Feel free to add new points of comparison or supportive examples as they come to you during your writing. Don't limit yourself only to your prewriting ideas.

5. Your thesis for this paper and the conclusion you draw are one and the same: the main point you are leaving with your readers regarding your subjects for comparison.

6. As you write, keep in mind the audience you have decided to
write to and your purpose in writing to them: what you want
them to think or do.

CAR STEREO SYSTEMS

If you are in the market for a car stereo, there are a lot of options available. I've put in a few systems myself over the years, and basically you get what you pay for. However, there are some good buys out there, depending on what your particular needs are.

Three car stereo brands that represent the high-price to low-price range are Alpine, Pioneer, and Sanyo. Nakamichi ranks with Alpine in the high range; Kenwood, Panasonic, and Sony are in the medium range with Pioneer; and Kraco, Craig, and Realistic join Sanyo in the lower-priced range.

In sound quality, there's not much difference between Alpine and Pioneer. Their frequency response, sound/noise ratio, and dynamic range are similar. If I listened to one and then the other using the same speakers, I couldn't tell which was which. The Sanyo, however, and its lower-priced cousins, don't sound as good. You get more noise with them as the volume increases, and their sound range isn't as great as the others.

In terms of features, all of the stereos offer cassette decks and CD player. Digital display and programming are standard on the Alpine and Pioneer, but not on the Sanyo. Alpine and Pioneer also offer pull-out models, remote control, and channel memory, not available with Sanyo and other cheaper brands.

The warranty on the different brands has to do with the quality of components and construction. As might be expected, the Alpine has the longest warranty of three years on parts and service while the Pioneer has a one-year parts-and-service warranty and Sanyo a 90 day to one year parts-only warranty. Clearly, the Alpine is better constructed, whereas the Pioneer and Sanyo are not going to hold up as well for as long a time.

The prices on the three models differ considerably. The Alpine models are priced from $500 to $1500, Pioneer from $200 to $500, and Sanyo from $50 to $200. The range of prices within each brand reflects the different quality of models each offers. A $1500 Alpine model would represent a state-of-the-art stereo of the finest craftsmanship, highest quality components, and the optimal number of features.

If I had money to burn, it would be great to have the $1500 Alpine, knowing I've got about the best car stereo money can buy. However, not many people I know can afford one. For the money, I believe the best buy would be a mid-priced brand like the Pioneer pull-out model with cassette and CD player, which you could get for under $300. You'd have good quality sound, the option to use tapes or CD's, and the security of being able to remove your stereo when you're parked. You could get the Pioneer even cheaper if you went with just a cassette or CD player and without the pull-out, if security isn't a problem.

Personally, I wouldn't recommend one of the lower-priced stereos like the Sanyo unless you aren't going to be in your car much or you really don't care about the quality of sound. Given the short warranty and lack of quality construction, you probably aren't going to be better off financially in the long run than if you'd bought a mid-priced stereo.

Finally, whatever you decide on, I'd recommend shopping around and looking for a good sale. Sale prices are more common on the mid-priced stereos since people who buy the more expensive ones aren't that price conscious and the cheaper stereos don't have much of a profit margin to discount. The only other consideration is whether you buy an American or foreign brand stereo--both are available at every price range--and that's an individual choice. Happy shopping.

■ ■ ■ ■ ■ ■ ■ ■ ■ ■ ■ ■

REVISIONS

Now that you have written the first draft, your next step is to look at it through "new" eyes to see what you've done well and what you might do better. Often the best way to evaluate your writing objectively is to set it aside for a day and return to it. Then you can read your draft much like another reader would rather than like someone who has just put much time and energy into it.

As you read and evaluate your draft, consider the following questions for revision:

1. Do I have a definite opening that introduces my topic in some manner and creates interest for readers? What, if anything, in the opening will inspire readers to continue reading?

2. Have I presented the important points of comparison in such a way that readers can clearly see the differences (and similarities) among subjects? Do I cover each subject on each point of comparison? (Sometimes a writer covers one subject on a particular point and forgets to cover the other one(s).)

3. Does the organization for my comparison work? Do I present the subjects in the best way for readers to make distinctions between (or among) them for each point of comparison?

4. Is my conclusion a strong part of the paper? Does it follow logically from my comparison, and does it take into account differences among readers or specific conditions or limitations on subjects? Do I leave readers with a clear viewpoint to consider (rather than just saying, "I've made the comparison. Now you decide.")?

5. Have I paragraphed the draft so that the opening, the points of comparison, and the conclusion stand out clearly? Do I have any

overly long paragraphs that should be divided or groups of short
paragraphs that should be combined or further developed?

6. **What questions might this draft raise among the readers that I
    could answer in my next draft?**

7. **Do any sentences need rewording to make them clearer, tighter,
    or stronger?**

8. **Have I accomplished my purpose?**

ACTIVITY *4.13*

Read the following student draft, and with a partner evaluate the paper,
applying the questions for revision. Come up with specific revision plans
for the draft.

Next, read and evaluate your own draft. If you'd like a second
opinion, exchange drafts with a classmate and raise questions that come
to you as you read the draft. When you are ready, write the next draft
of your paper, including all revisions that you think will improve it, and
continue the drafting and evaluating process until you are satisfied with
your final draft.

STUDENT FIRST DRAFT

DORMS AND APARTMENTS

The first semester of college, I lived in the dorms. The next semester I moved out into an
apartment with a friend. I've lived in the dorms, and I've lived in apartments.

Dormitories are definitely cheaper than apartments. When you pay for a dorm room,
you pay for an entire semester including your room, three meals a day, and laundry
service. You get five months of room and board for about $1,000, or about $200 a
month. Apartment living is much more expensive. You also have a lot more room in
apartments. You have a living room, a kitchen, a couple of bedrooms, and a bathroom.
You have more space to move around in and to be by yourself. Dorm space·is less. But
three paid meals a day really help.

I really enjoy the freedom of apartment living. I can come and go whenever I want
to, and I can eat when I want. I'm entirely on my own. In the dorms, I had to be in at
curfew, I had to eat each meal at a certain time, and I was watched by a dorm
attendant who acted like a warden. The dorms were like a minimum security prison. And
the dorm rooms were really small--a twelve-foot-by-twelve-foot cell.

I also prefer the quiet and privacy of apartment life. In the dorms, people stream in
and out of the rooms constantly. There is no privacy. And it's always noisy because of the
small rooms and thin walls. Sometimes it feels like living with one hundred girls in one
big room. You also have to share a bathroom and shower at the end of the hall with
twenty others. If you want privacy or quiet, you have to go elsewhere. An apartment is
sure different.

All in all, the dorms and apartments both have their good points and their bad points. Which would you choose? I think I'll take the dorms.

. . . .

PARAGRAPH TRANSITIONS

In Unit 2 you learned to use transitions within a paragraph. A second important use of transitional wording is to tie the paragraphs within a composition together. Here are some suggestions for doing that effectively:

1. Transitions are important for showing the relationship between paragraphs, for tying each individual paragraph to the whole essay, and for moving the reader smoothly and clearly from one idea to the next.

2. Transitional wording that ties paragraphs together is usually most effective in the first sentence of a paragraph. Aside from the opening paragraph, each paragraph in a paper usually contains some kind of transitional wording in its opening sentence.

3. Transitional wording is often simple; transitions like *another, the next step, second, also,* or *finally* in a paragraph's opening sentence can effectively tie it to the previous paragraph.

4. Without transitional wording, a composition loses the cohesiveness that transitions provide, and readers may not understand clearly how the writer's ideas relate to one another.

ACTIVITY 4.14

The following essay contains transitions in most paragraphs. With a partner, identify the transitional wording and its function in tying paragraphs together. Also evaluate how well the writer accomplishes his purpose, and why. Be prepared to discuss your findings with the class.

AUDIENCE   college administrators and others who establish grant qualification rules

PURPOSE   convince them to change the rules

SAMPLE DRAFT

THE INEQUITY OF COLLEGE GRANTS

When I walk through the business services office at school, I often notice a line of students getting their grant checks for the month. I don't begrudge them their checks be-

cause I know they need the money. But when I see them, I'm reminded that I applied for
every local and state grant I could, and I didn't qualify for anything.

Because I get no financial aid, I have to work at least thirty hours a week to help
pay for my college and living expenses. I work at least four hours a day during the week
and ten hours on weekends. With college expenses so high, something needs to be
done for lower-middle-income students like myself who are caught in between: too "well
off" for aid but too poor to survive without working long hours.

As an example, my mother and father's combined income is $25,000. That may
sound pretty good, but when there are four kids in the family, house payments, and the
usual bills, there's not much left for college expenses. My parents can't come close to
paying for my tuition, books, fees, and living expenses. Yet because of their salary
bracket, I didn't qualify for any grants. To stay in school, I have to make at least $500
a month.

Having to work long hours, I'm at a real disadvantage. Most students on grants don't
work a lot, and many students from middle- and upper-income families don't work at all.
While I'm working thirty hours a week, they can be putting those hours into studying. I never
feel there's enough hours in the day to get my reading and studying done.

Another problem is I usually end up taking only the 12-unit minimum per semester to
maintain full-time student status because I don't have time for more classes. This means I'll
have to put in an extra semester or year of college to graduate or go to summer school
every summer, which is even more expensive than regular semesters. I also have to cram
all of my classes into the morning hours so I can be at work by one o'clock on week-
days, limiting my choice of courses and instructors.

The most aggravating thing is I know I could do so much better in school. When I
was at home and going to high school, my grades were good because I only worked a
few hours a week. Now I feel that I have two full-time jobs--school and work--and I don't
have the time or energy to do my best in school. I end up settling for C's when I know I
could be getting A's and B's. If I decide one day to apply for graduate school, my
grades are going to be a problem.

However, I know I'm not in this alone. There are a lot of students caught in the same
dilemma, and they have the same problems that I have. It just doesn't seem fair that
going to college has to be made so much more difficult for some students than for others.
In America, everyone has the right to a college education, but having the right and
being given a fair opportunity to succeed are two different things. With some financial
aid and a reduced work load, I know I could succeed.

In the future, I don't realistically see college expenses going down. Therefore, I feel
that for students like myself, the salary limit for grant qualification should be raised. I'm
not saying I should have the full grant status that poorer students have, but I feel that I
should be entitled to at least a partial grant. Why couldn't someone in my position
receive a half or quarter grant rather than being shut out completely? And why has the
salary qualification level remained the same the last four years when the cost of college
has gone up tremendously? The ceiling should be raised annually with the increase in
college and living expenses.

Don't get me wrong. I don't mind working to help pay for my college education.
And I know my parents are helping me out as much as they possibly can. But I resent

having to work practically full time to stay in school. It puts me in a poor position to compete with classmates who are on grants or don't need to work, and it makes it impossible for me to really excel in my classes or carry the units I'd like to. I don't think this is fair, and I think the rules for grant eligibility should be changed to allow students in my financial situation to get some help so that we have as good a chance of excelling in college as the next person.

■ ■ ■ ■ ■ ■ ■ ■ ■ ■ ■ ■

ACTIVITY 4.15

Each of the following entries contains a thesis statement for a composition and four topic sentences that would begin paragraphs for that composition. Fill in the blanks in the topic sentences with appropriate transitional wording that would tie the paragraphs of the composition together.

EXAMPLE

THESIS   Rita is the busiest person I know.

___*First*___, she is a housewife with three small children.

Rita is ___*also*___ a paramedic on call four days a week.

Beginning last spring, Rita ___*added*___ college night classes ___*to her*

*responsibilities*___.

___*To top it off*___, she is helping her husband get his bookkeeping business started.

1. THESIS   Tim's old Volkswagen needs a lot of work before he sells it.

    _____ , he has to do a lot of body work.

    _____ , the car needs to be painted.

    When _____ , he can begin working on the interior.

    _____ , the engine is going to need a lot of work.

2. THESIS   There are advantages and disadvantages to renting a home.

    The _____ advantage is not needing a down payment.

    _____ advantage is maintenance and upkeep expenses.

    _____ , there's the problem of escalating rent.

    There's _____ the disadvantage of not building equity.

3. THESIS   Bowe should have no trouble defeating Holyfield for the heavyweight championship.

Bowe has age on his side.

Bowe _____ has a big quickness advantage.

_____ age and quickness, Bowe is the stronger boxer.

_____ , Bowe is a more skilled fighter than Holyfield.

4. THESIS   We need more stop signs on the corners of Brawley's suburbs.

_____ is that the intersecting streets are the same size.

_____ is that the amount of traffic in the suburbs has doubled in the past five years.

_____ is the number of small children living in the suburbs.

If _____ , the city council is running the risk of someone getting killed in a neighborhood intersection.

5. THESIS   The blue whale population is making a comeback.

_____ is the number of blue whales sighted off the Alaskan coastline.

_____ of the population increase is the number of blue whale calves found in the whale pods.

Perhaps the _____ is the first-ever success marine biologists have had in breeding blue whales in captivity.

If _____ , there is a chance they will be off the endangered species list by the year 2000.

6. THESIS   Weather patterns in the Western hemisphere are undergoing significant changes.

_____ , winters are becoming milder.

_____ is the shortening periods of spring and fall.

_____ winters _____ , summers are instead growing cooler.

_____ is the dramatic decrease in the amount of annual precipitation.

. . . .

SENTENCE REVISION

In each ''Sentence Revision'' section, you are introduced to some new wording and structural considerations and then review what you learned in earlier units. The new features in this section include revising misplaced or dangling modifiers and using appositives in your writing.

MISPLACED AND DANGLING MODIFIERS

Two common wording problems that can confuse readers involve *misplaced* and *dangling modifiers*. While the misplaced modifying phrase is located in an awkward position in a sentence, a dangling modifying phrase has nothing in the sentence to modify.

Follow these suggestions for identifying and correcting problems with misplaced and dangling modifiers:

1. A misplaced modifying phrase is usually some distance from the word it modifies, creating confusion about what the modified word is supposed to be.

   EXAMPLES   (modifying phrases underlined)

   The man applied for a job in Chicago from Toledo.

   The students can't hear the lecture sitting in the back of the room.

   The house is for sale for fifty thousand dollars across the street.

   The girl chased the elephant through the house in pigtails.

   The young man was brought into the emergency room bitten by a snake.

2. To correct most misplaced modifiers, place the phrase directly after the word it modifies. Occasionally the phrase will fit more smoothly directly before the modified word.

   EXAMPLES   The man from Toledo applied for a job in Chicago.

   The students sitting in the back of the room can't hear the lecture.

   The house across the street is for sale for fifty thousand dollars.

   The girl in pigtails chased the elephant through the house.

   The young man bitten by a snake was brought into the emergency room.

3. Dangling modifiers usually begin sentences, often start with words with *-ing* and *-ed* endings, and are followed by a subject they don't modify. The modifiers are "dangling" because they clearly don't modify the subject.

   EXAMPLES   (dangling phrase underlined)

   Driving to work yesterday, the road was very slippery. *(The subject, road, can't drive.)*

   Worried about her daughter's whereabouts, the police were called immediately. *(The subject, police, weren't "worried about her daughter's whereabouts.")*

   Grounded for three weeks for bad grades, John's sister got to use his car. *(The subject, sister, wasn't the one who was grounded.)*

Running through the park, the cool breeze felt great on our faces.
(The subject, breeze, can't run through the park.)

4. To correct a dangling modifier problem, either (a) change the subject of the sentence so that it goes with the modifying phrase or (b) add a subordinating conjunction and subject to the modifying phrase to form a complex sentence.

EXAMPLES   Driving to work today, I noticed how slippery the road was.

or

While I was driving to work today, the road was very slippery.

Worried about her daughter's whereabouts, Gretchen called the police immediately.

or

Because Gretchen was worried about her daughter's whereabouts, the police were called immediately.

Grounded for three weeks for bad grades, John couldn't drive his car so his sister got to.

or

Because John was grounded for three weeks for bad grades, his sister got to use his car.

Running through the park, we felt the cool breeze on our faces.

or

As we were running through the park, the cool breeze felt great on our faces.

ACTIVITY 4.16

Each of the following sentences has a misplaced modifier. Rewrite each sentence and put the misplaced modifier in a more appropriate location. The result will be clearer, smoother sentences.

EXAMPLE   The girl showed up in a trenchcoat from the dorms

REVISED   The girl from the dorms showed up in a trenchcoat.

1. The movie is very dull showing at the drive-in.
2. I was born in New Mexico of about one hundred families in a small town.
3. He didn't know that well how to drive a stick shift.
4. The cigarette that you finished smoking for your health is very bad.
5. He is a man used by God of many talents, for he is a pastor.

6. The girl was very wet from perspiring from Texas after the race.

7. The van was stolen from the front of the gym belonging to the school.

8. The jelly is from your knife in the peanut butter.

9. The candy bars have melted with nuts in the heat.

10. The patient has great courage in room 301.

- - - - - - - - - - -

ACTIVITY *4.17*

Each of the following sentences begins with a dangling modifier. Rewrite the sentence to correct the problem either by changing the subject so that it goes with the modifying phrase or by adding a subordinating conjunction and subject to the dangling phrase to form a complex sentence. In each case, use the correction method that generates the smoothest, clearest sentence.

EXAMPLE   Working in the backyard all morning, my clothes got very dirty.

REVISED   While I was working in the backyard all morning, my clothes got very dirty.

EXAMPLE   Thrilled by his semester grades, everyone John knew got a phone call.

REVISED   Thrilled by his semester grades, John phoned everyone he knew.

1. Sitting on the sofa in the living room, my feet got very cold.

2. Bothered by a sore throat, Mary's doctor suggested that she stay home.

3. Angered over an unfair speeding ticket, the judge got a lecture from Ned.

4. Driving down Manning Avenue, the grape vineyards are beautiful in the spring.

5. Locked out of the house, the only way for John to enter was through a window.

6. Waiting for a taxi on "G" Street, four taxis drove right by me.

7. Bored by the movie on TV, the channel was changed by Gladys.

8. Trying for a school record in the high jump, the bar was raised for Marie to 5 feet 10 inches.

- - - - - - - - - - -

REVISION REVIEW

Tinkering with sentences to improve their effectiveness is a lifetime practice for most writers. The more experience you have shaping and honing sentences, the more skilled you become at catching and

revising the awkward phrase, the inappropriate word, or the misplaced modifier.

Here is more practice revising first draft sentences. Their problems include wordiness, awkward phrasing, poor word choices, misplaced phrases, and nonparallel construction. Rewrite the sentences to make them smoother and clearer.

EXAMPLE   I didn't even hardly notice the spot on your collar that you got.

REVISED   I hardly noticed the spot that you got on your collar.

1. The incident took place where I am from, and it was the Philippines.
2. We wanted to laugh at the way she looked but yet not laughing at her.
3. When she landed, she was full of leaves and dirt at the bottom of the hill.
4. The truck was white, and it had four doors, and was very clean.
5. During the years from six to twelve were mostly the years that the only child felt the loneliest.
6. One child thought that the reason why he was spoiled was that he thought his parents had no one more to buy stuff for, so they gave him better gifts.
7. I figured that since I know that working full time and going to school full time was hard on me, and I wondered how others handled it.
8. We left the house and got to the river that was so low the water went up to our ankles.
9. Before you play Parcheesi, find a likable place to play like a table.
10. Freda walked across the road in a fast way to avoid the truck.
11. Charlotte detested people who made her feel subconscious and without the proper IQ.
12. At the moment dad saw her, he decided it would be love at first sight.
13. Claude doesn't mind math but hating English passionately.
14. That dog is intelligent, coordinated, and a coat of sleek black fur.
15. I've never met a more fascinated person than you and not wanting to.

• • • • • • • • • • • •

This practice provides you with more experience using transitions, such as *first, second, next, then, another, in addition, therefore, however, nevertheless,* *on the other hand, despite,* and *moreover.* **Fill in appropriate transitional words and phrases in the blanks in the following sentences. Notice how the transitions help the paragraph flow smoothly for the reader.**

EXAMPLE   _____*Despite*_____ John's weakness for sweets, he has kept his weight in check. _____*However*_____, you never know when he will go on his next binge.

_____ Rita didn't like eating in the cafeteria, she ate there on Friday. _____ , she ordered a barbecued beef sandwich. _____ she got an order of fries. _____ , she got a glass of iced tea and paid the cashier. _____ sitting down, she scanned the tables for a friend. Right in front of her, she spotted Lionel, so she joined him. _____ , she bit into her sandwich, which looked delicious. _____ , it was tough and rubbery. _____ , she had some french fries. They were _____ a disappointment, all hard and crunchy. _____ the lousy food, she did enjoy talking to Lionel; _____ , the lunch wasn't an entire waste. _____ , she vowed never to eat in the cafeteria again, and _____ nine months, she's _____ keeping her word.

■ ■ ■ ■ ■ ■ ■ ■ ■ ■ ■

ACTIVITY *4.20*

Here is a paragraph without transitions to tie sentences together. Rewrite the paragraph and insert transitional words and phrases wherever they will improve the effectiveness of the paragraph.

EXAMPLE   John went to town. He cruised around without ever parking.

REVISED   Last night, John went to town. However, he cruised around without ever parking.

Making tacos is easy. Get out the ingredients. Break up your hamburger meat and brown it. Add some chopped onions and spices. Get out your tortillas and heat some grease. Fry each tortilla on both sides, but don't get them too hard. Slice up your tomatoes, lettuce, and cheese. Fold a tortilla in half, put in a tablespoon of meat, and add your toppings. You can add hot sauce. It tastes just as good without it. Sit down and enjoy your taco. They taste delicious, and they are easy to make.

■ ■ ■ ■ ■ ■ ■ ■ ■ ■ ■

APPOSITIVES

Another useful structure for combining sentences or adding structural variety to your writing is the *appositive*. Here is some basic information on its use.

1. **An appositive is a word or group of words that provides additional information about the person or thing it follows in a sentence. The appositives here are underlined.**

   EXAMPLES   John Smith, <u>a lumberjack for forty years</u>, still lives at Dinkey Creek.

   I'd like you to meet Thelma, <u>the woman I love</u>.

   That gun, <u>a 1942 German Luger</u>, is a deadly weapon.

2. **Appositives are set off from the rest of a sentence by commas.**

   EXAMPLES   Fred Gomez, <u>the youngest of six brothers</u>, is the tallest of his family.

   Natalie Curry, <u>a mild-mannered woman</u>, married Thad Jones, <u>a violent-tempered man</u>.

   "The Equalizer," <u>a violent TV show</u>, is not for young children.

   Black bears, <u>usually peace-loving animals</u>, become enraged and violent if their cubs are endangered.

As you can see, an appositive provides information about the word it follows, comes directly after the word, and is separated from the rest of the sentence by commas. An appositive differs from other modifiers in that it provides a second way of expressing the word it modifies and structurally it is usually interchangeable with the modified words(s).

ACTIVITY *4.21*

Rewrite the following sentences by inserting the appositives in parentheses after the words they modify. Place commas before and after the appositives to indicate the pauses in the sentences.

EXAMPLE   Hawaii is the place most mainlanders dream about visiting some day. (the exotic island state)

REVISED   Hawaii, the exotic island state, is the place most mainlanders dream about visiting some day.

1. Monday always slips up on me. (the worst day of the week)
2. Your new hat is unusual looking. (the one with the lobster on it)
3. The new biology book contains over fifty overlays of the human body. (<u>Looking Inward</u>)
4. Your pectoralis majors are underdeveloped. (the major chest muscles)
5. The play <u>Leeward Isles</u> was successful on the road. (a flop on Broadway)

6. The Camry is selling better than any recent Toyota model. (Toyota's competitor with the Honda Accord)

7. John Matthew married my sister. (a short, dark-haired man with a goatee)

8. I'm really looking forward to Thanksgiving. (my favorite eating day of the year)

- - - - - - - - - - - - -

ACTIVITY 4.22

Insert the following appositives in your own sentences. Separate the appositive from the rest of the sentence with commas, and place it directly after the word it modifies.

EXAMPLE   an ugly sight
               Thick smog, an ugly sight, is terrible for your respiratory system.

1. the largest state in the United States

2. a horrible disease

3. the weirdest person in the class

4. a movie I've seen before

5. a most difficult class

6. the hottest car on the road

7. a terrible disappointment

8. the one with the thick eyebrows

- - - - - - - - - - - - -

ACTIVITY 4.23

Appositives can be useful for combining sentences. Combine the following pairs of sentences to form single sentences containing appositives. You'll find the appositive in the second sentence to insert in the first sentence. Eliminate unnecessary words.

EXAMPLE   Ted is an outstanding accountant. He was once a drunken loser.

REVISED   Ted, once a drunken loser, is an outstanding accountant.

1. Loretta flunked her history final. She is an excellent student.

2. Harry Smeds is a good bowler. He is our garbage collector.

3. Red coral is endangered in the Mediterranean. It is an underwater prize of great value.

4. Levi's sell for over $50 in Russia. They are America's best-selling jeans.
5. Samuel Hornby broke Gladys Ruther's big toe. He is a horrible dancer.
6. Jack the Ripper was never caught by the police. He was England's most terrifying and bizarre murderer.
7. Will Clark is one of baseball's wealthiest athletes. He was a virtual unknown a few years ago.
8. I ate that piece of strawberry pie. It was the one you were saving for dessert.

■ ■ ■ ■ ■ ■ ■ ■ ■ ■ ■ ■ ■

COMBINING SENTENCES REVIEW

Let's quickly review what you have learned about sentence combining.

1. **Combine sentences only when the newly created sentence is an improvement over the existing structures.**
2. **Check your drafts for groups of short sentences and for sentences with very similar structures. These sentences may offer combining possibilities.**
3. **Are you using compound and complex sentences? If not, consider combining possibilities that will include those sentence forms.**
4. **If it takes you three sentences to describe one thing, you may be spreading out descriptive words unnecessarily. Consider joining them and forming single sentences.**

ACTIVITY 4.24

Combine the following sentences to form single sentences using the combining methods you have learned. Here is an example of each method.

DRAFT   The desk is in the corner. It is walnut. It is for studying. It is twelve years old.

REVISED   The walnut study desk in the corner is twelve years old. *(repeated words eliminated, modifying words moved in front of word they describe)*

DRAFT   I never had problems with my hearing. Lately I don't hear the television well.

REVISED   I never had problems with my hearing, but lately I don't hear the television well. *(compound sentence formed by using coordinate conjunction* but *to join sentences)*

DRAFT   She is really tired of school. She'll stick it out for her last semester.

REVISED   Although Sue is really tired of school, she'll stick it out for her last semester. *(complex sentence formed by adding subordinate conjunction* although *to join sentence)*

DRAFT   Josephine finally went to an acupuncturist. She was bothered by nagging headaches.

REVISED   Bothered by nagging headaches, Josephine finally went to an acupuncturist. *(introductory phrase used in place of second sentence and unnecessary words eliminated)*

1. The lake is full of golden trout. It lies at the foot of Mt. Cirano. They will rise to any bait.

2. I don't think anyone was injured in the accident. I could tell from the looks of the cars involved. I couldn't say for certain.

3. Maria is tired of working. She is looking forward to school. Helena feels the same way as Maria. Joleen is enjoying working. She isn't looking forward to school.

4. The debate team swept through every match. They did it easily. They were from Des Moines. They competed against some of the best teams in the state.

5. You can take English 6 this semester. You can wait for summer school. It's easier in the summer. You don't learn as much.

6. Hilda is very friendly. She is generous with her time. She is generous with her money. She doesn't like to be used.

7. My German shepherd is six months old. It is being trained as a Seeing Eye dog. The Nunnley School for the Blind is training it. They will place it with a blind person. They will do this when the training is completed.

8. Freddie got a C− on his biology report. He worked very hard on the report.

9. The liquidambar is a tree. It is a good source of shade. It grows well in most climates. It fares best in warm weather. It fares worst in cold weather.

10. Please get ten more boxes of gingersnaps. Get the same brand. Do it this morning. Do it before I leave for work.

11. Mary has a terrible toothache. It's keeping her from eating. She should see a dentist. It could get even worse.

12. That man is mysterious looking. He has a patch over his left eye. He keeps looking at you. He seems to know you.

▪ ▪ ▪ ▪ ▪ ▪ ▪ ▪ ▪ ▪ ▪ ▪

ACTIVITY 4.25

Revise and rewrite the following paragraph by combining pairs and groups of sentences. Use any of the combining methods you've learned. Combine sentences only when your new sentence is an improvement.

EXAMPLE   Howard walked around the open field. He did this to avoid a bull. It was very ferocious.

REVISED   Howard walked around the open field to avoid a ferocious bull.

Lucinda was tired of school. She was also tired of work. She didn't have a major. She didn't care for any of her classes. She worked at a large chemical plant. She poured chemicals into large vats. The chemicals were smelly. She did this every day. Her work had nothing to do with her education. It had nothing to do with her future. Her friend Sarah was graduating from school. She had a nursing degree. She had a job waiting at Lafayette Hospital. It was two blocks from the school. Lucinda envied Sarah. She wished her life had direction. She decided to quit school. She decided to quit work. She felt relieved. She worried about the future.

Share your revised paragraph with a group of classmates. Compare sentence combining strategies. Share the most effectively written paragraphs with the class. What do the better paragraphs have in common regarding combining techniques?

■ ■ ■ ■ ■ ■ ■ ■ ■ ■ ■

ACTIVITY *4.26*

Write a paragraph or short paper for classmates comparing two or three types of something: walks, laughs, noses, feet, sneezes, hairdos, mouths, voices, ears, and so on. The intent is to keep your paper on the light and humorous side—a "just for fun" assignment.

When you finish your first draft, read it carefully and make sentence revisions to improve the clarity and smoothness of each sentence, to include a variety of compound and complex sentences, and to eliminate problems with nonparallel structures or misplaced or dangling modifiers. Write a second draft to share with classmates.

STUDENT WRITING SAMPLE

There are all kinds of interesting feet. There are very small, dainty ones that look great on small, dainty girls. There are also short, wide feet that look like catchers' mitts but are great for keeping upright in a strong wind. Then there are the long, narrow kind that look like some kind of fish flopping down the street. Some feet are huge pads that look like snowshoes and are great for stamping out fires or skiing barefooted. Most any foot looks good if it's in proportion to its owner's body. What looks funny is tiny feet on a six-foot bruiser or flippers on a petite girl. I've got the problem of my size seven feet trying to hold up a 6-foot, 3-inch, 200-pound body. It's embarrassing when my feet aren't much bigger than my twelve-year-old daughter's! But basically, feet are feet, and they get you where you want to go.

■ ■ ■ ■ ■ ■ ■ ■ ■ ■ ■

WRITING REVIEW

For your final paper for this unit, compare two or three groups of people. For individuals, you might compare specific friends, teachers, bosses, parents, political candidates or office holders, counselors, athletes, actors, singers, musicians, or models. For groups of people, you might compare mothers and fathers, Democrats and Republicans, dentists and doctors, two or three different rap groups (or country or rock groups), Catholics and Protestants, atheists and agnostics, city and country dwellers, divers and gymnasts, alcoholics and drug addicts, people with HIV positive and people with AIDS, and so on.

Select a topic that you know something about and is interesting. Also consider your purpose in comparing particular subjects and who your audience would be.

STUDENT SAMPLE TOPIC SELECTION

I think I'll do some kind of comparison with students. I could compare high school and college students, but the differences seem too obvious. I could compare different types of college students on campus--athletes, aggies, student council members, slide rule whizzes--but I think I'd end up stereotyping groups since I don't know that much about them.

I have met a number of foreign students from Southeast Asia at school and have gotten to know some of them fairly well. They sure have a different perspective on going to college than most American students I know. I could compare foreign students and American students, or more specifically Asian students and American students. I think I'll give it a try.

Since most American students don't mix much with foreign students, and vice versa, I think my best reading audience would be college students in general. I'm not sure what my purpose would be yet. I'll have to think about it some more.

Once you have selected a topic, consider the *criteria* you want to use for comparison; then do some type of prewriting to generate ideas for your paper: asking and answering questions, brainstorming, free writing, clustering, or a combination of activities. Finally, consider a possible *thesis* for your paper, that is, the main point you want to make through your comparison.

STUDENT SAMPLE PREWRITING

TOPIC   Asian and American students

CRITERIA FOR COMPARISON   1. attitude toward going to college
                               2. reasons for attending
                               3. difficulties faced
                               4. pressure to succeed

PREWRITING   I've decided to free write on the subjects to get some thoughts down.

FREE WRITING

I'd never given much thought to the foreign students on campus until I had a few in class. They seemed so quiet and kept to themselves. They always seemed to be studying and were so serious. American students were so different--casual about school, basically outgoing, and much less studious. The better I got to know some Asian students, the more I understood some of the differences. They are really intent on doing well. They're not in school for anything but to succeed. All the extracurricular and social stuff isn't what they're here for. They're here to get an education and eventually a degree. American students have different agendas, though the same bottom-line goals. Asian students also have more to cope with--language difficulties, adjusting to a different culture, feeling like outsiders, feeling as if they have to work harder to do well. American students don't even think about these things. As I'm writing, I'm understanding what I want to get at in the paper--that American students don't really understand what Asian students are going through by comparison. Maybe the comparison will help bring that out for them. That could be my thesis.

When you finish your prewriting work, write the first draft of your paper, keeping in mind your purpose for making the comparison and your audience. When you finish, set aside your draft for a while. Then consider the following questions for revision:

1. **What have I accomplished in my opening? How have I engaged my readers' interest in the topic? What is in the opening that will inspire readers to read further?**

2. **Have I compared my subjects on the most important points? Do I use good examples from my experience and observations and/or the experiences of others to provide support for each point?**

3. **Have I organized the comparison so that readers can follow it easily? Do I go back and forth between subjects in an effective manner?**

4. **Is my paragraphing effective? Do I change paragraphs as I move from one point of comparison to the next? Do I have any overly long paragraphs that should be divided or groups of short paragraphs that should be combined or further developed? Have I used transitions to tie my sentences and paragraphs together?**

5. **What have I accomplished in the ending? Do readers understand why I wrote the paper? Have I left them with a conclusion that follows logically from my comparison and helps accomplish my purpose?**

6. **Do I need to revise some first draft sentences that are wordy, awkwardly phrased, weakly worded, nonparallel, or have**

misplaced or dangling modifiers? Can I combine sentences to make them stronger and improve the sentence variety? Have I used a combination of compound and complex sentences to express myself?

7.   When I read my draft through the "eyes" of my audience, what questions does it raise that I can answer in the next draft?

Read the following student draft, and with a partner evaluate it by applying the questions for revision. Then evaluate your own draft. If you want a second opinion, exchange drafts with a classmate or two, and make note of questions the draft raises in your mind that you want to share with the writer. When you are ready, write the second draft of your paper, and continue the evaluating and drafting process until you are satisfied.

STUDENT DRAFT

COLLEGE AND FOREIGN STUDENTS

America may be the great "melting pot," but at this college, not much "melting" has taken place yet with the newest wave of foreign students, most typically Southeast Asians. These students are easily distinguished from their American counterparts, both by the way they stick together on campus and by their relative seriousness. They seem to have a determination that is often lacking in American students.

I've gotten to know a few Asian students, not very well, but at least enough to get beyond "How ya doin'?" One thing I've learned is that they don't take college for granted like Americans. In their countries, like Cambodia, Laos, and Viet Nam, college was restricted to the well-to-do, so the opportunity for a college education is a great thing for them. While most Americans take college for granted, many foreign students consider it a rare opportunity that shouldn't be wasted.

Many foreign students are attending college for different reasons than American students. They have come to America with hope but little else. Many are living in over-crowded apartments, their parents eeking out a living the best they can. These students realize that their passport out of poverty is a college degree, so they are highly motivated to succeed. Many American students come from relatively comfortable backgrounds, and they feel no urgency to change their living conditions or improve their lives. They want to eventually graduate, but in the meantime, life isn't so bad.

Foreign students are also going through tremendous transitions that American students can't relate to. While they are going to school, they are at the same time learning a new language, adjusting to a different culture, and trying to fit into a foreign society. It is little wonder that they stick together on campus and seem to be quiet and shy.

As my friend Latana said (in broken English), "You're never quite sure how Americans feel about you, so you feel uncomfortable a lot. You don't talk much because you feel you talk very poorly and are afraid of sounding stupid." On the other hand, American students have no such transitions to make. As Latana said, "Foreign students have to learn how to walk and run at the same time. American students have been walking all their lives."

A final difference between American and foreign students is the pressure they feel. With Asian students, according to math professor Dr. Lum Cho, there is first the traditional fear of failing in college and "losing face," causing the family disgrace. Second, there is pressure to succeed and help the family, who is counting on you. Third, there is pressure not to "blow" a great opportunity for an education, perhaps the only opportunity you will have. Most American students feel no such pressures, and without the pressures, they are more relaxed and carefree about school.

The more I get to know a few Asian students on campus, the more I like them. They are bright, funny, politically aware, and very nice. And now that I've gotten beyond "How ya doin'," I can begin to understand their seriousness, their determination, their shyness, and their sense of isolation in a strange land. They don't have a lot in common with the typical American students of today who take education for granted. They probably have a lot in common with the children of Irish, Italian, and German immigrants who, in the 1920s and 1930s, were sent to college with their families' hopes and blessings. In a way I envy them. For foreign students, the American dream is alive and shimmering in the future.

READINGS

. . . .

NEAT PEOPLE VS. SLOPPY PEOPLE

by Suzanne Britt

1   I've finally figured out the difference between neat people and sloppy people. The distinction is, as always, moral. Neat people are lazier and meaner than sloppy people.

2   Sloppy people, you see, are not really sloppy. Their sloppiness is merely the unfortunate consequence of their extreme moral rectitude. Sloppy people carry in their mind's eye a heavenly vision, a precise plan, that is so stupendous, so perfect, it can't be achieved in this world or the next.

3   Sloppy people live in Never-Never Land. Someday is their métier. Someday they are planning to alphabetize all their books and set up home catalogs. Someday they will go through their wardrobes and mark certain items for tentative mending and certain items for passing on to relatives of similar shape and size. Someday sloppy people will make family scrapbooks into which they will put newspaper clippings, postcards, locks of hair, and the dried corsage from their senior prom. Someday they will file everything on the surface of their desks, including the cash receipts from coffee purchases at the snack shop. Someday they will sit down and read all the back issues of *The New Yorker.*

4   For all these noble reasons and more, sloppy people never get neat. They aim too high and wide. They save everything, planning someday to file, order, and straighten out the world. But while these ambitious plans take clearer and clearer shape in their heads, the books spill from the shelves onto the floor, the clothes pile up in the hamper and closet, the family mementos accumulate in every drawer, the surface of the desk is buried under mounds of paper and the unread magazines threaten to reach the ceiling.

5   Sloppy people can't bear to part with anything. They give loving attention to every detail. When sloppy people say they're going to tackle the surface of the desk, they really mean it. Not a paper will go unturned; not a rubber band will go unboxed. Four hours or two weeks into the excavation, the desk looks exactly the same, primarily because the sloppy person is meticulously creating new piles of papers with new headings and scrupulously stopping to read all the old book catalogs before he throws them away. A neat person would just bulldoze the desk.

6   Neat people are bums and clods at heart. They have cavalier attitudes toward possessions, including family heirlooms. Everything is just another dust-catcher to them. If anything collects dust, it's got to go and that's that. Neat people will toy with the idea of throwing the children out of the house just to cut down on the clutter.

7   Neat people don't care about process. They like results. What they want to do is get the whole thing over with so they can sit down and watch the rasslin' on TV. Neat people operate on two unvarying principles: Never handle any item twice, and throw everything away.

8   The only thing messy in a neat person's house is the trash can. The minute something comes to a neat person's hand, he will look at it, try to decide if it has immediate use and, finding none, throw it in the trash.

9   Neat people are especially vicious with mail. They never go through their mail unless they are standing directly over a trash can. If the trash can is beside the mailbox, even better. All ads, catalogs, pleas for charitable contributions, church bulletins and money-saving coupons go straight into the trash can without being opened. All letters from home, postcards from Europe, bills and paychecks are opened, immediately responded to, then dropped in the trash can. Neat people keep their receipts only for tax purposes. That's it. No sentimental salvaging of birthday cards or the last letter a dying relative ever wrote. Into the trash it goes.

10   Neat people place neatness above everything, even economics. They are incredibly wasteful. Neat people throw away several toys every time they walk through the den. I know a neat person once who threw away a perfectly good dish drainer because it had mold on it. The drainer was too much trouble to wash. And neat people sell their furniture when they move. They will sell a La-Z-Boy recliner while you are reclining in it.

11   Neat people are no good to borrow from. Neat people buy everything in expensive little single portions. They get their flour and sugar in two-pound bags. They wouldn't consider clipping a coupon, saving a leftover, reusing plastic non-dairy whipped cream containers or rinsing off tin foil and draping it over the unmoldy dish drainer. You can never borrow a neat person's newspaper to see what's playing at the movies. Neat people have the paper all wadded up and in the trash by 7:05 A.M.

12   Neat people cut a clean swath through the organic as well as the inorganic world. People, animals, and things are all one to them. They are so insensitive. After they've finished with the pantry, the medicine cabinet, and the attic, they will throw out the red geranium (too many leaves), sell the dog (too many fleas), and send the children off to boarding school (too many scuffmarks on the hardwood floors).

Questions for Analysis

1. What thesis does Britt present on neat and sloppy people? Do you agree with her that a "moral" distinction can be made between the two?

2. What support does Britt provide to support her thesis? What kinds of evidence does she use?

3. How is the comparison organized? How effective is the organization?

4. Analyze the opening and conclusion of the essay. What is accomplished in each? How does each affect you?

5. What audience might the essay be written for? What is Britt's purpose in writing the essay? How well is the purpose accomplished?

6. Do you agree with the essay's thesis? Why? Do you consider yourself a sloppy or neat person? How does your motivation for being neat or sloppy correspond to Britt's theory? What other motivational theories are possible?

Vocabulary

stupendous (2), heirlooms (6), inorganic (12)

THROUGH THE ONE-WAY MIRROR

by Margaret Atwood

1 The noses of a great many Canadians resemble Porky Pig's. This comes from spending so much time pressing them against the longest undefended one-way mirror in the world. The Canadians looking through this mirror behave the way people on the hidden side of such mirrors usually do: they observe, analyze, ponder, snoop and wonder what all the activity on the other side means in decipherable human terms.

2 The Americans, bless their innocent little hearts, are rarely aware that they are even being watched, much less by the Canadians. They just go on doing body language, playing in the sandbox of the world, bashing one another on the head and planning how to blow things up, same as always. If they think about Canada at all, it's only when things get a bit snowy or the water goes off or the Canadians start fussing over some piddly detail, such as fish. Then they regard them as unpatriotic; for Americans don't really see Canadians as foreigners, not like the Mexicans, unless they do something weird like speak French or beat the New York Yankees at baseball. Really, think the Americans, the Canadians are just like us, or would be if they could.

3 Or we could switch metaphors and call the border the longest undefended backyard fence in the world. The Canadians are the folks in the neat little bungalow, with the tidy little garden and the duck pond. The Americans are the other folks, the ones in the sprawly mansion with the bad-taste statues on the lawn. There's a perpetual party, or something, going on there—loud music, raucous laughter, smoke billowing from the barbeque. Beer bottles and Coke cans land among the peonies. The Canadians have their own beer bottles and barbecue smoke, but they tend to overlook it. Your own mess is always more forgivable than the mess someone else makes on your patio.

4 The Canadians can't exactly call the police—they suspect that the Americans are the police—and part of their distress, which seems permanent, comes from their uncertainty as to whether or not they've been invited. Sometimes they do drop by next door, and find it exciting but scary. Sometimes the Americans drop by their house and find it clean. This worries the Canadians. They worry a lot. Maybe those Americans will want to buy up their duck pond, with all the money they seem to have, and turn it into a cesspool or a water-skiing emporium.

5 It also worries them that the Americans don't seem to know who the Canadians are, or even where, exactly, they are. Sometimes the Americans call Canada their backyard, sometimes their front yard, both of which imply ownership. Sometimes they say they are the Mounties and the Canadians are Rose Marie. (All these things have, in fact, been said by American politicians.) Then they accuse the Canadians of being paranoid and having an identity crisis. Heck, there is no call for the Canadians to fret about their identity, because

everyone knows they're Americans, really. If the Canadians disagree with that, they're told not to be so insecure.

6   One of the problems is that Canadians and Americans are educated backward from one another. The Canadians—except for the Quebecois, one keeps saying—are taught about the rest of the world first and Canada second. The Americans are taught about the United States first, and maybe later about other places, if they're of strategic importance. The Vietnam War draft dodgers got more culture shock in Canada than they did in Sweden. It's not the clothing that is different, it's those mental noises.

7   Of course, none of this holds true when you get close enough, where concepts like "Americans" and "Canadians" dissolve and people are just people, or anyway some of them are, the ones you happen to approve of. I, for instance, have never met any Americans I didn't like, but I only get to meet the nice ones. That's what the businessmen think too, though they have other individuals in mind. But big-scale national mythologies have a way of showing up in things like foreign policy, and at events like international writers' congresses, where the Canadians often find they have more to talk about with the Australians, the West Indians, the New Zealanders and even the once-loathed snooty Brits, now declining into humanity with the dissolution of empire, than they do with the impenetrable and mysterious Yanks.

8   But only sometimes. Because surely the Canadians understand the Yanks. Shoot, don't they see Yank movies, read Yank mags, bobble round to Yank music and watch Yank telly, as well as their own, when there is any?

9   Sometimes the Canadians think it's their job to interpret the Yanks to the rest of the world; explain them, sort of. This is an illusion: they don't understand the Yanks as much as they think they do, and it isn't their job.

10   But, as we say up here among God's frozen people, when Washington catches a cold, Ottawa sneezes. Some Canadians even refer to their capital city as Washington North and wonder why we're paying those guys in Ottawa when a telephone order service would be cheaper. Canadians make jokes about the relationship with Washington which the Americans, in their thin-skinned, bunion-toed way, construe as anti-American (they tend to see any nonworshipful comment coming from that gray, protoplasmic fuzz outside their borders as anti-American). They are no more anti-American than the jokes Canadians make about the weather: it's there, it's big, it's hard to influence, and it affects your life.

11   Of course, in any conflict with the Dreaded Menace, whatever it might be, the Canadians would line up with the Yanks, probably, if they thought it was a real menace, or if the Yanks twisted their arms or other bodily parts enough or threatened a "scorched-earth policy" (another real quote). Note the qualifiers. The Canadian idea of a menace is not the same as the U.S. one. Canada, for instance, never broke off diplomatic relations with Cuba, and it was quick to recognize China. Contemplating the U.S.–Soviet growling match, Canadians are apt to recall a line from Blake: "They became what they beheld." Certainly both superpowers suffer from the imperial diseases once so noteworthy among the Romans, the British and the French: arrogance and myopia. But the bodily-parts threat is real enough, and accounts for the observable wimpiness and flunkiness of some Ottawa politicians. Nobody, except at welcoming-committee time, pretends this is an equal relationship.

12   Americans don't have Porky Pig noses. Instead they have Mr. Magoo eyes, with which they see the rest of the world. That would not be a problem if the United States were not so powerful. But it is, so it is.

Questions for Analysis

1. What are the main points of comparison between Canadians and Americans in the essay? Why do you think Atwood selected these particular points?

2. Based on the points of comparison, how do Canadians and Americans differ, and how are they similar? What evidence does Atwood use to support her contentions?

3. How is the comparison organized? Outline the organization using A and B for Canada and America and 1, 2, 3, 4 and so on for the points of comparison. How effective is the organization?

4. What audience do you think the essay is intended for? What is Atwood's purpose for writing the essay? How well is the purpose accomplished?

5. How does your viewpoint of Canada and Canadians compare to how Atwood feels Americans view them? How accurately does Atwood capture America's world view (Americans have "Mr. Magoo eyes")?

6. What, if anything, did you learn from the essay?

Vocabulary

decipherable (1), raucous (3), construe (10), protoplasmic (10), myopia (11)

AMERICAN SPACE, CHINESE PLACE

by Yi-Fu Tuan

1   Americans have a sense of space, not of place. Go to an American home in exurbia, and almost the first thing you do is drift toward the picture window. How curious that the first compliment you pay your host inside his house is to say how lovely it is outside his house! He is pleased that you should admire his vistas. The distant horizon is not merely a line separating the earth from sky, it is a symbol of the future. The American is not rooted in his place, however lovely: his eyes are drawn by the expanding space to a point on the horizon which is his future.

2   By contrast, consider the traditional Chinese home. Blank walls enclose it. Step behind the spirit wall and you are in a courtyard with perhaps a miniature garden around a corner. Once inside his private compound you are wrapped in an ambiance of calm beauty, an ordered world of buildings, pavement, rock, and decorative vegetation. But you have no distant view: nowhere does space open out before you. Raw nature in such a home is experienced only as weather, and the only open space is the sky above. The Chinese is rooted in his place. When he has to leave, it is not for the promised land on the terrestrial horizon, but for another world altogether along the vertical, religious axis of his imagination.

3   The Chinese tie to place is deeply felt. Wanderlust is an alien sentiment. The Taoist classic *Tao Te Ching* captures the ideal of rootedness in place with these words: "Though there may be another country in the neighborhood so close that they are within sight of each other and the crowing of cocks and barking of dogs in one place can be heard in the other, yet there is no traffic between them; and throughout their lives the two peoples have nothing to do with each other." In theory if not in practice, farmers have ranked high in Chinese society. The reason is not only that they are engaged in a "root" industry of producing food but that, unlike pecuniary merchants, they are tied to the land and do not abandon their country when it is in danger.

4   Nostalgia is a recurrent theme in Chinese poetry. An American reader of translated Chinese poems may well be taken aback—even

put off—by the frequency, as well as the sentimentality, of the lament for home. To understand the strength of this sentiment, we need to know that the Chinese desire for stability and rootedness in place is prompted by the constant threat of war, exile, and the natural disasters of flood and drought. Forcible removal makes the Chinese keenly aware of their loss. By contrast, Americans move, for the most part, voluntarily. Their nostalgia for home town is really longing for a childhood to which they cannot return: in the meantime the future beckons and the future is "out there," in open space. When we criticize American rootlessness, we tend to forget that it is a result of ideals we admire, namely, social mobility and optimism about the future. When we admire Chinese rootedness, we forget that the word "place" means both a location in space and position in society: to be tied to place is also to be bound to one's station in life, with little hope of betterment. Space symbolizes hope; place, achievement and stability.

Questions for Analysis

1. What is being compared in the essay? Why do you think Tuan is interested in the topic?

2. What are the main points of comparison? How do Americans and Chinese differ on these points?

3. How is the essay organized? Outline the organization using A and B for the subjects being compared and 1, 2, 3, and so on for the points of comparison. How effective is the organization?

4. What conclusion does Tuan draw based on the comparison? Do you agree with the conclusion? Why?

5. What audience might the essay be intended for? What is Tuan's purpose in writing the essay? How well is the purpose accomplished?

6. Compare your living circumstances with those that Tuan ascribes to the American home. How are they similar or different? Do you agree with his theory on what the American home symbolizes? Why?

Vocabulary

ambiance (2), terrestrial (2), wanderlust (3), nostalgia (4), recurrent (4)

EXPLORING NEW TERRITORY

In the first four units, you wrote on familiar topics while learning to use the writing process for developing your papers. Writing is also a voyage of discovery where you explore new topics and share what you learn with your readers. In this unit, you write on topics that will require some investigation.

What is the best way to learn more about an unfamiliar topic? Let's say you are curious to know what it is like to go on a fat-free diet. You could put yourself on such a diet, you could observe someone on a diet, you could talk to dieters or former dieters, or you could read about fat-free dieting. If you did all four things, that combination of experiencing, observing, interviewing, and reading would give you much insight into the subject. The methods of investigation you use for a paper depend on your topic, the availability of information, and what you want to accomplish. The more sources you use for gathering information, the broader your perspective on a subject will be.

PREWRITING

Writing usually begins with what we know and how we feel about something. However, our thoughts and feelings are not enough for us to write effectively about everything that may interest us. Sometimes we need to go beyond our own experience and knowledge to become better informed before writing.

INVESTIGATING YOUR SUBJECT

There are many ways to learn more about a topic: read about it, experience it, or talk about it with knowledgeable people. For your first "investigative" assignment, you will be talking to people, perhaps on campus or at work, who know a lot about the topic you choose. They will provide you with information on which to build your paper.

ACTIVITY 5.1

The following criteria will help you select a topic for your next paper:

1. Pick something you're interested in and would like to explore.
2. Pick something that you can find knowledgeable people to interview.
3. Pick something that may be of interest to some group of readers.

Following the criteria presented, select any topic beginning with the following query, "What is it like _____ (being a foreign student in an American college, being an "older" student returning to school after many years, growing up in a large family, being an only child, living in the college dormitories, working as a _____ , being a single parent, being raised by a single parent, skydiving, scuba-diving, being in a gang, being a devout Catholic, being an atheist?" Select a topic about which you know little or nothing.

STUDENT TOPIC SELECTION

Let's see, there are lots of things I'm interested in, but they are things I know something about. What do I know little about that interests me? I wonder what it's like to be a really famous model or movie star. That's out since I don't know any to interview. That big rubber plant I drive by going to school always has foul-smelling smoke coming out of its stacks. I've always thought that would be a lousy place to work, but I really have no idea. That sort of interests me.

What's it like to be mayor of Glenburg? Naw, I don't really care. A lot of my friends' folks are divorced, probably more so than not. I've never really asked them what it's like to go through all that. I've just felt lucky my parents are together. I do have some curiosity about that, and it sure affects a lot of people. Maybe I'll write on what it's like on children to deal with their parents' divorce. I think I'd write this to a rather general audience although I'll make that decision after I talk to some of my friends.

■ ■ ■ ■ ■ ■ ■ ■ ■ ■ ■ ■

CONDUCTING INTERVIEWS

The best way to talk to people about your topic is one on one so that they can be most candid and won't be influenced by what others say. Here are some suggestions for conducting your informal interviews:

1. Let the interviewees know your exact purpose for interviewing them, and assure them that, if requested, their names will be kept confidential. Make your interviewees feel comfortable enough to talk freely.

2. Interview one person at a time, and select a time and place where you can talk privately and comfortably; allow at least a half hour for an interview.

3. For each interviewee, generate a list of questions that you feel covers the most important (and interesting) aspects of the topic. Have six to eight general questions ready, and begin by asking the easiest, least controversial questions to get the interviewee talking.

4. Don't expect each interviewee to gush forth with information. Be prepared to ask a number of follow-up questions to get the kind of examples and details you'll need to write an interesting paper. Think of yourself as an investigative reporter who must do some digging to get to the information beneath the surface responses. Ask questions like, "Why do you feel that way about . . . ?" "Can you give me an example of what you consider . . . ?" "How would you define . . . ?" "What details do you remember about the incident?" "How did that experience feel?" Understand that interviews often begin slowly and that most interviewees will speak in generalities. Your follow-up questioning will help you get interesting information.

5. Allow the interview to go in unexpected directions. Since the interviewee knows more about the topic than you do, he or she may get into subjects you hadn't considered. Be flexible in letting your interviewees respond, and be open to integrating new ideas into your research.

6. Don't expect every interview to go marvelously. Some interviewees simply won't offer as much or know as much as others, and that is

why you need to be prepared to interview, say, six or seven people to get four good interviews.

7. **Take detailed notes as you go, and feel free to ask your interviewees to slow down or repeat things at times. Don't rely on your memory to recall the specific examples and details that will be important when you write the paper.**

ACTIVITY 5.2

Generate six to eight questions to ask your interviewees about the topic you have selected. Then find some people who are knowledgeable about your topic and who are willing to talk to you. Conduct six to eight interviews so that you will get a number of perspectives on the subject. Take notes as your interviewees answer questions, and ask them to give examples whenever possible to support and clarify their statements. Your notes and interview recall will provide the basis for your paper.

STUDENT SAMPLE INTERVIEW QUESTIONS

Children of Divorce

1. What was it like when your parents first got divorced? What thoughts and feelings did you have?

2. Who did you live with after the divorce, and how did you feel about each of your parents?

3. In what different ways did the divorce affect your life?

4. What have been the hardest things to deal with? What, if any, positive things have come from the experience?

5. Now that you are an adult, how do you view the situation? What is your family life like now?

6. What advice would you give to children who like yourself had to go through their parents' divorce?

7. In what ways, if at all, has the experience affected your attitude toward marriage and family?

The following excerpts are from an interview based on the preceding questions.

INTERVIEW #1   *(in interviewer's words)*

The divorce was awful. She couldn't believe it was happening, had never thought of the possibility. She remembers crying for days and being embarrassed to tell anyone. She felt a great loss when her dad left the house because they were close. Their relationship has never really been the same. She hoped for a long time that her parents would get back together.

Everything was harder after the divorce. She was alone more and didn't get as much attention. Her mother had to work more and wasn't home as much. She only saw her dad on weekends. She and her brother grew closer as a result and she had someone to talk to about everything.

She could find nothing positive about the divorce. It still affects her now, some eight years later, because she and her dad have grown further apart and she is not close to her stepfather. She doesn't blame her mom for remarrying, but she doesn't feel as comfortable in her home anymore. Holidays are no longer a time of joy, because they bring back memories of a happy family life that no longer is there. She has real doubts about marriage and would hate to put children of her own through what she's been through.

. . . .

FIRST DRAFTS

. . . .

At this point in the writing process, you have a topic and a set of notes from your interviews. Your next step is to consider how to use your interview material in your paper.

FROM NOTES TO DRAFT

As you read over your notes and consider your first draft, keep the following in mind:

1. What similarities run through the interviews, that is, are there aspects of the topic that most interviewees agree with or have in common?

2. What differences run through the interviews, such as different viewpoints that reveal different perspectives?

3. In what general categories might you group the interview information to help organize the draft for yourself and your readers?

4. What specific examples can you use from the interviews to support the main points the interviewees made?

5. What potential thesis does the interview material support: the main point you derived from the interviews that you want to share with your readers?

ACTIVITY 5.3

Review your interview notes and apply the preceding questions to help you make the most sense of the notes. Then make a list of general categories that you might use to organize the information. Next, write a potential thesis statement that the interview material supports.

SAMPLE STUDENT LIST OF CATEGORIES

1. initial reactions to divorce

2. effects on children's lives

3. perspective as an adult

4. effects on attitude toward marriage and family

POSSIBLE THESIS STATEMENT

Divorce can be devastating to children and can have lasting effects.

■ ■ ■ ■ ■ ■ ■ ■ ■ ■ ■ ■

WRITER'S VOICE

As you write your draft, you are doing more than merely recording the thoughts and opinions of the people you interviewed. As your audience reads the paper, they should be strongly aware of your writing presence. The following suggestions will help put you in control of your paper:

1. Create your opening without using material from the interviews. Engage your readers' interest in the topic and reveal your own interest in some manner.

2. Have a clear thesis that the interview material supports in the paper. You may present the thesis in your opening or raise a thesis "question" that your paper will answer, such as "We are often concerned with what a divorce does to husbands and wives, but perhaps more important, what does it do to children?"

3. Rather than just presenting the interview material, use it to make certain points. Following the sample on the effects of divorce on children, the writer might open a paragraph with the point, "The effects of divorce last long beyond childhood." Then he or she would support the statement with examples from the interviews showing how college-age adults are still dealing with their parents' divorce. From the interviews, you can draw a number of general conclusions (like the one just presented in quotations) that you can support with the interview material.

4. Integrate the interview material in your paper. By presenting the material through different categories (initial reactions to divorce, effects on one's life, perspective as an adult, effects on attitude toward marriage and family), you integrate material from all of the

interviews throughout the paper. The other less effective option—to present each interview separately—diminishes the writer's role and may lead to a less insightful paper.

5. Have a clear purpose for writing the paper that you transmit to readers. If you were writing about the effects of divorce on children, you may be writing to make readers more aware of and sensitive to the things that such children go through, even into their adult years. As you write the paper, you would do your best to make your readers understand that.

6. When you present interview material in the paper, put it in your own words. An occasional direct quote from an interviewee is effective, but otherwise the paper should sound like you.

ACTIVITY 5.4

Read the essay "When Television Is a School for Criminals" on page 158, and make a list of ways in which the writer "controls" the paper, keeping in mind the six suggestions just presented.

■ ■ ■ ■ ■ ■ ■ ■ ■ ■ ■ ■

ACTIVITY 5.5

Write the first draft of your investigative essay, remembering the following:

1. *Your audience*, and your purpose for writing to them.

2. *Your thesis for the paper:* your viewpoint on the topic that you will support with the interview material.

3. *Your opening:* introducing your topic in a way that creates reader interest, inspiring them to read further.

SAMPLE STUDENT FIRST DRAFT

The parents of many of my friends are divorced, and have been for some time. We've never talked much about it. It's so common that it's not something I'd ever given much thought to. However, once I decided to find out more about how divorce has affected my friends' lives, and undoubtedly the lives of thousands of others, I began to realize how different things have been for them than for me.

Divorce is very traumatic on children. All my friends agreed that it changed their lives forever. Their emotions at the time of divorce run the gamut: sadness, anger, fear, regret, embarrassment. Some blamed themselves in some way for their parents' divorce while others blamed the parent that left the house, invariably the father. Their family lives as they had always known them were torn apart, and for the most part with little fore-warning. Their all-encompassing thought was, "What's going to happen to me now?" Insecurity invaded their lives, and sometimes stayed with them for years.

Divorce changes a child's life in hard ways. Generally, they see much less of their fathers, and those who were close to them feel abandoned and sometimes unloved. "If he really loved me, he would never have left" was a common thought. Mothers often have to work more out of the home after a divorce to make ends meet, so children are on their own more. Loneliness sets in, and siblings often grow closer, looking to each other for support. It's not surprising that children frequently hold out hope that their parents will get back together: "For years, I held the illusion that things would go back as they used to be. It was hard to give up that dream."

As the years go on after the divorce, a sense of order is usually established in the children's lives, but often at a price. Some children are raised by their mothers and establish good relations with their fathers. Some have stepfathers, and stepmothers as well, and feelings for stepparents run from love to indifference to hatred. Some also have stepbrothers or stepsisters they live with. Children of divorce are forced to cope with many things, including adjusting to living with new people and working out relationships with steprelatives. Said one girl, "In some ways it's like a foster situation. You can be moved to a different home and live with different people, except for your mom being there. The new situation can be bad or it can be alright, but it's never like it was."

My friends had little positive to say about divorce, except in situations where the family life was bad before the divorce. In instances where mothers and fathers argued constantly or where the father was distant or even abusive to the children, divorce improved the situation. Said one friend, "I was a lot happier when my dad left. He was mean to mom and mean to us kids, and it was better when he wasn't around." How-ever, even in marriages that were rocky, most children would still have preferred the family to stay together. "Sure, things were far from perfect, but at least we were a family, and families are supposed to stay together," said one guy.

Adulthood does not make everything okay for former children of divorces. Most of my friends still have fond memories of their family that will be with them forever. Some think that if their parents hadn't divorced, their lives would have been better than they were. Some still think about being children of divorced parents, like a stigma they carry with them. They somehow feel less worthy or less complete than their friends who have families intact. "I've always felt some embarrassment about my folks being divorced, and it's made me less secure about myself," said one friend. Said another, "Even today events that are supposed to be happy, like birthdays and Christmas and Thanksgiving and family weddings, are often sad. You can't be with both your father and mother, and you feel that sense of loss the most on special days."

Finally, children of divorce are often uncertain about their own marital futures. They've seen the effects of divorce, and some wonder if marriage is worth it. Others are determined that if they get married, they'll never do to their children what was done to them. Some don't see marriage as a permanent situation anymore. Said one friend, "I'm not going to have children because who knows how long the marriage will last. Why take the chance?"

After talking to my friends, I realize how much most of them lost through their parents' divorce: stability, security, confidence, innocence, and a part of their former lives. They don't want anyone feeling sorry for them, and they don't care much for sitting around and talking about their situations. But they do carry with them a certain burden that children whose parents remain together don't have. They've had it tougher as kids, and they have it tougher as young adults. Things that I take for granted every day with my family they only have distant memories of. Divorce is a real American tragedy, and children of divorce often hurt the worst and the longest.

- - - - - - - - - - -

REVISIONS

- -

Now that you have written the first draft of your investigative paper, you can look at it afresh, much like a different reader would. Although it is impossible to distance yourself completely from its authorship, the more objectively you can look at your draft, the more likely you will be to identify both its strengths and weaknesses.

When evaluating your draft, consider the following questions for revision:

1. What does the opening offer the reader in the way of interest and content? Is the topic clearly introduced? Is the thesis (or a thesis-related question) for the paper included? What is there to the opening that would attract the readers' attention?

2. What supporting points for the thesis are included in the middle paragraphs? Are examples provided from the interview material to clarify and develop each point?

3. Is the draft paragraphed so that readers can follow the writer's thoughts easily? In most paragraphs, do all the sentences relate to a main idea? Are there overly long paragraphs that need to be divided or groups of short paragraphs that need to be combined or further developed?

4. Is the draft organized effectively? Does the reader get a sense of moving from opening to middle to conclusion? Are there any sentences that would sound better in different paragraphs?

5. Are there any overly wordy, awkward, or unclear sentences that need rewording?

6. What do you think readers will learn from the paper that you learned from your interviews? Have you left anything important out?

7. What four or five questions might the draft raise among readers that you could answer in the next draft?

8. Given your purpose for writing to the audience you selected, how well do you think the draft accomplishes your intentions? What might you do to accomplish your purpose even more effectively?

9. As the writer, are you clearly in charge of the paper from beginning to end? Do you use the interview material to help make your points rather than merely present it without comment? Do you use quotations from the interviews effectively? Does the conclusion leave readers something to think about that you learned through your investigation?

ACTIVITY 5.6

Read the following first draft, and with a partner evaluate it by applying the questions for revision. Then evaluate your own draft similarly, making changes that you feel will improve it. When you are ready, write the next draft of your paper, and continue the drafting and evaluation process until you are satisfied with your final draft.

STUDENT DRAFT

BACK TO COLLEGE

When I went to my first college night class last semester, I was surprised to find I was one of the younger students in the class. At least a dozen of the students were women ranging from thirty to fifty years of age. The last thing I pictured myself doing at their age was being in college, so I wondered why so many older women were there.

As the semester progressed, I got to know several of the women, and I really enjoyed being in class with them. I also found out more about their background and their reasons for being in school. Judging from their comments, the experience of being back in school is different for each of them.

Women come back to school for a lot of reasons. Some are filling a void in their lives created when their children grew up and left home. Some are picking up on career ambitions that were put aside when they got married. Many are back out of necessity: some are divorced and need training for a good-paying job; others need to contribute to new house payments.

Some women are returning just to prove something to themselves. They may have a low self-image from earlier school years that they want to improve, or they may want to know if they have what it takes to graduate. Some just enjoy the challenge; they want to test their wits against the younger generation or see how much they can learn about all kinds of subjects.

Women's first impressions on returning to school also varied. Some were relieved to see so many people their age in school, and they felt comfortable right away. Some were depressed by the amount of reading and studying they would have to do, and they wondered how they'd find time. Many were apprehensive about their ability to succeed, and they were intimidated by the younger students' abilities.

One woman's experience was seconded by some of the others. She was in a biology class with mainly younger students who asked lots of questions in class and appeared much abler than she was. She studied like mad for the first test, hoping just to pass and not score lowest in the class. She ended up with the third highest grade on the test, which surprised and thrilled her. She began to realize that college students hadn't changed much--most of them just do enough to get by--and she knew then that she could succeed.

Most of the women had positive things to say about being in school. One woman enjoyed making friends with other students her own age. Another loved being around the younger students, some of whom called her "Mom." Another woman found she had a real aptitude for computer work, and she couldn't wait to take more computer classes. Still another felt good about how kind her teachers were to her. Many of them said it felt good to have a goal to be shooting for, and one woman in her fifties said, "This is the first time I've really used my brain for twenty years!"

All was not rosy, however, for these women. They had their share of problems, too.

One of the biggest complaints was the lack of time. Women who had jobs or who had children at home never felt they had enough time to get everything done. Many had to stay up late studying every weeknight, and some had to drop classes that required too much homework. One woman said she felt exhausted all week long, and all she did was sleep on weekends to recuperate.

Some women had trouble at home; their husbands complained that dinner was never ready and they were neglected. The women whose husbands didn't really support their being in school suffered the most. Then there were the problems with failed tests and bad grades that all students occasionally face. There were also those who couldn't see the end of it all. One woman said, "If I keep taking my six units a semester, I won't graduate for eight years. I'll never last that long." Finally, a few women didn't really know what they were doing in school or what direction they were heading. One said, "I'm not really accomplishing much, but maybe if I just hang on another semester, I'll get my act together."

From what I observed from the older women in my night class, some will graduate and go on to universities, some will complete two-year programs and get jobs, some will get a few basic skills and be a little better for it, some will keep taking classes just because they enjoy it, some will drop out in frustration, and some will be dropped because they can't make it. There are probably as many ways for these women to exit college as there were reasons for them to enter.

However, succeed or fail, few women have regrets about being back in school. As one woman put it, "If I don't learn anything else, I'll have learned some things about myself that I wanted to know." And as another said, "This is my one last chance to give school a try. It's now or never."

■   ■   ■   ■   ■   ■   ■   ■   ■   ■   ■   ■

SENTENCE REVISION

In the "Sentence Revision" sections, you work on first draft sentences to make them clearer, smoother, tighter, more interesting, and more structurally varied. In this section, you are first introduced to a revision technique for creating livelier-sounding sentences, and later you add some new sentence structures to your writing repertoire.

Active Sentences

Most readers enjoy sentences that are lively and active. One way writers bring their sentences to life is to have the subjects doing something. For example, in each of the last two sentences, the subject is doing something: readers are enjoying lively sentences, and writers are bringing sentences to life.

Sentences that have their subjects doing something are called *active* sentences. *Passive* sentences, on the other hand, place the "doer" at the end of the sentence instead of the beginning. Compare the following active and passive sentences:

ACTIVE   Most readers enjoy sentences that are lively and active.

PASSIVE   Sentences that are lively and active are enjoyed by most readers.

ACTIVE   Writers bring their sentences to life by having the subjects do something.

PASSIVE   Sentences are brought to life by writers who have their subjects do something.

ACTIVE   In Wyoming, bears sometimes sneak into campers' tents and steal the food.

PASSIVE   In Wyoming, campers' tents are snuck into by bears and the food is stolen.

ACTIVE   Monroe hit a home run over the stadium scoreboard.

PASSIVE   A home run was hit over the stadium scoreboard by Monroe.

ACTIVE   Maria and Fran rode on the giant roller coaster, and soon after they regurgitated their lunches.

PASSIVE   The giant roller coaster was ridden on by Maria and Fran, and their lunches were soon after regurgitated.

As you can see, the active sentences are more interesting to read because something is happening in each sentence.

ACTIVITY 5.7

Change the following passive sentences to active ones by making the actor the subject.

EXAMPLE

Tickets were purchased by John for the MC Hammer concert.
John purchased the tickets for the MC Hammer concert.

1. A new route was taken by the Gonzaleses to their cabin in the Black Hills.

2. A discovery was made by Jack that when calculus was studied late at night, very little knowledge was retained by him.

3. A wallet was left at the train depot by a short man with a cane.

4. Sarah's feelings were deeply hurt by Jonathan Jones because she wasn't invited by him to the premiere of his one-man theater production.

5. The carrot cake was eaten by one of the twins, but which one is unknown to me.

6. A resolution was passed by the Russian state parliament declaring that Russian international trade could not be restricted by Soviet national policy.

7. Flags of their countries were unfurled by representatives of 110 nations when the Olympics were hosted by Canada in 1980.

8. The Hewlett-Packard plant was toured by college senior computer majors the semester before their diplomas were received by them.

*   *   *   *   *   *   *   *   *   *   *

ACTIVITY 5.8

The following paragraph contains a number of passive sentences. Rewrite the paragraph and create active sentences wherever you feel they would improve the paragraph.

In 1991, a major breakthrough in combating the Asian flu virus was made by American scientists at the Brooks Institute. One strain of the virus was isolated by Drs. Selkirk and Gulander, and a vaccine was created from the strain. The vaccine was given to two chimpanzees; they were successfully immunized against the disease. However, caution should be taken by all against undue optimism. The vaccine was created for only one of three strains of the virus, and although the chimps were successfully immunized, the vaccine may not work on humans. And even if the vaccine proves successful with humans, ten to fifteen years may be taken to get it approved for use in the United States. Approval for new drugs is granted cautiously by the FDA, so immunizations against the Asian flu might be given to people in Europe long before the drug is legal in the United States.

*   *   *   *   *   *   *   *   *   *   *

ACTIVITY **5.9**

For revision practice, rewrite the following paragraph to make the sentences clearer, smoother, or less wordy. Eliminate any problems with nonparallel construction or dangling or misplaced modifiers, and replace passive sentences with active ones.

At first, I felt sorry for my roommate because she was lonely. I did things with her, tried to cheer her up when she was depressed, and my clothes she could borrow anytime. Nothing seemed to help out the situation for long though because I'd come back to the dorm after class and there she'd be just staring at the ceiling or just crying for no reason on the bed. I couldn't be with her all the time. One night a dance was put on by the college and I met a guy who seemed really nice. We started going out, and my roommate was made very angry by that. She wouldn't talk to me or say anything to me when I came back from dates. It was like as if she was being betrayed by me for having a boyfriend. On top of that, my clothes were now borrowed by her without asking, and she was even getting into my make-up. Finally, I'd had enough. Anxious to get out of that room, the dorm adviser told me when another dorm room became vacant. I moved out of that room and into a single room, and even though I had to pay more for it, having to pay the extra money was worth the freedom that I received from my old roommate. I hope some psychological counseling can be gotten by her both for her own good and before she drives another roommate crazy.

■ ■ ■ ■ ■ ■ ■ ■ ■ ■ ■ ■ ■

COMPOUND AND COMPLEX SENTENCES: COMBINATIONS

Combinations of compound and complex sentences, called *compound-complex sentences* and *complex-complex sentences*, are among the most sophisticated patterns for expressing yourself. They are also very useful for showing relationships that require a more complicated sentence structure. These sentence forms are combinations of forms you have been using throughout the book, so they shouldn't be difficult to learn. (Remember, a *compound sentence* is formed by combining two complete sentences with a coordinate conjunction. A *complex sentence* is created by combining two complete sentences with a subordinate conjunction.) Here are the basic structures:

1. *Compound-complex sentence:* a compound sentence with a complex sentence in one or both of its halves. Here are some examples, with subordinate conjunctions and coordinate conjunctions underlined.

EXAMPLES   Hal couldn't eat after the operation <u>because</u> his mouth was wired, so the nurse fed him intravenously for a week. *(Because is the subordinate conjunction identifying the complex sentence, and so is* the coordinate conjunction joining the two halves of the compound sentence.)

Meg hates horror movies, but she watched Mausoleum since she paid her admission. (But *is the conjunction joining the two halves of the compound sentence, and* since *is the subordinate conjunction identifying the complex sentence.*)

Although Ed had a lazy streak, he did what had to bo dono, and that is how he kept his job. (Although *identifies the complex sentence, and* and *joins the compound sentence halves together.*)

2. *Complex-complex sentence:* **a sentence with** *three* **clauses,** *two of which begin with subordinate conjunctions.* **Here are some examples with the subordinate conjunctions underlined.**

EXAMPLES   Although the yard looks drab now, it will be bursting with color when the petunias start blooming. (Although *begins the first clause, and* when *begins the last clause. "It will be bursting with color" is the independent clause in the middle.*)

When Stanley drives up, we should be ready to go because he is usually a few minutes late. (When *identifies the first clause, and* because *identifies the last clause. "We should be ready to go" is the independent clause in the middle.*)

The gift that you brought to the party was misplaced before we got to open it. (The *relative pronoun* that *identifies one clause, and* before *identifies the last clause. The independent clause, which is split in the sentence, is "the gift was misplaced."*)

If you don't catch the five o'clock bus, you'll have to wait for the trolley that comes by at 5.30. (If *identifies the first clause, and* that *identifies the relative clause. "You'll have to wait for the trolley" is the independent clause.*)

ACTIVITY 5.10

Complete the following compound-complex and complex-complex sentences by adding appropriate words. The key coordinate conjunctions, subordinate conjunctions, and relative pronouns are underlined. Notice the use of commas in compound-complex combinations. Use them before the coordinate conjunction joining sentence halves and after all clauses starting with subordinate conjunctions.

EXAMPLE   The boy who saved our dog left ___*before we could reward him.*___

1. When you _____ , please

_____ , and

_____ .

2. Alice and Juan didn't go to the lake <u>because</u> _____

_____ , <u>so</u> _____ .

3. When _____ ,

Freddie _____ <u>because</u>

_____ .

4. As the car entered the freeway, it _____

_____ <u>until</u> _____

_____ .

5. <u>Because</u> the doors were locked, the burglar _____

_____ , <u>but</u> _____ .

6. <u>As</u> they entered the haunted house, _____

_____ , <u>but</u> _____ .

7. <u>After</u> you _____ ,

the water <u>that</u> _____ .

8. <u>As</u> _____ ,

he was tripped by a runner <u>who</u> _____ .

9. Unless _____ , we won't go

clamming, <u>and</u> _____ .

10. You can take a nap <u>while</u> _____ ,

<u>or</u> _____ .

11. <u>Even though</u> Alicia has a D average in health, she's _____

_____ <u>because</u> _____ .

12. The medicine <u>that</u> _____

spilled on the floor <u>when</u> _____ .

■ ■ ■ ■ ■ ■ ■ ■ ■ ■ ■

ACTIVITY *5.11*

Write your own compound-complex and complex-complex sentences
using the following conjunctions, subordinate conjunctions, and relative
pronouns as you wish. Use commas as you would in regular compound
and complex sentences.

EXAMPLE   compound-complex sentence using *because* and *and*

Because you need help in math, I'm going to get you a tutor, and I don't expect anything in return.

1. compound-complex sentence using *when* and *but*
2. compound-complex sentence using *and* and *because*
3. compound-complex sentence using *after* and *but*
4. compound-complex sentence using *so* and *while*
5. complex-complex sentence using *when* and *since*
6. complex-complex sentence using *if* and *unless*
7. complex-complex sentence using *as* and *who*
8. complex-complex sentence using *until* and *because*

- - - - - - - - - - -

ACTIVITY 5.12

Revise the following paragraph by combining sentences to form more effective and informative ones. Your revised paragraph should include a variety of compound and complex sentences, including some with relative (*who, which, that*) clauses, as well as compound-complex combinations.

The drinking water in town is tasting awful. The city is chlorinating it. They are doing this to kill bacteria. The bacteria count is higher than the allowable level. The level is established by the county health department. The water now has a strong aftertaste. It is safe. It is practically undrinkable. Most people are opting for bottled water. They can buy it in any supermarket. It costs about a quarter a gallon. There is another option. Some people are installing water-treatment units. These units have carbon filters. The filters take out all of the chlorine. The water tastes normal. It tastes just like bottled water. Both options are better than drinking chlorinated water. I prefer the water-treatment unit. It's more convenient. It still allows me to drink tap water. It's sad that the untreated city water isn't safe enough to drink. This is the result of underground contaminants polluting the water system. The contaminants come from agricultural pesticide spraying.

- - - - - - - - - - -

ACTIVITY 5.13

Write a paragraph or short paper for your classmates about something you learned in life "the hard way," in other words, by something you did wrong. Relate the experience and what you learned from it.

When you finish your first draft, read each sentence carefully to see how you might improve it. Work on the sentences until they are as clear and smooth as possible. Pay particular attention to revising any passive sentences and to varying your sentence structure by including some compound-complex sentence combinations. Write a second draft with all of your sentence improvements to share with classmates.

STUDENT SAMPLE FIRST DRAFT

My freshman year I really enjoyed the freedom that came with college. After having been in "prison" for four years of high school, it felt great not having classes every hour of the day and even greater being able to miss a class now and then.

The problem was the "now and then" became more frequent as the semester went on. I mostly had large lecture classes, and the teachers didn't take roll or worry about who was there and who wasn't. So I started sleeping in more and more often and relying on the notes that friends would take in class.

My grades starting slipping more and more, but I was determined to make up for it all by doing well on my finals. The trouble was, I had missed so much class and gotten so far behind that I tried to do about a month's studying in a few nights. I vowed to stay up all night studying before each final, but it never worked out. I was hopelessly behind, and did terrible on my finals.

For the semester, I ended up with one C and the rest D's and F's. I was so ashamed that I lied to my parents and my friends. I'd basically blown my first semester of college. I'd learned that the freedom of college was deceptive. In college, they give you enough rope to hang yourself, and that's what I had done.

In college, if you don't learn to take the responsibility to go to class and put your free time to good use, you'll end up in a hole. This semester I'm having to dig myself out, including taking two classes over again. I'll also have to go to summer school if I want to end up with 30 units for the year. I'm going to class regularly, taking my own notes, and keeping up on my reading better. So far I'm doing okay, but there's still twelve weeks to go. I hope I've learned my lesson.

■ ■ ■ ■ ■ ■ ■ ■ ■ ■ ■

WRITING REVIEW
■ ■

A second way to investigate a particular topic is to observe something firsthand. For your final paper, write about the behavior of a particular group of people, which may also include yourself: shoppers at a mall or supermarket, spectators at an athletic event, students in the cafeteria, people at a dance or party, people on a subway, tourists at an amusement park, and so on. Observe your group of people closely to analyze their behavior.

The following are general suggestions for observing a situation you might write about:

1. Make use of all your senses. Be aware of not only what you *see* but also what you *hear, smell,* and *feel.*

2. Look for both *patterns of behavior* and *unusual behavior.* For example, at a college football game, different groups might be identified by their behavior: rowdy alumni, carefree students, anxious parents, critical townspeople. Then there might be some individuals who fit no group: the aging hippie sitting in the middle of the band, for example.

3. Find examples of specific behavior that typify a group or individual: an alumnus calling the referee a "blind turkey"; students dancing in the stands; parents silently chewing their nails; some businessmen booing the coach's play selection; the hippie reading a magazine during the fourth quarter.

4. Pay attention to detail. For example, at a supermarket you might notice different ways people evaluate watermelons: lifting them, thumping them, pushing on their stem, squeezing them.

Once you have selected a topic, make your observations, taking into account the four suggestions just presented. Then do some type of prewriting activity—free writing, brainstorming, clustering—to put what you've observed on paper. Finally, decide on an audience to write for, a purpose for writing to them, and a tentative thesis for your paper—the main idea that your observation left you with.

STUDENT SAMPLE TOPIC SELECTION/PREWRITING

Since I'm going to a rock concert this weekend, I think I'll write about it. I can't think of anything else that might be more interesting. Besides, this is my first rock concert, so it should be interesting. I don't know what to expect.

I'm not sure who my audience will be for the paper or what my thesis might be. I'll figure all that out after I do the observation. I'll watch the concert and then free write on it the next morning.

FREE WRITING

The arena was packed with people. There were so many bodies I wondered if there was enough air to breathe. It was hot and stuffy and I got a feeling of claustrophobia. Then the group came out and a roar went up around the arena. It was really loud. The group went into one of their latest hits and everyone went crazy. The sound of the guitars was unbelievably loud. I'd never heard anything as loud as those amplifiers. The sound bounced off the walls and filled my head. Once I got used to it, it seemed like it had taken over my body. It was a mindless experience that is unreal. You become a part of this great, wild crowd. You lose all personal control. It is a group experience. The crowd was good. You hear all this stuff about the crazies everywhere, but I didn't see many. There was a lot of pot going around and you could smell it and see this cloud hanging over the arena, and there were some drunk people, but everyone was having a good time and not bothering people. A lot of girls were on top of the boys' shoulders, and some people were dancing. Most were just clapping their hands over their heads and screaming wildly after each song. The time went very fast. I didn't once think about how long I'd been there. Time didn't seem to matter at all. It just began and then it was over. The group was great. They played with great energy, and they really came to entertain. You could tell they were here to give everyone his money's worth. Their energy carried to the audience and kept it on a high. They never stopped playing long enough to break the trance. It was the closest thing to hysteria I'd been around, but it wasn't a bad hysteria. It was happy and wild and joyful. I loved the experience. The light show was also great. It added to the magic, to the fantasy of the experience; it put you in another world. It helped create the experience--the flashing strobes, the lightning bolts of reds and greens and blues, the fiery explosions. It was the Fourth of July on Mars. It took me a long time to come down from the emotion after the concert. I had really been pumped up and excited by everything. Maybe it was partly because it was my first concert. Maybe it seemed routine to some people. But the way everyone was responding, I'll bet it's the same wild time whenever a good group comes in.

From attending the concert and doing the free writing, the student made the following decisions for his paper:

AUDIENCE   I want to write to people about my age who have never gone to a concert.

PURPOSE   I want them to see what they're missing.

THESIS   Attending a rock concert can be a powerful emotional experience.

MAIN POINTS

1. first impressions
2. the music
3. the crowd
4. the rock group
5. the total experience

After you have done your observation and prewriting, write the first draft of your paper, keeping in mind your tentative thesis. When you finish, set it aside for a while. Then reread your draft and apply the following questions for revision:

1. **What have I accomplished in the opening? Is my topic clearly introduced? Have I presented my thesis (or indicated where my paper was heading)? Have I included anything that will inspire my audience to want to continue reading?**

?   What main points have I included to support my thesis? How have I used examples from my observation to support these points? How have I used visual details to help the readers see what I saw?

3.   Have I paragraphed my paper effectively? Do I change paragraphs as I move to something new in the paper? Have I used transitions to tie sentences and paragraphs together? Do I need to divide any overly long paragraph or combine or develop any short paragraphs?

4.   How can I improve sentences by making them clearer, smoother, more interesting, or more structurally varied? Are there sentences that can be combined effectively? Are there overly wordy sentences that need tightening?

5.   What have I accomplished in my ending? Do readers understand my purpose for writing? Are they left with a definite sense of conclusion? What might they remember from my ending?

6.   After reading the draft through my readers' eyes, what questions might it raise that I can answer in the next draft?

Write the second draft of your paper, and continue the drafting and evaluation process until you are satisfied that your paper is ready for its reading audience.

STUDENT DRAFT

ROCK CONCERT

Here I was twenty-one years old and carrying a terrible secret around. You see, I figured I was the only twenty-one-year-old in the country who had never been to a rock concert. In high school I didn't live close enough to a big city to attend a concert, and three years of army duty in South Korea presented no opportunities. Now I was back in the States, back in school, and anxious to lose my concert "virginity."

After waiting in line for over an hour to get into the arena where Huey Lewis and the News were playing, I passed my bottle-frisking by a security guard and went in. My first impression on being inside was frightening. There were so many people packed into the dimly lit arena that I began to panic. What if a fire broke out? What if these thousands of people sucked up what breathable air was left in the smoke-filled room? I took air in large gulps and felt my body getting hot and clammy.

As my eyes adjusted to the light, I began to relax a bit. As the blur of bodies took on form, I realized that there was enough space between people standing on the floor for survival. Looking around the arena, I saw thousands of people in the rows of seats rising toward the ceiling on all sides. And there was plenty of air to breathe in the spacious, high-ceiling arena. I was also struck by how quiet 20,000 rock fans could be, only a low hum of expectation rising and falling. This could be a Billy Graham crusade crowd, I began thinking, until a strong whiff of marijuana smoke dispelled that notion.

All of a sudden, the arena got pitch dark, a dozen spotlights danced wildly around the room, and a throaty roar went up from the crowd, followed by 20,000 voices chanting in unison, "Huey, Huey, Huey, Huey, Huey." It was impossible not to get caught up in the excitement, and I was chanting as loudly as anyone.

I heard Huey and his group before I saw them. A guitar blast shot from the massive honeycomb of speakers and filled every inch of the arena. The heavy beat of the drummer accentuated by the bass guitar hit people like an electrode, throwing thousands of arms and legs involuntarily into rhythmic motion, including my own. Then the stage lit up to reveal Huey and the News jumping enthusiastically into "Hip to Be Square," a rocker for all ages. The sound was unbelievably loud and the pounding beat literally shook the floor. The music joyfully invaded every pore of my body like a fantastic drug. Nothing had ever carried me away as delightfully as this high-amp rock 'n' roll.

And the entire audience was responding as one. Here were all ages of people, from teenyboppers to couples in their thirties, and all types, from punks to preppies, molded into one enthusiastic body. Differences were forgotten, and everyone was enjoying everyone else having a great time. We sang, clapped, our arms stretched above our heads, and danced to the beat for a solid two hours. Huey's music was the common denominator; we were all rock lovers caught up in a great performance, forgetting everything but the music and the sheer joy it brought with it.

Huey Lewis was terrific in concert. He and his band played with great enthusiasm, and they seemed to enjoy playing as much as we enjoyed listening. His style was no-frills, straight-at-you rock 'n' roll, and he gave us every minute of the two hours: no breaks, no small talk, no cute stuff. Yet, when he finally left stage, a strange hush fell over the arena in place of a wild ovation.

Then, suddenly, the darkness glowed with thousands of fireflies, actually matches and cigarette lighters, silently calling Huey back to stage in an eerily religious gesture. Then an explosion came from the audience; Huey was back on stage for one last rocker, a quick, "Thanks folks, it was great," and a final roar of appreciation to which I added what was left of my vocal chords. I slowly filed out with the crowd, sweat drenched, emotionally wired, and very happy. "Man, that was great," said one dude with spiked hair and a safety pin in his ear. "Yeah, man," I said. "That was great."

READINGS

WINNERS, LOSERS, OR JUST KIDS?

by Dan Wightman

1   If I envied anyone in high school, it was the winners. You know who I mean. The ones who earned straight A's and scored high on their Scholastic Aptitude Tests. The attractive ones who smiled coyly, drove their own sport cars and flaunted those hard, smooth bodies that they kept tan the year round.

2   By contrast, my high-school friends were mostly losers. We spent a lot of time tuning cars and drinking beer. Our girlfriends were pale and frumpy, and we had more D's than B's on our report cards. After graduation, many of us went into the Army instead of to a university; two of us came back from Vietnam in coffins,

three more on stretchers. On weekends, when we drank Colt 45 together in my father's battered Ford, we'd laughingly refer to ourselves as the "out crowd." But, unless we were thoroughly blotto, we never laughed hard when we said it. And I, for one, rarely got blotto when I was 16.

3   The reason I mention this is that last month 183 winners and losers from my Northern California high-school graduating class got together at a swank country club for a revealing 15-year reunion.

4   Predictably, only happy and successful people attended. The strange thing, though, was that the people I once pegged as losers outnumbered the winners at this reunion by a visible margin. And, during a long session at the bar with my informative friend Paula, I got an earful about the messy lives of people I'd once envied, and the remarkable metamorphoses of people I'd once pitied.

5   Paula reported that Len, a former class officer, was now a lost soul in Colorado, hopelessly estranged from his charming wife. Tim, one of the sorriest students I'd ever known, was a successful sportswriter, at ease with himself.

6   Estelle, who was modestly attractive in her teens, was now a part-time stripper in the Midwest, working to support her young son. Connie, a former car-club "kitten," had become a sophisticated international flight attendant.

7   Paula told me that Gary, a college scholarship winner, was overweight, underemployed and morose. Ron, who had shown little flair for music, had become a symphony violinist.

8   Sipping a piña colada, I thought to myself how terribly mistaken my senior counselor had been when she told me that high-school performance indicates how one will fare later.

9   I looked at Paula, a high-school troublemaker with a naughty smile, whose outgoing personality and rebellious spirit had endeared her to me so long ago. Together, we once stole a teacher's grade book, changed some of our low marks, then dropped the book in the lost-and-found box. The savvy teacher never said a word about the incident, but at the end of the year, when report cards were issued, gave us the D's we deserved.

10   Now Paula was a housewife, a volunteer worker and the mother of two sons. She wore a marriage-encounter pin on her modest dress, and sat at the bar tippling Perrier on ice.

11   She shook her head when I reminded her of the grade-book escapade, and the sheepish look on her face reminded me how presumptuous it is to anticipate the lives of others.

12   It also got me thinking about my own life since high school—how I'd gradually shaken my loser's image, gotten through college, found a decent job, married wisely, and finally realized a speck of my potential.

13   I thought about numerous situations where I could have despaired, regressed, given up— and how I hadn't, though others had—and I wondered why I was different, and had more luck, less guilt.

14   "The past is fiction," wrote William Burroughs. And, although I don't subscribe to that philosophy entirely, the people I admire most today are those who overcome their mistakes, seize second chances and fight to pull themselves together, day after day.

15   Often they're the sort of people who leave high school with blotchy complexions, crummy work habits, fingernails bitten down to the quick. And of course they're bitterly unsure of themselves and slow to make friends.

16   But they're also the ones who show up transformed at 15-year reunions, and the inference I draw is that the distinction between winners and losers is often slight and seldom crucial—and frequently overrated.

17   In high school, especially, many people are slow getting started. But, finding their stride, they quickly catch up, and in their prime often return to surprise and delight us—their lives so much richer than we'd ever imagined.

Questions for Analysis

1. What groups of people are being compared by Wightman? What group does he identify with?

2. How does Wightman investigate his subject? Was this a good way to make a comparison? How else could he have studied his groups?

3. What conclusion does Wightman make about his former classmates? What is his thesis on winners and losers? Do you agree?

4. How does Wightman support his thesis in the essay? Find examples of such support. Is it convincing? Are there enough examples?

5. Discuss the essay's organization: the opening, middle, and concluding paragraphs. Where does each section begin and end? What is accomplished in each section? How effective is this organization?

6. What kind of an audience is this essay intended for? How does Wightman try to relate to this audience in the essay? Who else might benefit from this essay? Why?

Vocabulary

flaunted (1), frumpy (2), metamorphoses (4), morose (7), savvy (9), presumptuous (11)

WHEN TELEVISION IS A SCHOOL FOR CRIMINALS

by Grant Hendricks

1   For years, psychologists and sociologists have tried to find some connection between crime and violence on television and crime and violence in American society. To date, no one has been able to prove—or disprove—that link. But perhaps the scientists, with their academic approaches, have been unable to mine the mother lode of information on violence, crime and television available in our prison systems.

2   I'm not about to dismiss the scientists' findings, but as a prisoner serving a life sentence in Michigan's Marquette maximum-security prison, I believe I can add a new dimension to the subject. Cons speak much more openly to one of their own than to outsiders. And because of this, I spent three weeks last summer conducting an informal survey of 208 of the 688 inmates here at Marquette, asking them what they felt about the correlation between the crime and violence they see on television and the crime and violence they have practiced as a way of life.

3   Making this survey, I talked to my fellow prisoners in the mess hall, in the prison yard, in the factory and in my cell block. I asked them, on a confidential basis, whether or not their criminal activities have ever been influenced by what they see on TV. A surprising 9 out of 10 told me that they have actually learned new tricks and improved their criminal expertise by watching crime programs. Four out of 10 said that they have attempted specific crimes they saw on television crime dramas, although they also admit that only about one-third of these attempts were successful.

4   Perhaps even more surprising is the fact that here at Marquette, where 459 of us have television sets in our individual cells, hooked up to a cable system, many cons sit and take notes while watching "Baretta," "Kojak," "Police Woman," "Switch" and other TV crime shows. As one of my buddies said recently: "It's like you have a lot of intelligent, creative minds—all those Hollywood writers—working for *you*. They keep coming up with new ideas. They'll lay it all out for you, too: show you the type of evidence the cops look for—how they track you, and so on."

5   What kinds of lessons have been learned by TV-watching criminals? Here are some examples.

6 One of my prison-yard mates told me he "successfully" pulled off several burglaries, all patterned on a caper from "Police Woman."

7 Another robbed a sporting-goods store by following the *modus operandi** he saw on an "Adam-12" episode.

8 By copying a *Paper Moon* scheme, one con man boasts he pulled off a successful bunco fraud—for which he has never been caught (he's currently serving time for another crime).

9 Of course, television doesn't guarantee that the crime you pull off will be successful. One inmate told me he attempted to rip off a dope house, modeling his plan on a "Baretta" script. But the heroin dealers he tried to rob called the cops and he was caught. Another prison-yard acquaintance mentioned that, using a "Starsky & Hutch" plot, he tried to rob a nightclub. But to his horror, the place was owned by underworld people. "I'm lucky to still be alive," he said.

10 On the question of violence, however, a much smaller number of Marquette inmates feel they were influenced by watching anything on television. Of the 59 men I interviewed who have committed rape, only 1 out of 20 said that he felt inspired or motivated to commit rape as a result of something he saw on television. Forty-seven of the 208 men I spoke to said that at one time or another they had killed another person. Of those, 31 are now serving life sentences for either first- or second-degree murder. Of these 31, only 2 said their crimes had been television-influenced. But of the 148 men who admitted to committing assault, about 1 out of 6 indicated that his crime had been inspired or motivated by something he saw on TV.

11 Still, one prisoner after another will tell you how he has been inspired, motivated and helped by television. And crime shows and

---

* *Modus operandi* is Latin for *method of operation.*

TV-movies are not the only sources of information. CBS's "60 Minutes" provides choice viewing for Marquette's criminal population. One con told me: "They recently did a segment on "60 Minutes" on how easy it was to get phony IDs. Just like the hit man in *Day of the Jackal,* but on "60 Minutes" it wasn't fiction—it was for real. After watching that show, you knew how to go out and score a whole new personality on paper—credit cards, driver's license, everything. It was fantastic."

12 Sometimes, watching television helps you learn to think on your feet. Like an old friend of mine named Shakey, who once escaped from the North Dakota State Penitentiary. While he hid in the basement of a private residence, they were putting up roadblocks all around the city of Bismarck. But Shakey was smart. He knew that there had to be some way for him to extricate himself from this mess. Then, all of a sudden it occurred to him: Shakey remembered a caper film he'd seen on television once, in which a fugitive had managed to breach several roadblocks by using an emergency vehicle.

13 With this basic plan in mind, he proceeded to the Bismarck City Hospital and, pretending to be hysterical, he stammered to the first white-coated attendant he met that his brother was lying trapped beneath an overturned farm tractor about 12 miles or so from town. He then climbed into the back of the ambulance, and with red lights blazing and siren screaming, the vehicle drove right through two roadblocks— and safely out of Bismarck.

14 Two days or so later, Shakey arrived back on the same ranch in Montana where he'd worked before his jail sentence. The foreman even gave him his job again. But Shakey was so proud of what he'd done that he made one big mistake: he boasted about his escape from the North Dakota state prison, and in the end he was turned over to the authorities, who sent him back to North Dakota—and prison. . . .

15 An 18-year-old inmate told me that while watching an old "Adam-12" show, he had

learned exactly how to break open pay-phone coin boxes. He thought it seemed like a pretty good idea for picking up a couple of hundred dollars a day, so he gave it a try. To his surprise and consternation, the writers of "Adam-12" had failed to explain that Ma Bell has a silent alarm system built into her pay phones. If you start tampering with one, the operator can notify the police within seconds—even giving them the location of the phone being ripped off. He was arrested on his first attempt and received a one-year sentence.

16   Another prisoner told me that he had learned to hot-wire cars at the age of 14 by watching one of his favorite TV shows. A week later he stole his first car—his mother's. Five years later he was in federal prison for transporting stolen vehicles across state lines.

17   This man, at the age of 34, has spent 15 years behind bars. According to him, "TV has taught me how to steal cars, how to break into establishments, how to go about robbing people, even how to roll a drunk. Once, after watching a 'Hawaii Five-O,' I robbed a gas station. The show showed me how to do it. Nowadays (he's serving a term for attempted rape) I watch TV in my house (cell) from 4:00 P.M. until midnight. I just sit back and take notes. I see 'em doing it this way or that way, you know, and I tell myself that I'll do it the same way when I get out. You could probably pick any 10 guys in here and ask 'em and they'd tell you the same thing. Everybody's picking up on what's on the TV." . . .

18   One of my friends here in Marquette says that TV is just a reflection of what's happening "out there." According to him, "The only difference is that the people out there haven't been caught—and we have. But our reaction to things is basically the same. Like when they showed the movie *Death Wish* here, the people reacted the same way they did on the outside—they applauded Charles Bronson when he wasted all the criminals. The crooks applauded Bronson!"

19   Still, my research—informal though it is—shows that criminals look at television differently than straight people. Outside, TV is entertainment. Here, it helps the time go by. But it is also educational. As one con told me, television has been beneficial to his career in crime by teaching him all the things *not* to do. Another mentioned that he's learned a lot about how cops think and work by watching crime-drama shows. In the prison factory, one guy said that he's seen how various alarm systems operate by watching TV; and here in my cell block somebody said that because of television shows, he's been kept up-to-date on modern police procedures and equipment.

20   Another con told me: "In the last five to seven years we've learned that the criminal's worst enemy is the snitch. TV has built that up. On 'Starsky & Hutch' they've even made a sympathetic character out of a snitch. So we react to that in here. Now the general feeling is that if you use a partner to commit a crime, you kill him afterwards so there's nobody to snitch on you."

21   For most of us cons in Marquette, it would be hard to do time without TV. It's a window on the world for us. We see the news shows, we watch sports and some of us take great pains to keep tuned into the crime shows. When I asked one con if he felt that watching TV crime shows in prison would be beneficial to his career, he just smiled and said, "Hey, I sit and take notes—do my homework, you know? No way would I sit in my cell and waste my time watching comedies for five hours—no way!"

Questions for Analysis

1. What subject did Hendricks explore in his survey? What thesis did the survey lead him to?

2. What sources does Hendricks use for his ideas? How does he incorporate source material in the essay?

3. Find specific examples supporting Hendricks's point of view on television viewing by criminals. Are the examples convincing? Is there enough evidence?

4. Discuss the essay's organization—the opening four paragraphs, the middle paragraphs, and the final paragraph. What is accomplished in each part? What one paragraph "qualifies" Hendricks's thesis? Why is it in the essay?

5. What groups of people might Hendricks be addressing in this essay? Why? What might his purpose be?

Vocabulary

mother lode (1), caper (6), bunco (8), extricate (12), consternation (15)

MEANWHILE, HUMANS EAT PET FOOD

by Edward H. Peeples, Jr.

1 The first time I witnessed people eating pet food was among neighbors and acquaintances during my youth in the South. At that time it was not uncommon or startling to me to see dog-food patties sizzling in a pan on the top of a stove or kerosene space heater in a dilapidated house with no running water, no refrigerator, no heat, no toilet and the unrelenting stench of decaying insects. I simply thought of it as the unfortunate but unavoidable consequence of being poor in the South.

2 The second time occurred in Cleveland in the summer of 1953. Like many other Southerners, I came to seek my fortune in one of those pot-at-the-end-of-the-rainbow factories along Euclid Avenue. Turned away from one prospective job after another ("We don't hire hillbillies," employers said), I saw my nest egg of $30 dwindle to nothing. As my funds diminished and my hunger grew, I turned to pilfering food and small amounts of cash. With the money, I surreptitiously purchased, fried and ate canned dog and cat food as my principal ration for several weeks.

3 I was, of course, humiliated to be eating something that, in my experience, only "trash" consumed. A merciless pride in self-sufficiency kept me from seeking out public welfare or asking my friends or family for help. In fact, I carefully guarded the secret from everyone, because I feared being judged a failure.

4 Except for the humiliation I experienced, eating canned pet food did not at the time seem to be particularly unpleasant. The dog food tasted pretty much like mealy hamburger, while the cat food was similar to canned fish that I was able to improve with mayonnaise, mustard or catsup.

5 The next time I ate dog food was in 1956 while struggling through a summer session in college without income for food. Again, I was ashamed to admit it, fearing that people would feel sorry for me or that others who had even less than I would feel compelled to sacrifice for my comfort. I never again had to eat pet food.

6 Later, while working as a hospital corpsman at the Great Lakes Illinois Naval Training Center in the late 1950s I had the opportunity to ask new recruits about their home life and nutrition practices. While I was not yet a disciplined scientist, I was able to estimate that about 5 to 8 percent of the thousands of young men who came to Great Lakes annually consumed pet foods and other materials not commonly thought to be safe or desirable for humans. Among these substances were baking soda, baking powder, laundry starch, tobacco, snuff, clay, dirt, sand and various wild plants.

7 My later experience as a public assistance caseworker in Richmond, a street-based community worker in South Philadelphia, and my subsequent travels and studies as a medical sociologist throughout the South turned up instances of people eating pet food because they

saw it as cheaper than other protein products. Through the years, similar cases found in the Ozarks, on Indian reservations and in various cities across the nation have also been brought to my attention.

8   While there do exist scattered scientific reports and commentary on the hazards and problems associated with eating such things as laundry starch and clay, there is little solid epidemiological evidence that shows a specific percentage of American households consume pet food. My experience and research, however, suggest that human consumption of pet food is widespread in the United States. My estimate, one I believe to be conservative, is that pet foods constitute a significant part of the diet of at least 225,000 American households, affecting some one million persons. Who knows how many more millions supplement their diet with pet-food products? One thing that we can assume is that current economic conditions are increasing the practice and that it most seriously affects the unemployed, poor people, and our older citizens.

9   There are those who argue that we do not have enough hard data on the human consumption of pet foods. Must we wait for incontrovertible data before we seriously seek to solve the problems of hunger and malnutrition in America? I submit that we have data enough. Isn't it sufficient to know that one American child or a single elderly person in this bountiful land is reduced to eating the forage of animals or exposed to unknown toxic levels of mercury, lead or salmonella to know that something very extraordinary must be done?

Questions for Analysis

1.   What is the subject of Peeples's essay? What are the various ways he gathered information on the subject?

2.   What examples does Peeples use to support his contention that people eat pet food? Are the examples convincing? Are there enough of them? Do you believe him?

3.   What is Peeples's thesis on the subject— the main point behind the essay? Where is his thesis found?

4.   Discuss the organization of the essay. In what order are the supporting examples presented? Why? What is the purpose of the next-to-the-last paragraph? Why does Peeples save his thesis for the end?

5.   Most of the paragraphs have topic sentences. Find the topic sentences and discuss each paragraph's development. Discuss other types of paragraphs in the essay.

6.   What audience might this essay be intended for? Why? How does the essay take into account its audience?

Vocabulary

unrelenting (1), stench, (1), pilfering (2), surreptitiously (2), merciless (3), compelled (5), epidemiological (8), incontrovertible (9), forage (9)

CONVINCING OTHERS

Just as travelers set sail for a variety of reasons, writers embark on writing voyages for different reasons: to inform, entertain, analyze, and, as we discuss in this unit, to persuade.

Persuasive writing challenges all writers. Since its purpose is to influence people's thoughts and actions, it is aimed at an audience whose initial viewpoints range from neutral to hostile. Audience awareness is crucial for persuasive writers, and when you write to persuade, you are dealing with the wariest, most skeptical readers.

Persuasive writing provides a fitting conclusion to your writing voyages in this text. It calls on all of the skills and resources you have developed through your earlier writing experiences, and it places even greater demands on your abilities to think logically, support your viewpoints, and "read" your audience accurately.

This final unit also provides a thorough review of all the revising skills that have been covered throughout the text. As you conclude this unit, you will take with you an effective, personalized writing process to apply to all future writing voyages, and a set of writing and thinking skills to build on throughout your life.

PREWRITING

■ ■

Taking a position on a controversial issue isn't that difficult. Most of us, for example, have an opinion on topics like gun control, capital punishment, pornography, abortion, or gay rights. However, supporting a position in a way that convinces readers of its validity or good sense is a challenge for any writer.

First, in analyzing our position, we sometimes discover that our viewpoint is based more on emotion than on rational thought, or on beliefs we hold but have never questioned or examined. We may even find that our viewpoint isn't ours at all, but rather that of parents or friends whose opinion we've adopted.

Second, while it's easy to write for readers who have the same opinion, they are not the target audience. There's no point in writing persuasive papers for people who don't need to be persuaded. We need to engage readers who disagree or are sitting on the fence. Such an audience will not accept our viewpoint just because we believe in it strongly.

ACTIVITY 6.1

Select a writing topic that is controversial. It may be a campus-related issue, a topic in your hometown, county, or state, or a national or international issue. It can come from any field—politics, education, business, sports, medicine, music, science, religion, and so on. Use the following criteria to help you choose a topic:

1. Select a current controversial issue—one that readers would recognize.

2. Select a topic that interests you and that you know something about. However, you may also want to broaden your knowledge of the topic by doing some investigative research.

3. You don't necessarily have to have a clear opinion right now. Your position may develop as you learn more about the topic.

4. Although no topic is off-limits, be cautious in selecting "traditional" controversial issues, such as abortion, capital punishment, euthanasia, or gun control. They have been written and talked about so much that it is sometimes difficult to get beyond the pro and con arguments that almost everyone has heard.

5. Select a topic that can be investigated through interviews and personal experience as you did in Unit 5. This is *not* intended to be a library research paper where you have to do extensive reading and reporting.

Once you have chosen a topic, which will probably take some time and thought, consider two other things:

1.   Who is the best audience for your paper?
2.   What is your purpose in writing to them?

STUDENT SAMPLE

What's controversial these days? The state legislature voted to double community college tuition beginning next semester. That's sure controversial with students. The city council is debating on whether to spend a couple hundred thousand dollars to "beautify" the downtown area, and people are split on the issue. Multibillionaire Ross Perot's running for President, and there are all kinds of opinions on what his chances are. On campus, there's a controversy on whether condom vending machines should be installed in the bathrooms. There are also the continuing complaints over the price of textbooks at the bookstore and the lousy food in the cafeteria.

What to write about? How about the instant replay debate in professional football? What about steroid use? Trouble is, there's not much to debate there. Most people agree that steroids are bad. What about beer being sold in eating places on college campuses. It's happening a lot, and it seems controversial. Then there's the question of whether campus police should be allowed to carry guns. I don't know what I want to write about yet. I'm going to give it a rest and think some more about my options during the day.

After I gave them further thought, none of the topics I'd mentioned really grabbed me. Then I remembered the rumor that the college newspaper would shut down after this year. I checked it out and it's true. The school is planning on discontinuing the paper after next semester. That I don't like, and it's something I think I'd like to write about. It's sure going to be controversial.

As for my audience, it's got to be the people who favor shutting down the paper. That wouldn't be many students. I need to write to the people at the school who are going to make the decision. I'll have to find out who they are.

My purpose is pretty clear: to convince people to keep the paper going. It's important to the students.

■   ■   ■   ■   ■   ■   ■   ■   ■   ■   ■

GENERATING IDEAS

Now that you have selected a topic, an audience, and a tentative purpose for your writing, the next step is to use some prewriting technique to generate ideas. Rather than learn a new technique in this last unit, feel free to use any prewriting strategy, or combination of strategies, that have been useful during the course: asking and answering questions, brainstorming, free writing, clustering, or just thinking and reflecting.

ACTIVITY *6.2*

Generate some ideas for your paper by doing some type of prewriting activity. Use whatever strategy, or combination of strategies, you feel will work best for this particular paper.

STUDENT SAMPLE PREWRITING

The most important thing I need to do is think of all the reasons I can for saving the school paper. I'm going to make a list of everything that comes to mind, and later decide which ideas would be the best to use for my audience.

- students enjoy reading it--something to look forward to
- provides school news that students wouldn't otherwise get
- puts student accomplishments in print
- presents controversial issues that students should know about
- only source of outside news for some students
- important for journalism students
- creates sense of togetherness for students
- wouldn't seem like a "real" college without it
- publicizes important school activities
- presents good movie/book/TV/music reviews for students
- gives students something in common to talk about
- helps students understand more about their college
- gets students in the habit of regular newspaper reading

∎ ∎ ∎ ∎ ∎ ∎ ∎ ∎ ∎ ∎ ∎ ∎

SEEING THE OTHER SIDE

When you consider the reading audience for your persuasive paper, you can assume that most of them already have a viewpoint and reasons for believing as they do. In your paper, if you only present the reasons supporting your opinion, you may do little to shake their faith in their own beliefs.

In most cases, effective persuasive writing involves two focuses: presenting the reasons you believe as you do, and discrediting the reasons that support your readers' viewpoint. If you can present credible, well-supported reasons for your position *and* raise doubts in your readers' minds about the legitimacy of their reasons, you may change some minds.

To help you cast doubt on your readers' viewpoint, consider the
following questions:

1. What position would most of my readers have on the topic?
2. What do I think their main reasons for supporting this position are?
3. How might I refute, or get my readers to question, their main
   supportive reasons?

ACTIVITY *6.3*

For each of the following positions, come up with two probable
supporting reasons. Assuming for the sake of argument that you do not
agree with the position, explain how you might try to refute or undermine
each reason.

SAMPLE RESPONSE

Students should be allowed to park free on college campuses.

SUPPORTING REASONS

a. Students have to pay enough money for college without the added expense of a
   parking permit.
b. Students should have the right to park free at public institutions they attend. Since no
   high school students are charged parking fees, why should college students be
   charged?

REFUTATION

a. Parking fees are a small expense compared to the benefits that they provide: security
   protection for vehicles, clean, well-maintained parking areas, and insurance against
   noncollege vehicles taking up valuable parking space.
b. It is a common practice across the country to charge students and employees for
   parking rights at public institutions. There is no guaranteed right to free parking in
   any state or national education code. Paying for parking at college is consistent
   with all other college charges, while not paying for high school parking is consistent with not charging high school students for tuition, books, health care, and
   so on.

1. Drugs like cocaine and marijuana should be legalized and sold in pharmacies at
   affordable prices.
2. The maximum speed limit throughout the United States should be 55 mph.
3. The welfare system in the United States should be abolished.

4. Going to grade school (1–12) in the United States should be voluntary.

5. The drinking age in the United States should be lowered to 18 in all states.

■ ■ ■ ■ ■ ■ ■ ■ ■ ■ ■ ■ ■

ACTIVITY *6.4*

Read the essay "The Death Penalty is a Step Back" on page 193, and identify the opposing arguments that King introduces. How does she refute each argument, and how effective are her refutations?

■ ■ ■ ■ ■ ■ ■ ■ ■ ■ ■ ■

ACTIVITY *6.5*

For your writing topic, consider a few of the main reasons that readers would take an opposing viewpoint. (Some investigation of your topic may help you uncover very definite reasons.) Then decide how you might refute those reasons.

STUDENT SAMPLE

TOPIC   Saving the school newspaper

SUPPORTING REASONS

1. The school has budget problems, and doing away with the paper will save money.

2. The professor who taught journalism is retiring and his position isn't being filled.

3. Student interest in writing for the paper has been low, and it has gotten more and more difficult to produce a weekly paper.

REFUTATION

1. There are lots of ways to cut the budget at the college without doing away with the paper. (I'll provide examples in the paper). Why pick on the paper? You can also make the paper more cost effective: print it on campus in the reproduction department instead of at a print shop and have the paper staff push harder for advertisements to help cover expenses.

2. You don't need to hire a full-time instructor to put out a paper. Hire a part-time professor, someone from one of the local newspapers or a recent journalism masters graduate, to teach the one journalism and one newspaper class. Other colleges have done the same, like . . .

3. The problem wasn't the lack of interest, it was the instructor who's retiring. He had lost interest in the paper and was doing a lousy job of recruiting students and maintaining interest in the program. A young enthusiastic journalist could turn the program around and make it as popular as it was in the 1980s. There are plenty of students who would be interested in working for the paper today if Mr. _____ weren't in charge.

■ ■ ■ ■ ■ ■ ■ ■ ■ ■ ■ ■ ■

SOURCES

The topic for your persuasive essay may require you to go beyond your own experience and knowledge to generate the support needed to convince your audience. You may need to investigate your topic as you did in Unit 5 to get the information to write a well-informed essay.

For example, if your topic is local student government, you may want to interview student council members, other students, a faculty adviser, and your college president to get their impressions. If you want to know if your school's student government situation is similar to others, you may also want to interview students from other local colleges.

If your topic is the deteriorating condition of the downtown area of your hometown, you may want to interview city council members, downtown businesspeople, shoppers who frequent the downtown area, and shoppers who refuse to go downtown. If your topic is the need for more recreational facilities in your community, you might interview local youths and their parents, recreation leaders at existing facilities, local educators, and local police to get support for your position.

The essay topics for this unit do not require you to rely on library research. The intent is for you to base your essay on your own experience and knowledge and whatever information you can obtain from *primary sources:* people you can interview or survey. This "limited investigation" approach serves as a lead-in to more comprehensive research papers you may write in later courses.

The following suggestions will help you investigate your primary sources.

1. *Personal experience and observation:* You may use personal experience in a number of ways in developing your essay:

   a. to decide on a tentative thesis that, based on your experience, you feel is the right, best, or fairest position

   b. to provide background information to help your audience understand the topic or its importance

   c. to provide personal examples that support your thesis or support other sources' contentions

A consideration in using personal experience is that it not be seriously limited--based on a single, nonrecurring incident or situation. For example, if you decide that Mexican food is terrible based on having eaten a microwaved enchilada TV dinner, you have drawn your conclusion from too limited an experience. If you conclude that college is easy based on only your first semester, you may be in for a surprise later.

2. *The experience of friends/acquaintances:* You may use the experience of friends and acquaintances in all the ways listed in suggestion 1 for using personal experience. In addition, you may use the experience of others as evidence to support a particular point. For example, if you find that nineteen of the twenty dormitory residents you interviewed agree that the dorms are too noisy at night, you have strong evidence to support that claim. However, if only four out of twenty agree, you have a pretty weak claim.

3. *Expert opinion:* Local "experts" on your topic provide a great source of information. The following suggestions should help you use them effectively:

   a. Seek out individuals who would be most knowledgeable on your topic: people who have direct experience with or an educational background in the topic.

   b. Seek out a range of individuals to gain the best perspective. For example, if you think the bookstore is overcharging students for textbooks, you might talk to a number of students, bookstore employees, faculty members, and administrators. If you are concerned about the lack of on-campus parking, you might talk to students, faculty, the campus police, the college president, and the facilities' manager.

   c. Follow the basic suggestions for interviewing people that you used in Unit 5.

ACTIVITY *6.6*

In the essay "The Death Penalty Is a Step Back," what sources does King use, and how does she incorporate them in her essay?

■ ■ ■ ■ ■ ■ ■ ■ ■ ■ ■ ■

ACTIVITY *6.7*

Do whatever investigative research you need to do before writing your first draft. You might interview knowledgeable people who hold different viewpoints on your topic. Your research can help you answer any of the following questions that you don't feel qualified to answer:

1. What position do I want to take on the topic? If you aren't sure on what side of the issue you stand, talking with other people and getting their viewpoints may help.

2. What are the best reasons in support of my position? If you know how you feel about an issue but don't have some convincing supportive arguments, your research can help you.

3. What examples or other support can I provide to substantiate my supportive reasons? Your research may help provide you with the "proof" you need to convince readers that your arguments are sound.

4. What reasons do my readers have for taking a contrary position? The best way to find this out is to talk with people who disagree with you.

FIRST DRAFTS

Now that you've selected a controversial topic and done substantial prewriting work, you're ready to write your first draft. Although persuasive writing involves a number of considerations, it's best to keep your focus relatively simple when writing the first draft. Trying to think of too many things at once can lead to writing paralysis.

For your first draft, consider focusing on the following:

1. Keep your readers—those people whose viewpoint you are trying to change—in mind as you write.

2. Your thesis for the paper is the position you are taking on the topic. Readers should know where you stand on the issue from early on in the paper.

3. Present your best reasons for believing as you do, and support each reason as strongly as possible. Readers will evaluate that support carefully.

4. After presenting your reasons, present and refute at least one or two of the main reasons that support your readers' position.

5. Leave the readers with a clear sense of why you are writing to them.

ACTIVITY 6.8

Before writing your first draft, read the following student first draft, written to the college school board, and answer these questions:

1. **What is accomplished in the opening?**

2. **What are the main reasons the writer presents to defend her position? How does she substantiate each of her reasons?**

3. **What opposing points does the writer bring up and refute? How does she attempt to refute them?**

4. **How is the essay paragraphed? What is contained in each paragraph, and when does the writer move from one paragraph to the next?**

STUDENT FIRST DRAFT

I can't believe the school board is thinking about dropping the newspaper. It's been around since the school began. It's as much a part of the school as the football team, the band, or anything else. I know a lot of students who read the school paper. In fact, that is the only paper they ever read, so they would be losing their one newspaper source.

I know the paper isn't exactly the New York Times, but it serves a purpose. It keeps students interested in what's going on around school. We don't have much involvement in activities and government as it is. Without a newspaper keeping us in touch with sports, activities, meetings, and rallies, there would be even less involvement.

The newspaper also brings in some news of the outside world--things that are happening in education, some world events, things that are happening in state politics. As I said, it's not like major news coverage, but for me and other students, it is the only news we read regularly.

The paper also gives students a chance to put in their two-bits. I like reading letters to the editor and student editorials, and sometimes students do get involved in issues and take sides--for example, when they were considering changing the name of the college. There was some real student involvement, and a lot of it came out of the coverage the paper gave the issue. Students don't get involved in many issues at the college. Without the paper, they wouldn't know any issues to get involved in.

The paper also gives some people a chance for a little attention. It's fun getting your name or picture in the paper. I don't know any student who doesn't like that. A lot of students get their pictures and opinions in when they ask a weekly question like "How do you feel about the new early semester calendar?" That's one of my favorite weekly regulars in the paper, and a lot of others too.

The paper also provides some journalism training for a lot of students. Without a paper, where would the journalism majors go? That would wipe out a program.

Finally, the paper can't be a big expense. It doesn't look as though it's expensively done up. What's the big cost to justify dropping the program? Why don't you look for other things to cut that are less important? Why don't you look for ways to save the paper? I'd really miss the paper. It's important to the school. What's a school without a newspaper? Even my old junior high still runs a weekly newspaper. And this college can't?

■ ■ ■ ■ ■ ■ ■ ■ ■ ■ ■ ■

ACTIVITY *6.9*

Write the first draft of your paper, keeping in mind the four focus points presented.

■ ■ ■ ■ ■ ■ ■ ■ ■ ■ ■

REVISION

Now that you have written your first draft, the next step is to read it carefully to see how it might be improved. This section presents a few new writing suggestions that are best considered after you've gotten your basic thoughts on paper.

As you read your draft, consider the following questions for revision:

1. What have I accomplished in the opening? Do readers know what the topic is and where I stand on it? How have I engaged the readers' interest and inspired them to read further?

2. Have I presented the reasons supporting my position clearly? What "proof" (examples, facts, other support) have I provided to substantiate each of my reasons?

3. What *opposing* argument or arguments have I presented? Have I refuted each of them effectively?

4. Have I concluded my draft so that readers understand my purpose and are left with something to think about?

5. Do readers know when I am presenting information from my investigations rather than sharing my personal experience or beliefs? To introduce interview material, have I used references such as "Several students agreed that . . . ," "Most working mothers I talked to . . . ," "Local environmental expert Albert Watts believes . . . ," "After talking with several instructors about beer being sold on campus, . . . ," "Not even the president of the college had a good argument against . . . ," or "After talking with four club officers, I concluded that . . . ." (For examples of such *source references* within a paper, read the student draft on pages 174 and 175.

6. Does my paragraphing help the reader move clearly from point to point? Do I present my supportive reasons in different paragraphs? Do I have any overly long paragraphs that need to be broken up or groups of short paragraphs that need to be combined or developed further.

7. **Is my draft organized effectively? Is there a clear opening, middle, and conclusion? Could any sentence(s) or paragraph(s) be moved to a more effective location?**

8. **Can I reword any sentence(s) to make it clearer, smoother, or less wordy?**

ACTIVITY *6.10*

Read the following student draft, and with a classmate, analyze it by applying the revision questions. Make a list of things the writer does well along with any suggestions you have.

Then read and evaluate your own draft, noting possible changes for your next draft. However, don't write the draft until you go over the upcoming section on *persuasive pitfalls*.

DOWN WITH THE GREEKS

Early Sunday morning, the whole place looked like a disaster area. Windows were broken out, bottles were strewn all over the floors, bodies were lying around, and a goat was on a sofa munching pretzels. The effects of an earthquake? A Chicago gangland massacre? A scene from a bombed-out Italian village in a World War II movie? None of the above. Just another Saturday night bash at the Sigma Nu frat house.

Over the years, fraternities have completely lost sight of why they were created, if there were any good reasons in the first place. Today's fraternities represent a lot of the worst things about our society. They should be disbanded once and for all.

First of all, fraternities are elitist outfits, each one catering to its own kind. For example, while I was at Landsford State, the Theta Chi's wanted nothing but doctors and lawyers-to-be, the Sigmas wanted nothing but jocks, the SAE's nothing but rich party boys, and the Lambda Nu nothing but young Republicans. Each group hung around campus in a big clique, either ignoring or looking down their noses at outsiders. Fraternities aren't for everyone, as they would have you believe.

And once in a fraternity, previously nice guys turned into egotistical snobs, including Tom Anderson from my old high school. Tom, a year ahead of me in school, had always been a friendly, decent guy. When I went to Landsford State as a freshman, I passed by Tom in his AGR sweatshirt with some of his frat friends, and he looked right through me, like I didn't exist. Later I asked a couple of other friends about good old Tom, and they said that he'd "gone frat" and was now a total jerk. So much for the myth that fraternities build character.

Aside from the elitism, fraternities have become a place where bad behavior is valued. For example, the Sigmas have their annual March 31st belching contest, where the guy with the loudest, longest belch wins a case of beer. At the Theta house, there is the legend of Josh the Vomiter, the legendary Theta who came into a frat meeting totally bombed, walked to the front of the room, and regurgitated a half gallon of wine all over the visiting Grand Deacon from Klamath Falls.

Then there's the cheating. I have seen the SAE "testing file" in their basement: a filing cabinet full of hundreds of stolen tests from every department on campus. The new pledge class each year shows their courage by stealing as many tests as possible, a great start on their fraternity careers. And the campus police have their records: over 80 percent of the vandalism reports in the college apartment area west of campus are traced back to fraternity houses, according to campus Police Chief George Shrum.

A lot of the fraternities' problems occur because of all the drinking. Fraternities are basically boozing clubs, and by the fraternities' own admission in the school newspaper, over 200 kegs of beer are consumed in fall pledge week activities alone. Most of the social fraternities have at least three parties a week: a mid-weeker to kill the boredom, a TGIF, of course, and an elaborate drunk on Saturday nights.

With all the emphasis on partying and drinking, it's not surprising that the overall GPA for frat members at Landsford State, according to the school registrar, is a 2.15, just high enough to stay in school. And the school president, Dr. Kirtch, had this to offer after the latest police raid on a frat party: "If some fraternities put half as much effort into encouraging studying as into encouraging drinking, they could do their members some good."

Finally, fraternities are sexist, racist organizations, and the facts speak for themselves. First, women cannot belong to fraternities, but each fraternity has a "little sisters' auxiliary," which is used, according to an ex-little sister, to clean up after parties, to get members dates, to console them when they're depressed, and to be their hostesses at parties. They are college geisha girls, in other words. As to racism, at Landsford College, 96 percent of the frat members are white, 2 percent are oriental, and 2 percent are black. And that is with a school population that is 70 percent white, 20 percent black, and 8 percent oriental. It is no wonder that the Black Student Union on campus has petitioned the college to start a new fraternity; they know the present fraternities aren't for them.

I know what happens to many fraternity types when they get older. We have a number of service clubs in town and one club called the Order of the Eagles. They aren't civic minded; they just like to party: an open bar at every meeting, plus casino nights, stag nights, and trips to Las Vegas. And they don't care about their public image. In fact, they're proud of it. So fraternity types never die; they just join the Order of the Eagles somewhere and continue their self-centered, purposeless ways. If Landsford abolished all fraternities tomorrow, I wonder what negative effects that might have on students or the college. After two hours, I'm still thinking.

* * * * * * * * * * *

PERSUASIVE PITFALLS

Sometimes writers get so caught up in defending their position that they inadevertently write things that may hurt their purpose more than help it. Such problems have been lumped together under *persuasive pitfalls*. Here are some of the more common ones:

1. *Inappropriate tone:* **If you write in a manner that offends the very readers that you are trying to convince, you have a problem. If in defending your position you belittle your readers or their opinions, or you anger them so that they quit listening to you, you may have defeated your purpose.**

   EXAMPLE   "I can't believe how you school board members can be so stupid as to consider dropping the school paper. Obviously you don't really care about students or education or you wouldn't consider such a ridiculous proposal." *(How would you respond as a school board member?)*

   REMEDY   Treat your readers and their beliefs with respect. You may certainly refute their arguments, but in a well-reasoned and courteous manner.

2. *Overgeneralization:* **When you state that "everyone" feels the same way or believes the same thing, you are overgeneralizing. Since it is impossible to speak for "everyone" on any issue, it is wise to avoid such generalities.**

   EXAMPLES   *Everyone* knows that democracy is the best form of government.

   Nobody really believes that capital punishment is not a deterrent to would-be murderers.

   Deep inside, *all* Americans are true patriots.

   REMEDY   When talking about large groups of individuals, use qualifiers like "some," "most," or "a majority," or refer to a certain percentage:

   Over 80 percent of Americans polled supported some form of gun control legislation.

3. *Loaded language:* **When you use emotionally charged language to label persons or situations negatively, you can turn off readers.**

   EXAMPLES   The *pigs* came into our yard and arrested my brother for no good reason.

   Congress is full of nothing but *idiots, liars,* and *fornicators.*

   Welfare recipients are the *scum of the earth.*

   REMEDY   Avoid using inflammatory language that makes a writer sound biased and unreasonable. The only readers that may be impressed are those who share those biases.

4. *Hasty conclusion:* **If you base a conclusion on very limited experience or data, readers will doubt its worth.**

   EXAMPLES   The food at the cafeteria is terrible. I ate lunch there yesterday, and my hamburger was burnt and cold. *(One bad hamburger doesn't necessarily mean all cafeteria food is bad.)*

   Gwen Smith is going to be a big tax-and-spend liberal in the Senate. Yesterday, she voted in favor of doubling funds for the educational Head Start program. *(One vote is not enough to base a conclusion on.)*

A River Runs Through It is a great movie. The reviewer in our college paper gave it four stars. *(One reviewer's opinion does not ensure the greatness of a movie.)*

REMEDY   Make sure that your conclusions are based on adequate support (for example, five consecutive bad eating experiences in the cafeteria, fifty congressional votes by Ms. Smith, or basic agreement among a dozen movie reviewers).

5. *Red herring:* **When a writer gets off the topic and diverts attention from the real issue, he is using a "red herring." When readers notice that a writer has veered off course, they wonder what his motive is.**

EXAMPLE   I couldn't really help running that red light on 10th Street. It's only a two-lane road, and there are parked cars along the curb. There's barely enough room for cars to drive. Besides, the speed limit isn't posted in that area. *(What do the two lanes, parked cars, limited driving space, and lack of posted speed limit have to do with running a red light? Presumably nothing.)*

REMEDY   Stick to the issue and your support for it. Getting off on side roads will only confuse readers or make them question your logic or motives.

6. *Ad hominem attack:* **When a writer attacks the person rather than the issue, he or she is attempting to discredit the person's viewpoint by discrediting the person. Perceptive readers will see that the writer is really avoiding the issue.**

EXAMPLES   John Felstead has no right to support pro-choice. He's not a woman and has no idea what it's like to have a living being growing inside you. *(Writer is attacking John for being a man rather than attacking his pro-choice position on its lack of merits.)*

Don't go to Dr. Janet Adams for marriage counseling. She's been divorced herself. *(Writer is attacking Dr. Adams for being divorced rather than evaluating her ability as a marriage counselor.)*

REMEDY   Attack the opposition's *position* on an issue rather than the person. An attack on the person is unfair and misleading, diverting readers from the issue.

ACTIVITY 6.11

Read the following sample essay. With a partner, find examples of various persuasive pitfalls in the draft and analyze how they may affect readers. Discuss the kinds of revisions that would be needed to make the writer's next draft more reasonable sounding and effective.

THE WELFARE SCAM

If you see a guy driving around in a Cadillac with a big smile on his face and a back-seat full of merchandise, he may be a hard-working American who's made it honestly. On the other hand, that guy in the Cadillac may be one of millions of welfare chiselers who rake in the bucks and sit on their butts all day. He's smiling because he's ripping us taxpayers off and getting away with it.

Millions of able-bodied men and women are on welfare because they are too lazy to work, and the government pays them for being lazy. These people make so much money from welfare that they are better off sitting home and waiting for those checks on the first and fifteenth of the month than they would be drawing honest wages. And they are laughing all the way to the bank.

What's more, they are producing thousands of welfare chiselers of the future. They have eight or nine kids so they can get more and more money, and then these kids grow up seeing how great their parents have it, and they learn to play the welfare game too. And it's an easy game: pretend you are looking for work occasionally, pay off a couple of people to say you couldn't get employment with them, and then go back to making more welfare babies.

These people would rather be on welfare than work or they'd be working. I've seen some of these guys sitting around the park across from the police station all day and loving it. I say they should be across the street locked up in jail, for they are ripping off the hard-working taxpayer worse than most crooks. And a lot of government officials are obviously getting kickbacks, or they wouldn't keep this outrageous scam going. Everyone's getting his palm greased, and we've all had enough of it.

I'm calling on all of you to write your congressman and demand that he start legislation to destroy the welfare system or at least drastically change it. If a man or woman has two arms and two legs, he or she should not be on welfare under any circumstances. And if you make them work, they'll quit having so many babies because all they have them for is the welfare money. Then we can start a real welfare system for the ten thousand people in America who really need it: the crippled Vietnam veterans whom we've all been giving the shaft to for twenty years. I say turn some of these Vietnam veterans loose on the welfare chiselers and we wouldn't have a problem for long.

■ ■ ■ ■ ■ ■ ■ ■ ■ ■ ■

ACTIVITY 6.12

Read your own first draft a last time for any persuasive pitfalls it may contain, and consider how you can eliminate them in the next draft. Then write your next draft, including all revisions noted for improving your persuasive paper, and continue the evaluation and drafting process until you are satisfied with your final draft.

■ ■ ■ ■ ■ ■ ■ ■ ■ ■ ■

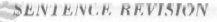

SENTENCE REVISION

This final "Sentence Revision" section reviews the most typical sentence problems and sentence variety options covered in the book.

WORDING PROBLEM REVIEW

To help you improve first draft sentences, here is a summary of the different kinds of sentence problems that writers often revise.

1. *Wordiness:* Sentences often contain more words than necessary to express a writer's thoughts. These sentences contain repeated words and phrases or unnecessarily complicated wording to make simple statements. To revise wordy sentences, eliminate words that are not needed, and replace complicated phrases with simpler ones.

WORDY SENTENCE	We were out in the rays of the sun for six hours of daylight, but we didn't burn due to the fact that we wore a sunscreen that kept us from burning.
REVISED	We were out in the sun for six hours, but we didn't burn because we wore a sunscreen.

2. *Awkward phrasing:* First draft sentences often contain awkward wording that occurs when a writer first tries out his or her thoughts on paper. If a sentence sounds odd to a writer, it will probably give a reader problems. To correct awkward wording, find a better way to express the thought. Changing a word or two may make the difference, or you may have to revise the entire sentence.

AWKWARD SENTENCE	There is a square cement floor with trees and bushes that are around the cement.
REVISED	Oak trees and a few bushes surround the cement patio.

3. *Poor word choices:* First draft sentences sometimes contain words that don't say quite what the writer wants. You can often tell when you've used a word in a first draft that doesn't sound right, but you can't think of a better choice. On returning to a draft after a few hours or days, the poorer word choices stand out even more, and often better choices come to you. To correct poor word choices, replace them with more appropriate words.

POOR WORD CHOICE	The clown made the boy full of fear instead of enjoying him.
REVISED	The clown frightened the boy instead of entertaining him.

4. *Misplaced and dangling modifiers:* Misplaced modifiers occur when a modifying phrase is placed some distance from the word it modifies. Dangling modifiers occur when an introductory phrase is

followed by a subject that it *doesn't* modify. To correct misplaced modifiers, put them directly after (or occasionally before) the modified word. To correct dangling modifiers, change the subject so that it goes with the modifying phrase, or add a subordinating conjunction and subject to the beginning of the phrase to form a dependent clause.

DANGLING PHRASE	Walking to school this morning, a car almost hit me.
REVISED	Walking to school this morning, I almost got hit by a car.
	or
	As I was walking to school this morning, a car almost hit me.
MISPLACED MODIFIER	That student looks rather strange with red hair standing by the door.
REVISED	That student with red hair standing by the door looks rather strange.

5. *Parallel construction:* Groups of words joined together in a sentence should be similar, or *parallel*, in structure. When you write, "John is tall, clumsy, brown hair, and intelligence," you are mixing your word forms in an awkward manner. When you write, "John is tall, clumsy, brown-haired, and intelligent," you have improved the sentence by using four modifying words that are parallel in structure. To correct a parallel construction problem, change the structure of any word in the series that is not parallel with the rest.

FAULTY PARALLEL CONSTRUCTION	The crook divided up the loot among his accomplices, left the largest share for himself, and for the crooked cop he saves $1,000.
REVISED	The crook divided up the loot among his accomplices, left the largest share for himself, and saved $1,000 for the crooked cop.

6. *Concrete language:* Vague, general wording should be replaced by *concrete language* that *shows* the reader what the writer sees, hears, and feels.

VAGUE WORDING	The boy works one part of the year.
REVISED	My ten-year-old neighbor, Jim Jones, works all summer at his father's feed store.

ACTIVITY *6.13*

The following sentences contain all the different sentence problems you have covered. Revise these first draft sentences to make them as clear and smooth as possible.

EXAMPLE   The militants they returned to campus after their release from jail for nuclear disarmament.

REVISED   The militants for nuclear disarmament returned to campus after their release from jail.

1. The drafting I did in high school was really the only thing that I knew.

2. I knew there would be some responsibilities I would have to make for college that would be economical for my parents.

3. For college students, succeeding or failing is a challenge.

4. Waiting for my aunt at the bus stop, two policemen started harassing me.

5. Do you think that it is worth all the effort that you're putting into school really worth it?

6. The woman is a great speaker in a blue jumpsuit and pink sandals.

7. What I found most difficult were the classes by which you arranged the time to meet with the instructor and you met with him individually.

8. Depressed by poor quarter grades, a visit from Julie's boyfriend cheered her up.

9. The court told him to go back to India, and that he cannot return to Malaysia.

10. There is no bell that rings for classes in college, and not like in high school.

11. There is a great difference in college life than when I was in high school.

12. This is an experience that happened to me in the summer of my freshman year, and I had just gotten my driver's license that summer when it happened.

13. We usually take the dog to the mountains every time we go hunting for animals in the mountains.

14. We became really good friends in our freshman year, and from then on we've become the best of friends since our freshman year.

15. Rhonda has blonde hair, a cute smile, about five feet tall, and blue-eyed.

16. The dog played in the house with a family member.

■ ■ ■ ■ ■ ■ ■ ■ ■ ■ ■

ACTIVITY 6.14

The following paragraph needs revising for sentence improvement. Rewrite the paragraph making each sentence as clear and smooth as possible.

It was a hot day for a parade. The band of the school had a five-mile walk through the middle of the town. Before the parade began, the band members standing at attention for an hour. Most band members were wet with sweat before they had walked one step. One tuba player he passed out from the heat and is taken to the hospital. Finally, the band began marching and starts playing "When the Saints Go Marching In." Every one of the members of that band was sick of that song "When the Saints Go

Marching In" before they got even halfway through the parade route they were marching along. By the time the band reached the judges' stand, their lips were too parched to suck, their march was a stagger, and their white uniforms are colored by sweat. The band finally went to the park and on the lawn collapsed. They stripped off their hats, coats, and shoes that they wore for the parade. They drank gallons of lemonade and compare blisters on their feet and compare scuffed up shoes.

. . . .

ACTIVITY 6.15

As you learned in earlier units, transitions are words and phrases that tie sentences and paragraphs together so that the readers can understand relationships of time, action, and thought. Fill in the blanks in the following paragraph with appropriate transitions. Some of the most common transitions include *first, second, next, then, now, finally, on the other hand, however, therefore, despite, nevertheless, on the contrary, last, another, still,* and *also*.

EXAMPLE   ___*After*___ Alice backed out of the driveway, her car stalled.

___*Then*___ it wouldn't start again. She ___*finally*___ pushed it to the curb and went back into the house. She didn't go to school.

___*Fortunately*___, she only had one class on Friday.

_____ Louie looked back on the semester, he felt good.

_____ , he'd passed his English class. He'd _____ passed history, Spanish, and mechanical drawing. He _____ had a total of 30 units of college credit; _____ , he wouldn't have to go to summer school to make up any units. _____ , Louie _____ had one regret about the semester. He hadn't gotten to know Delma as well as he had wanted to. He'd have to wait until next semester to do that. _____ that one setback, Louie felt it had been a good year. _____ he was ready for an easy summer.

. . . .

COMBINING SENTENCES

The purpose of joining sentences is to create strong single sentences out of two or more short, weaker ones. As you combine sentences, you also add variety by using different combining methods. Let's review the combining methods you have been using throughout this book.

1. **Eliminate repeated words and group similar words together, often by using the joining word *and*.**

DRAFT SENTENCES	Marie is a freshman. She is thirty-five years old. She is from Chicago. She now lives in Akron.
COMBINED	Marie is a thirty-five-year-old freshman from Chicago now living in Akron.
DRAFT SENTENCES	Joseph enrolled in college. Then he dropped out. Then he re-enrolled in the spring. This time he stayed.
COMBINED	Joseph enrolled in college, dropped out, re-enrolled in the spring, and stayed.

2. **Join sentences with coordinate conjunctions (*and, or, but, so, for, yet*) to form compound sentences.**

DRAFT SENTENCES	Mildred used to love to fly across country. Now you can't get her in a plane.
COMBINED	Mildred used to love to fly across country, but now you can't get her in a plane.
DRAFT SENTENCES	Harold has lived alone for thirty years. He likes it that way.
COMBINED	Harold has lived alone for thirty years, and he likes it that way.

3. **Join sentences with subordinate conjunctions (*because, since, unless, although, if, when, after, until*) or with relative pronouns (*who, whom, which, that*) to form complex sentences.**

DRAFT SENTENCES	I'm not crazy about my history instructor. I'm not going to drop the class because of that.
COMBINED	Although I'm not crazy about my history instructor, I'm not going to drop the class because of that.
DRAFT SENTENCES	Ramona is engaged to Raphael now. She used to be engaged to Armando.
COMBINED	Ramona, who used to be engaged to Armando, is engaged to Raphael now.

4. **Join sentences by using an introductory phrase and eliminating unnecessary words from the second sentence.**

DRAFT SENTENCES	Gwen had to quit the chess team. She was bothered by nagging headaches.
COMBINED	Bothered by nagging headaches, Gwen had to quit the chess team.
DRAFT SENTENCES	Take Route 42 to the bridge. That will get you to Muskegee.
COMBINED	To get to Muskegee, take Route 42 to the bridge.

DRAFT SENTENCES   Harold caught a hard right hand on the jaw. He was not worrying about defense.

COMBINED   <u>Not worrying about defense</u>, Harold caught a hard right hand on the jaw.

5. **Join sentences by inserting an appositive into the first sentence and eliminating unnecessary words.**

DRAFT SENTENCES   Fred likes to open beer bottles with his teeth. He's an old friend of mine.

COMBINED   Fred, <u>an old friend of mine</u>, likes to open beer bottles with his teeth.

DRAFT SENTENCES   The new parents named their baby girl Neptunia. That is an unusual name.

COMBINED   The new parents named their baby girl Neptunia, <u>an unusual name.</u>

ACTIVITY *6.16*

Here is an opportunity to use all of the combining methods just reviewed. Combine each group of sentences to form a single sentence by eliminating, adding, and moving words.

EXAMPLE   Melba likes to listen to her stereo. Thad likes to listen to his. They both enjoy using their headphones. They are brother and sister.

COMBINED   Melba and Thad, <u>who are brother and sister</u>, enjoy listening to their stereos and using their headphones.

1. Sheri is an interesting girl. She is a freshman in college. She is a practicing minister. She is an assistant manager of a shoe store.

2. The spaniel ran all over the hills. He was delighted to be in the open. He is owned by Mr. Jacobs. Mr. Jacobs turned him loose for an afternoon.

3. The Keystone Building is old. It is on 52nd Street. It is going to be demolished. It will be replaced by a high rise. It will happen by the end of summer.

4. Some children in town will be bused to school. They live on the northeast side of town. This will only be for one semester. Their school is being refurbished. It was damaged in an earthquake.

5. Clyde rushed to school. He opened his locker. He removed his notebook. He ran to his biology lab. He was late.

6. We found thousands of cockroaches in the old house. We found them behind the refrigerator. We found them this summer. They were dead. They had starved to death.

7. Greta is young. She is naive. She is impressionable. She is quick to learn.

8. The house is for sale. It's a dark brown. It's on the east corner of 5th Street. It's listed for $55,000. That is a real steal.

9. Jonathan is going bald. He's a nineteen-year-old fireman. He couldn't care less about going bald. He is not vain.

10. Ann rooms with Helen. Marie rooms with both of them. They are sophomores from Natchez. They live in off-campus housing. They live there during the semester. They move home in the summer.

11. Freda is friendly. She acts this way with everyone. She is only friendly on Fridays. There has to be a full moon.

12. Harley contemplates his future. He sits in his room. He forgets his past. It is troubled.

13. Mary likes to win. She isn't afraid of losing. She is the captain of the lawn bowling team. The team is from Friar Hill.

14. Teddy is my brother. He is younger than I am. He is bigger than I am. He doesn't weigh as much.

15. Kelly went skinny-dipping in the pond. Liza went with her. They did this despite the freezing water. They did it at midnight. It was pitch-dark.

16. Harold has trouble with allergies. He carries a box of tissues in his car. He goes through the box in a day. He does this in the springtime.

17. Mattie found her first grade class picture. She found it in the attic. It was among boxes of old albums. She was rummaging around for an old sweater.

18. Hank was attracted to Willifred. Willifred was attracted to Clyde. Clyde was attracted to Clementine.

19. Think of a way to get out of health science today. Come up with something new. Make it ingenious. I'm not prepared for the test. Neither are you.

20. Alexandra had to make a choice. She had to choose between beauty college and art school. She had to decide in the next week. Both schools enrolled students on Monday.

▪ ▪ ▪ ▪ ▪ ▪ ▪ ▪ ▪ ▪ ▪

COMPOUND-COMPLEX COMBINATIONS

In Unit 5, you learned that compound and complex sentence forms can be combined to form *compound-complex sentences* and *complex-complex sentences*. A compound-complex sentence is a compound sentence with a complex sentence in one or both of its halves. A complex-complex sentence has three clauses, two of which begin with subordinate conjunctions or relative pronouns. Since you have worked extensively with both compound and complex sentences, these combination forms should not be difficult to use.

Here are examples of compound-complex and complex-complex sentences.

EXAMPLES

Judy couldn't drive her car to school <u>because</u> the battery was dead, <u>so</u> she got a ride with her friend Tillie. *(compound-complex sentence)*

Meg didn't enjoy the concert, <u>but</u> she stayed until the end <u>since</u> her date had paid her way. *(compound-complex sentence)*

The teachers <u>who</u> were invited to tea were from the English department, <u>but</u> none of them went <u>because</u> they had papers to read. *(compound-complex sentence)*

<u>Although</u> the apartment looks barren now, it will be full of furniture <u>when</u> we bring in our parents' old chairs and sofas. *(complex-complex sentence)*

<u>When</u> Ralphie is in town, Marie, <u>who</u> works at the Bank of Pretoria, gives him free pens. *(complex-complex sentence)*

Ms. Anheimer, <u>who</u> teaches French and German, is fond of the man <u>who</u> owns the Greek delicatessen on Hope Street. *(complex-complex sentence)*

ACTIVITY 6.17

Fill in appropriate conjunctions, subordinate conjunctions, and relative pronouns to complete the following compound-complex and complex-complex sentences.

EXAMPLE   *After* Vinnie waxed his car, he put it in the garage *where* the birds couldn't get to it.

1. The stock market, _____ was healthy in July, took a dive in August _____ there was trouble in the Middle East.

2. The president was popular the first few months _____ everyone was giving him the benefit of the doubt, _____ soon after his popularity plunged.

3. _____ colleges are turning out more graduates today, there are fewer jobs available _____ people aren't retiring to create openings.

4. Murray Singleton, _____ waited tables at El Gazebo, never got a tip, _____ that didn't bother him _____ his salary had a 10 percent tip built in.

5. The building _____ you were in last night crumbled in a heap _____ the earthquake hit this morning.

6. _____ Sonya washes her hair, she sits and lets it dry for a while _____ it has set enough to blow dry.

7. _____ you want to succeed in college, pace yourself each semester

_____ you don't want to burn out early in your career.

8. _____ Willie cleans up his act, he'll get nowhere with Cecelia,

_____ likes a polished guy.

9. _____ we finish our geometry, let's take a four-day break

_____ you have a better suggestion.

10. _____ Hortensia talks, everyone listens _____ she has a

voice that would move Mt. Rushmore.

. . . .

ACTIVITY *6.18*

Write your own compound-complex and complex-complex sentences using the conjunctions, subordinate conjunctions, and relative pronouns provided. Follow the topics given.

EXAMPLE   **compound-complex sentence about a ship using *when* and *but***

When the ship pulled out of the harbor, it was barely moving, but in the open water it increased speed to 15 knots.

1. compound-complex sentence about fishing using *when* and *but*

2. compound-complex sentence about cleaning fish using *after* and *and*

3. compound-complex sentence about eating fish using *although* and *so*

4. complex-complex sentence about washing dishes using *as* and *because*

5. complex-complex sentence about setting a table using *after* and *until*

6. complex-complex sentence about mopping the floor using *if* and *unless*

7. compound-complex sentence about driving to school using *if, and,* and *because*

8. compound-complex sentence about finding a parking place using *since, but,* and *unless*

9. compound-complex sentence about studying for a test using *before, so,* and *until*

10. compound-complex sentence about watching television using *and* and *after*

11. complex-complex sentence about two teachers using *who* and *who*

12. compound-complex sentence about shopping using *that*, *but*, and *that*

. . . .

ACTIVITY **6.19**

Using your knowledge of effective persuasive writing, write a short essay convincing someone to break a bad habit. When you finish your first draft, check your sentences for wording problems and structural variety. Do you have any pairs or groups of sentences that would be more effective combined into a single sentence? How can you revise individual sentences to make them clearer, smoother, or more interesting? Write a second draft to share with the person you are writing to.

AUDIENCE   my sister Joselyn

PURPOSE   talk her out of eating so much at night

SAMPLE ESSAY

Joselyn, dear sister, you know what your worst habit is: stuffing your face all evening until you go to bed. You show great control during the day. You eat no breakfast, only a small lunch, and a reasonably sized dinner. But those 7:00-to-11:00 p.m. munchies are doing you in.

You know the results of your nighttime binging. You're a good ten pounds overweight; just take a good look at those love handles in the mirror. And you know you look a lot better with those pounds off. Your friends say you look better, you feel better, and you like yourself more. And you know how you usually forget to brush your teeth at night? All of that sugar and Dorito bits and pizza cheese hang out in your mouth all night long. Is it any wonder you have so many cavities every time you go to the dentist?

Let's analyze the problem, Joselyn. You don't eat in the morning because you're not hungry. You don't eat much lunch because you're rushing to get to your afternoon classes. You eat a good dinner because you haven't eaten much all day. So why do you go crazy at night? The main reason is that you're sitting in front of the TV relaxing, and you want to enjoy yourself and reward yourself for watching your diet during the day. And let's admit it: You love to eat junk food!

Okay, so you admit you're flabby and you're ruining your teeth with your evening eating habits. So what are you going to do about it? You might get more active in the evenings, do things to take your mind off food, but knowing you, you're just going to relax at night like you've done all your life. You could try replacing the junk food with health stuff like fruit and vegetables and cereal, but you don't really like that stuff, and you don't feel it fills you up. You could try toughing it out and going cold turkey for awhile, but I can guess how long that would last.

So this isn't an easy habit to break, I can see that. You've tried, I know. So let's try something different. First, try holding off and eating dinner about an hour later. You know that when you have a late dinner, say at about 7:00 or 7:30, you don't crave more food at night like you do when you eat at 5:30 or 6:00. So eat dinner later, even if it means eating a banana at 5:00 or so to keep the stomach under control.

Next, allow yourself one good snack a night—something you really like to eat. Everyone snacks a little at night, so choose one thing a night that you really love, and make that be enough for the evening. Eat that snack around 9:30 or 10:00 to have something to look forward to and so you won't be so tempted to eat again later.

So you're eating dinner later and snacking only once at night. Good for you. The pounds are starting to melt off, and now, after a month, you've dropped ten. Now go out and splurge. Buy yourself a new outfit, and pay for it on time, twelve months if possible, and make sure it fits the new you. Wear the outfit at least once a week, and be determined that it is going to keep fitting you until you have it paid off. That will give you a goal of going a year on your new plan. If you can last a year, you've got it made. You'll look great, you'll still get to eat your favorite junk food, you'll have some new clothes, and your teeth will be healthier. Get started tonight. If you put it off a day, you'll put it off a month.

WRITING REVIEW

ACTIVITY 6.20

For your final paper, select a topic that affects you personally, where your viewpoint differs with the person or persons in control on the issue: a boss, parent, teacher, school administration, club members, police department, store manager, insurance company, and so on. Write your paper to the person or persons in control in an attempt to change their minds.

After you select a topic, do some type of prewriting work to generate ideas for your paper, and decide on a tentative thesis. Do whatever investigation necessary to write the most persuasive paper. When you are ready, write your first draft, keeping the following in mind:

1. What is your purpose in writing to this particular audience, and how can you best accomplish it?

2. What are the most important points you need to present to support your viewpoint, and how can you weaken your reader's viewpoint?

STUDENT SAMPLE TOPIC SELECTION

Let's see, what issue affects me personally where someone else is calling the shots. My wife hardly ever lets me drive the good car, something I'd at least like to do at least once in a while. Then there's the insurance problem where they only reimbursed me $250 on $850 worth of property stolen from my car. They say I didn't read the coverage on the contract.

One thing that's bugging me right now is that two of my classes were canceled for lack of enrollment. What a hassle. Now I've got to scrounge around for classes during the third week. That's a lousy deal, and it's happened before. The administration is overscheduling classes and students are suffering. That's something I'd like to write to them about. I'll give it a try.

STUDENT SAMPLE PREWRITING

I think I'll brainstorm on the topic to get some ideas down. Then I'll consider a specific thesis statement, although I already know how I feel about the issue.

BRAINSTORMING

overscheduling hurts students

can't get into classes

not the students' fault

why do they do it?

wait too long to cancel class

should put out a warning

could change classes during registration

not considering effect on students

must be hoping for bigger enrollment

must screw up teachers too

teachers aren't even listed for some sections

playing games

could add classes if enrollment justifies

think of students, not funding

who's responsible if students can't find classes

need guarantee for students

no-fault for students if class is canceled

find out who does scheduling

find out school's rationale

TENTATIVE THESIS STATEMENT

The school's practice of overscheduling and then canceling courses is hurting students, and it should be stopped.

MAIN IDEAS FROM BRAINSTORMING

1. Explain college's practice as I see it.
2. Show the negative effects on students (plenty of examples).
3. Question the need (refute opposing viewpoint).
4. Offer alternatives.

STUDENT FIRST DRAFT

SCHEDULING WOES

Last semester I was lucky enough to enroll in all five classes that I needed for general education requirements. All the course sections I had in my schedule were still open when I registered. I didn't have to worry about back-up classes since I figured my schedule was set.

By the end of the second week of the semester, three of my five classes had been canceled, due to a lack of the "necessary" enrollment. Then I was forced, along with many other students, to scrounge around for other classes, which was frustrating and difficult. I ended up getting into only two other courses, neither of which I would have taken by choice. Clearly, there's something wrong with the scheduling practice at the college, and students are suffering.

For the second semester now, the college has scheduled significantly more sections of general ed courses than have been "made." It appears the school, or deans, or whoever makes the enrollment decisions waits to see which sections reach the magic minimum of twenty enrollees, and then cancels all those with fewer than twenty. Students caught in the smaller classes are then compelled to seek out other sections or courses, with no guarantees that they'll be allowed in.

To make matters worse, sometimes smaller sections are "carried" through the second week in hopes of late enrollments, leaving students desperately seeking classes in the third week of the semester. Some instructors have a policy of not accepting any students after the second week of the semester, and the students are often treated as if they have no business trying to get into classes late!

The effects of sections being canceled are obvious. First, students are lulled into believing that their schedules are set for the semester, so they don't worry about "double enrolling" in additional courses to cover themselves, a practice the college frowns on. Second, they are left, often for two weeks into the semester, with the uncertainty and anxiety of not knowing which of their classes will "make" and which will be canceled. Third, once classes are canceled, students are left with the responsibility of finding other classes to fill their schedules, and the college guarantees them nothing. Finally, and most damaging, they often end up taking classes they didn't want or need, and taking fewer classes than they had planned, which could jeopardize their grant eligibility and lengthen their stay at the college.

I'm sure the college has its reasons for overscheduling sections of courses. It can see which sections fill and then cancel the smaller sections that are more costly. It can also list the instructors for most sections as "staff" and then place teachers in sections where there are the best enrollments. And the college knows that with many small sections being canceled, the enrollment in the sections that "make" will only get better. In short, the administrators are doing what's best financially for the college at the expense of the students.

The college's current practice of overscheduling sections of courses is very unfair to students. The number of sections offered any semester should reflect the number of classes that realistically should fill with at least twenty students. That number can be pretty well determined by checking the number of sections of a course that "made" the same semester of the previous year. A two- or three-year study, taking college enrollment fluctuations into account, might provide an even more accurate indicator. The excuse that the college can't really predict how many sections to offer in any given semester just doesn't wash.

Last semester, according to the college admission's office, twenty-four sections of general ed pattern courses were canceled due to small enrollment. That is a scandalously high number. I think anyone could understand four or five sections needing to be canceled or added, based on enrollment fluctuations, but twenty-four canceled sections indicates a clearly intended practice of overscheduling and canceling classes, strictly for the financial benefit and convenience of the school and at the expense of the students.

This practice needs to be stopped immediately, and I am asking the administration to meet with a student committee before next semester's schedule is published. We want to ensure that all of the classes scheduled, based on current overall enrollment, have a realistic chance of reaching minimum enrollment figures. When that occurs, students' registration schedules will accurately reflect their load for the semester, students won't be forced to scrounge for classes after the semester begins, and students will have a better chance of getting the classes and the units they need. After all, the college is here for the students, and not the other way around.

▪ ▪ ▪ ▪ ▪ ▪ ▪ ▪ ▪ ▪ ▪ ▪

When you finish your first draft, read it over, applying the questions for revision on pages 173 and 174, and including the persuasive pitfall considerations on pages 175 through 178. If you want a second opinion, exchange papers with a classmate, asking him or her to react as if he or she held the viewpoint of the intended reading audience. When you are ready, write the second draft of your paper, and continue the evaluating and drafting process until you are ready to share your paper with your readers.

READINGS

THE DEATH PENALTY IS A STEP BACK

by Coretta Scott King

1   When Steven Judy was executed in Indiana [in 1981] America took another step backwards towards legitimizing murder as a way of dealing with evil in our society.

2   Although Judy was convicted of four of the most horrible and brutal murders imaginable, and his case is probably the worst in recent memory for opponents of the death penalty, we still have to face the real issue squarely: Can we expect a decent society if the state is allowed to kill its own people?

3   In recent years, an increase of violence in America, both individual and political, has prompted a backlash of public opinion on capital punishment. But however much we abhor violence, legally sanctioned executions are no deterrent and are, in fact, immoral and unconstitutional.

4   Although I have suffered the loss of two family members by assassination, I remain firmly and unequivocally opposed to the death penalty for those convicted of capital offenses.

5   An evil deed is not redeemed by an evil deed of retaliation. Justice is never advanced in the taking of a human life.

6   Morality is never upheld by legalized murder. Morality apart, there are a number of practical reasons which form a powerful argument against capital punishment.

7   First, capital punishment makes irrevocable any possible miscarriage of justice. Time and again we have witnessed the specter of mistakenly convicted people being put to death in the name of American criminal justice. To those who say that, after all, this doesn't occur too often, I can only reply that if it happens just once, that is too often. And it has occurred many times.

8   Second, the death penalty reflects an unwarranted assumption that the wrongdoer is beyond rehabilitation. Perhaps some individuals cannot be rehabilitated; but who shall make that determination? Is any amount of academic training sufficient to entitle one person to judge another incapable of rehabilitation?

9   Third, the death penalty is inequitable. Approximately half of the 711 persons now on death row are black. From 1930 through 1968, 53.5% of those executed were black Americans, all too many of whom were represented by court-appointed attorneys and convicted after hasty trials.

10   The argument that this may be an accurate reflection of guilt, and homicide trends, instead of a racist application of laws lacks credibility in light of a recent Florida survey which showed that persons convicted of killing whites were four times more likely to receive a death sentence than those convicted of killing blacks.

11   Proponents of capital punishment often cite a "deterrent effect" as the main benefit of the death penalty. Not only is there no hard evidence that murdering murderers will deter other potential killers, but even the "logic" of this argument defies comprehension.

12   Numerous studies show that the majority of homicides committed in this country are the acts of the victim's relatives, friends and acquaintances in the "heat of passion."

13   What this strongly suggests is that rational consideration of future consequences are seldom a part of the killer's attitude at the time he commits a crime.

14   The only way to break the chain of violent reaction is to practice non-violence as individuals and collectively through our laws and institutions.

Questions for Analysis

1. What is the essay's thesis on the topic of the death penalty? Where is it found?

2. What are King's arguments in support of the thesis? What evidence is provided for each argument? Evaluate each argument and its evidence.

3. What arguments in support of the death penalty are presented? How are they refuted?

4. What audience might the essay be intended for? What is King's purpose in writing the essay? How well is the purpose accomplished?

5. Do you agree with the thesis? If you do, what arguments and evidence in the essay are most convincing? If you don't, how would you refute King's arguments against the death penalty?

Vocabulary

deterrent (3), unequivocally (4), specter (7)

LIMITING HANDGUNS

by Robert deGrazia

1   We buried Donald Brown in May. He was murdered by three men who wanted to rob the supermarket manager he was protecting. Patrolman Brown was 61 years old, six months from retirement. He and his wife intended to retire to Florida at the end of the year. Now there will be no retirement in the sun, and she is alone.

2   Donald Brown was the second police officer to die since I became commissioner here on Nov. 15, 1972.

3   The first was John Schroeder, a detective shot in a pawnshop robbery last November. John Schroeder was the brother of Walter Schroeder, who was killed in a bank robbery in 1970. Their names are together on the honor roll in the lobby of Police Headquarters.

4   John Murphy didn't die. He was shot in the head last February as he chased a robbery suspect into the Washington Street subway station. He lived, but he will be brain-damaged for the rest of his life, unable to walk or talk.

5   At least two of these police officers were shot by a handgun, the kind one can buy nearly everywhere for a few dollars. Those who don't want to buy one can steal one, and half a million are stolen each year. There are forty million handguns circulating in this country; two and a half million are sold each year.

6   Anybody can get a gun. Ownership of handguns has become so widespread that the gun is no longer merely the instrument of crime; it is now a cause of violent crime. Of the eleven Boston police officers killed since 1962, seven were killed with handguns; of the seventeen wounded by guns since 1962, sixteen were shot with handguns.

7   Police officers, of course, are not the only people who die. Ten thousand other Americans are dead at the price of our promiscuous right to bear arms. Gun advocates are fond of saying that guns don't kill, people do. But guns do kill.

8   Half of the people who commit suicide do so with handguns. Fifty-four percent of the murders committed in 1972 were committed with handguns. Killing with handguns simply is a good deal easier than killing with other weapons.

9   Rifles and shotguns are difficult to conceal. People can run away from knife-wielding assailants. People do die each year by drownings, bludgeonings and strangulation. But assaults with handguns are five times more likely to kill.

10   No one can convince me, after returning from Patrolman Brown's funeral, after standing in the rain with hundreds of others from this department and others, that we should allow people to own handguns.

11   I know that many people feel deeply and honestly about their right to own and enjoy guns. I realize that gun ownership and self-protection are deeply held American values. I am asking that people give them up.

12   I am committed to doing what I can to take guns away from the people. In my view, private ownership of handguns must be banished from this country. I am not asking for registration or licensing or outlawing cheap guns. I am saying that no private citizen, whatever his claim, should possess a handgun. Only police officers should.

Questions for Analysis

1.   What is the topic of this essay? What is deGrazia's thesis? Where is the thesis specifically stated? Where is it implied?

2.   What is presented in the first five paragraphs? What impact do these paragraphs have on the reader? Why do you think deGrazia opened his essay this way?

3.   What are deGrazia's main arguments against handguns? Where do these arguments appear in the essay? Are they convincing?

4.   Discuss the organization of the essay: the opening five paragraphs, the middle paragraphs, and the final three paragraphs. What is accomplished in each part? Is the organization effective? How might the essay be organized differently?

5.   What audience do you think deGrazia is trying to reach in the essay? What might his purpose be in writing it? Do you agree with his viewpoint on handguns?

Vocabulary

promiscuous (7), wielding (9), assailants (9), bludgeonings (9), banished (12)

THE COLORIZATION OF FILMS INSULTS ARTISTS AND SOCIETY

by Woody Allen

1   In the world of potent self-annihilation, famine and AIDS, terrorists and dishonest public servants and quack evangelists and contras and Sandinistas and cancer, does it really matter if some kid snaps on his TV and happens to see *The Maltese Falcon* in color? Especially if he can simply dial the color out and choose to view it in its original black and white?

2   I think it does make a difference and the ramifications of what's called colorization are not wonderful to contemplate. Simply put, the owners of thousands of classic American black and white films believe that there would be a larger public for the movies, and consequently more money, if they were reissued in color. Since they have computers that can change such masterpieces as *Citizen Kane* and *City Lights* and *It's A Wonderful Life* into color, it has become a serious problem for anyone who cares about these movies and has feelings about our image of ourselves as a culture.

3   I won't comment about the quality of the color. It's not good, but probably it will get better. Right now it's like elevator music. It has no soul. All faces are rendered with the same deadening pleasance. The choices of what colors people should be wearing or what colors rooms should be (all crucial artistic decisions in making film) are left to caprices and speculation by computer technicians who are not qualified to make those choices.

4   Probably false, but not worth debating here, is the claim that young people won't watch black and white. I would think they would, judging from the amount of stylish music videos and MTV ads that are done in black and white, undoubtedly after market research. The fact that audiences of all ages

have been watching Charlie Chaplin, Humphrey Bogart, Jimmy Stewart, Fred Astaire—in fact, all the stars and films of the so-called Golden Age of Hollywood—in black and white for decades with no diminution of joy also makes me wonder about these high claims for color. Another point the coloroids make is that one can always view the original if one prefers. The truth is, however, that in practical terms, what will happen is that the color versions will be aired while token copies of the original black and white will lie around preserved in a vault, unpromoted and unseen.

5   Another aspect of the problem that one should mention (although it is not the crucial ground on which I will make my stand) is that American films are a landmark heritage that do our nation proud all over the world, and should be seen as they were intended to be.

6   One would wince at defacing great buildings or paintings, and, in the case of movies, what began as a popular entertainment has, like jazz music, developed into a serious art form. Now, someone might ask: "Is an old Abbott and Costello movie art? Should it be viewed in the same way as *Citizen Kane*?" The answer is that it should be protected, because all movies are entitled to their personal integrity and, after all, who knows what future generations will regard as art works of our epoch?

7   Yet another question: "Why were directors not up in arms about cutting films for television or breaking them up for commercials, insulting them with any number of technical alterations to accommodate the television format?" The answer is that directors always hated these assaults on their work but were powerless to stop them. As in life, one lives with the first few wounds, because to do battle is an overwhelmingly time-consuming and pessimistic prospect.

8   Still, when the assaults come too often, there is a revolution. The outrage of seeing one's work transformed into color is so dramatically appalling, so "obvious"—as against stopping sporadically for commercials—that this time all the directors, writers and actors chose to fight.

9   But let me get to the real heart of the matter and to why I think the issue is not merely one that affronts the parties directly involved but has a larger meaning. What's at stake is a moral issue and how our culture chooses to define itself. No one should be able to alter an artist's work in any way whatsoever, for any reason, without the artist's consent. It's really as simple as that.

10   John Huston has made it clear that he doesn't want *The Maltese Falcon* seen in color. This is his right as an artist and certainly must be his choice alone. Nor would I want to see my film *Manhattan* in color. Not if it would bring in 10 times the revenue. Not if all the audiences in the world begged or demanded to see it that way.

11   I believe the people who are coloring movies have contempt for the audience by claiming, in effect, that viewers are too stupid and too insensitive to appreciate black and white photography—that they must be given, like infants or monkeys, bright colors to keep them amused.

12   They have contempt for the artist, caring little for the moral right these directors have over their own creations.

13   And, finally, they have contempt for society because they help define it as one that chooses to milk every last dollar out of its artists' work, even if it means mutilating the work and humiliating the culture's creative talent.

14   This is how we are viewed around the world and how we will be viewed by future generations. Most civilized governments abroad, realizing that their society is at least as much shaped and identified by its artists as by its businessmen, have laws to protect such things from happening. In our society, merchants are willing to degrade anything

or anyone so long as it brings in a financial profit.

15 Allowing the colorization of films is a good example of our country's regard for its artists, and why I think the issue of moral rights requires legislative help and protection.

16 The recent Federal copyright decision says that if a human being uses a certain minimum amount of creativity in coloring a black and white film, the new color version is a separate work that can be copyrighted. In short, if a man colors *Citizen Kane*, it becomes a new movie that can be copyrighted. This must be changed. How? By making sure that Representative Richard A. Gephardt's film integrity bill is passed. It would legalize the moral rights of film artists and, in the process, make colorization without consent illegal.

17 It is, after all, a very short step to removing the score from *Gone With the Wind* and replacing it with a rock score under the mistaken notion that it will render it more enjoyable to young people.

Questions for Analysis

1. What is the topic of the essay? What is the essay's thesis? Where is it found?

2. What are Allen's main arguments in support of the thesis? What evidence is provided for each argument?

3. What arguments are presented in support of colorization? How is each refuted in the essay?

4. What comparisons are used to support the thesis? What effect do they have?

5. Analyze the opening and conclusion of the essay. What is accomplished in each? Why do you think Allen chose to open and conclude the essay as he did?

6. How is the essay organized? How effective is the organization? What other way could the arguments have been presented? Would it have been as effective? Why?

7. Do you agree with the thesis? How would the fact that many of the original artists who created the black and white films are dead affect Allen's argument?

Vocabulary

ramifications (2), diminution (4), appalling (8), affronts (9)

FINAL EDITING

The last step in completing a paper is to correct any errors in your writing. When you *proofread* an essay, you check it over carefully for errors in sentence structure, spelling, punctuation, and grammar. No matter how good your content is, readers will have problems if they must grapple with mistakes. The "Final Editing" section shows you common errors to look for in your writing, ways of correcting those errors, and suggestions for avoiding them.

Although proofreading for errors is considered the last step in drafting, it is also an ongoing process for most writers. While you are revising a draft to improve your sentences, you might run across mistakes in spelling or sentence structure. You might notice an *ed* left off a verb or an -s missing from a plural word. You might correct the errors then or you could circle the questionable words and sentences and correct them later. Any time you run across a possible error, it is a good idea to make note of it.

SENTENCE PROBLEMS

The two most common sentence structure problems are running sentences together and writing incomplete sentences. Two or more sentences run together are called a *run-on sentence*. An incomplete sentence is called a *fragment*. In most cases, run-on sentences and fragments are errors that confuse readers and make your writing harder to understand. The purpose of this section is to help you recognize the most common types of run-ons and fragments, to show you ways of correcting them, and to help you avoid them in your writing.

Run-on Sentences

Here are some common features of run-on sentences:

1. A run-on is usually two sentences run together without a period ending the first sentence or a capital letter beginning the second.

   EXAMPLE   June is a very spoiled child she expects to get her way at all times.

2. A run-on with a comma between the two sentences is called a *comma splice*. A comma by itself does not separate sentences, and it does not replace a period.

   EXAMPLE   We never go into town during the week, it is too far from our farm.

3. The sentences within a run-on are usually closely related in meaning.

   EXAMPLE   Maria is doing well in algebra she has gotten B's on all her tests.

Run-ons Involving Pronouns

Most run-on sentences follow certain patterns. A *pronoun* often begins the second sentence within a run-on. You will learn more about pronouns later, but for correcting run-on sentences, you need to know the following pronouns:

he	it	they
she	you	we
I		

Here are some examples in which the underlined pronoun begins the second sentence within the run-on sentence:

EXAMPLES   Ted's parents spoil him <u>they</u> give him money to brush his teeth.

Sylvia came to class early, <u>she</u> wanted to study her notes.

The history test was a cinch <u>it</u> took only fifteen minutes to complete.

The tides at the beach were unpredictable, <u>they</u> made swimming dangerous.

Annie wasn't eager to go home she knew the house was empty.

All of us drove to the supermarket, <u>we</u> rode in Charlie's van.

Each of these sentences is a *run-on*: two sentences run together without correct punctuation. Notice that the *pronoun* beginning the second sentence often replaces a word in the first sentence. *To correct the sentences, you need to either separate the sentences with a period or join them with a coordinate or a subordinate conjunction.* Here are the sentences correctly punctuated. When a joining word is added, it is underlined.

EXAMPLES   Ted's parents spoil him. They give him money to brush his teeth.

Sylvia came to class early <u>because</u> she wanted to study her notes.

The history test was a cinch. It took only fifteen minutes to complete.

<u>Since</u> the tides at the beach were unpredictable, they made swimming dangerous.

Annie wasn't eager to go home. She knew the house was empty.

All of us drove to the supermarket, <u>and</u> we rode in Charlie's van.

ACTIVITY *1*

Most of the following sentences are run together. Rewrite the run-on sentences correctly by putting a period after the first sentence and capitalizing the second sentence in each pair or by joining the sentences with a coordinate or subordinate conjunction to form one compound or complex sentence. *As a general rule, separate the longer run-ons with periods, and connect the shorter sentences with joining words.*

EXAMPLE   The bear backed into its cave, it was frightened by the flames.

REVISED   The bear backed into its cave because it was frightened by the flames.

EXAMPLE   I have tried to ignore your annoying habit of cracking your toes in class I must now ask you to stop before I go crazy.

REVISED   I have tried to ignore your annoying habit of cracking your toes in class. I must now ask you to stop before I go crazy.

1. The downtown bus is always late, I don't expect it to arrive for another twenty minutes.

2. Ronald Reagan lifts weights regularly you couldn't tell by looking at him.

3. Fred and Hilda have something special in common they were born in the back of the same taxi cab exactly one year apart.

4. Howard is never late for work, for he has an alarm that plays reveille.

5. The hurricane hit at midnight it brought winds of eighty miles an hour.

6. Most children seem to perform best when praised they often don't do as well when they are criticized.

7. Amelia always looks for the best in other people, she is one of the most positive individuals I've met.

8. The bassett hound yelped at the moon and awakened the neighborhood.

9. You should take advanced badminton next semester at the college you would be a whiz at it with your quickness and coordination.

10. Colette, my youngest sister, is only seventeen, she is married to the bouncer at the Kitten Club.

■ ■ ■ ■ ■ ■ ■ ■ ■ ■ ■ ■ ■

ACTIVITY **2**

Write eight pairs of sentences using the subjects provided to begin each sentence. Punctuate your sentences correctly to avoid run-ons.

EXAMPLE   The owls—they

The owls in the pine trees hooted all night. They didn't bother me, but they made Henry mad.

1. **The bookstore—it**
2. **The elephants—they**
3. **Mr. Kettlefish—he**
4. **Matilda—she**
5. **The entire class—we**
6. **The pool hall—it**
7. **The hand grenades—they**
8. **The frightened child—she**

■ ■ ■ ■ ■ ■ ■ ■ ■ ■ ■ ■

Other Run-on Patterns
Although pronouns are involved in many run-on sentences, other kinds of words frequently begin the second part of a run-on. These are some of the more common patterns:

1. *Names:* **Sam, Helen, Clyde, Leftie, Rose**
2. *Introductory words:* **then, there, here, the, this**
3. *Amounts and numbers:* **some, none, all, most, few, each, one**
4. *Command words:* **stop, don't, do, please**

Here are examples of run-on sentences involving these types of words:

EXAMPLES   Eighty runners began the marathon, all of them finished.

Harry ordered a milkshake and french fries at McDonald's then he ordered a tostada at Peco Pete's.

It is easy getting to the subway <u>there</u> are many streets you can take.

The X ray will be painless, <u>don't</u> be concerned.

Halbrook is worried about losing his job, <u>Al</u> is in no danger of losing his.

Please drive downtown after school <u>stop</u> at the bank and deposit my check.

Each of the example sentences is run together. The underlined word begins the second sentence. Here are the corrected versions with the sentences either separated by a period or joined to form a compound or complex sentence.

EXAMPLES   Eighty runners began the marathon, and all of them finished.

Harry ordered a milkshake and french fries at McDonald's. Then he ordered a tostada at Peco Pete's.

It is easy getting to the subway because there are many streets you can take.

The X ray will be painless, so don't be concerned.

Halbrook is worried about losing his job. Al is in no danger of losing his.

Please drive downtown after school, and stop at the bank and deposit my check.

ACTIVITY 3

The following sentences are run together. Rewrite and correct the sentences by placing a period after the first sentence and capitalizing the first letter of the second sentence, or by joining the sentences with conjunctions or subordinate conjunctions to form compound and complex sentences. Look for words from this section that often begin the second part of a run-on.

EXAMPLE   Let's get into some grubby clothes then we'll be ready for the mud fight.

REVISED   Let's get into some grubby clothes, and then we'll be ready for the mud fight.

EXAMPLE   John has been absent now for eight days in a row, there is really no excuse for his missing that much school.

REVISED   John has been absent now for eight days in a row. There is really no excuse for his missing that much school.

1. Go down the corridor and turn left at the "T" then enter the first door on your right.

2. Chess is a complicated game there are many options for each move.

3. Fishing was slow on Sunday morning most of the salmon had been caught Saturday evening.

4. The false teeth on the sink were for Aunt Hilda here yours are on the dresser.

5. You've been writing some exciting papers lately please send me some more as soon as you've finished.

6. Only five of the fifty contestants were selected to represent the college in the academic decathlon Naomi was one of the five selected.

7. The otter disappeared under the dam, then it surfaced fifty yards downstream in the middle of some lily pads.

8. The twins don't compete against each other each one has her own talents.

9. Samantha has been pushing herself hard this semester now it's finally over.

10. The political science students were active in the gubernatorial election in their state most of them walked precincts and made phone calls.

11. Let's go to the garage before noon tomorrow, Albert should have the radiator patched by then.

12. You've turned in every assignment this semester well in advance, keep up the good work!

■ ■ ■ ■ ■ ■ ■ ■ ■ ■ ■

Longer Run-ons

Although the majority of run-on sentences involve two sentences, it is not uncommon for a writer to run three or four sentences together without periods or joining words. Writers who have problems with longer run-ons usually have not mastered the concept of the sentence as a complete thought, so they are uncertain where to put their periods. Reading sentences aloud and looking for the ending of one thought and the beginning of another often helps writers understand the sentence concept. You can solve the problem of running sentences together if you understand the idea of separating complete ideas and scrutinize every draft sentence carefully to uncover those more elusive run-ons.

These examples of run-on sentences involve three or more sentences.

EXAMPLE   Ralph got to school early this morning he went to the library to study for his 9:00 Spanish test, then he went to class ten minutes early to ask his Spanish teacher about conjugating irregular verbs.

This run-on contains three sentences. It contains three complete thoughts, and if you read the run-on aloud, you will see how your voice drops and you pause after each sentence. Here is one way to correct this run-on, combining two sentences with a conjunction and separating the other sentence.

REVISED   Ralph got to school early this morning, so he went to the library to study for his 9:00 Spanish test. Then he went to class ten minutes early to ask his Spanish teacher about conjugating irregular verbs.

EXAMPLE   My sister lives with her husband in the apartment behind our house although they would like their own home, they can't afford one, they are putting some money away each month for an eventual down payment.

This run-on sentence has the common problem of having a clause beginning with a subordinate conjunction (*although*) in the middle. The writer isn't sure what sentence the clause belongs with, so he runs the sentences together. Here is a correctly revised version eliminating the three-sentence run-on.

REVISED   My sister lives with her husband in an apartment behind our house. Although they would like their own home, they can't afford one. They are putting some money away each month for an eventual down payment.

ACTIVITY 4

The following sentences are run together, and some contain three or four sentences. Rewrite and correct the sentences by separating some sentences with periods and joining shorter sentences with coordinate and subordinate conjunctions to form compound and complex sentences.

EXAMPLE   Freda lives next door she's lived there for thirty years, her husband lived with her until he died last November.

REVISED   Freda lives next door, and she's lived there for thirty years. Her husband lived with her until he died last November.

1. The willow tree is losing its leaves it's only the first part of the summer, it must have some kind of disease.

2. That snail hasn't moved it's been sitting in the driveway all morning, I've heard of moving at a "snail's pace" this is ridiculous.

3. Arvy ran from his home to the college and back, it took him a little over an hour, he was surprised how good he felt he had never run that far before.

4. The only way to lose weight is to eat less, it also helps to exercise regularly.

5. Hortensia was having problems with her eyes if she read for over an hour, she would get a bad headache, finally, she went to an eye doctor he prescribed some reading glasses.

6. Clyde took his dirty clothes to the laundromat on campus then he went to the grocery store for some bread and salami.

7. "Moonshoes" are very popular shoes, all the big-name athletes advertise them on television although the company used to manufacture only basketball shoes, now

Moonshoes Inc. has jogging shoes, track shoes, soccer shoes, and casual shoes, the advertisements have really helped sell them.

8.   Our new neighbors are private people I've never seen them in their yard I've also never seen any company at their house even though they've been in their home for a year, I still don't know how many people live there.

. . . .

Run-on Sentence Review

Let's review what you have learned about run-on sentences in this section:

1.   A run-on is usually two sentences run together without proper punctuation.

2.   A comma by itself does not correctly separate sentences.

3.   A pronoun (*I, he, she, it, you, they, we*) most commonly begins the second sentence within a run-on.

4.   Four other kinds of words also frequently begin the second sentence of a run-on: introductory words (*there, then, here, the*), amounts and numbers (*one, all, some, each*), names, and command words (*don't, do, please*).

5.   Writers who have difficulty recognizing complete sentences sometimes run three or more sentences together. Longer run-ons frequently involve subordinate conjunctions (*because, since, until, if, as, when, after*) as well as the words covered in numbers 3 and 4.

6.   Reading sentences aloud is a way to find where sentences end. Writers who have severe run-on problems often can identify the ends of sentences when they read them aloud.

7.   Run-on sentences can be corrected by placing a period after each complete sentence and beginning each new sentence with a capital letter or by joining the sentences with coordinate or subordinate conjunctions to form compound and complex sentences.

8.   Two or three very short sentences run together may be condensed into a single sentence rather than being separated by periods or joined with coordinate or subordinate conjunctions.

> EXAMPLE   Beth is smart she is outgoing she is a pest.
>
> REVISED   Beth is a smart, outgoing pest.

9.   Run-on sentences should be corrected because they confuse readers by running separate thoughts together and by eliminating the familiar signposts—periods, capital letters, and joining words—that readers rely on to follow a writer's thoughts.

ACTIVITY 5

The following sentences are run together. Some contain two sentences, and some contain three or more. Many of the run-ons are identified by the kinds of words that frequently begin the second sentence within run-ons. Rewrite and correct the run-ons by separating complete sentences with periods and capital letters and by joining sentences with coordinate conjunctions (*and, or, but, so, for, yet*) or subordinate conjunctions (*because, until, when, if, as, unless, since, while, where*). Use your own judgment regarding when to separate sentences and when to join them.

EXAMPLE   Freda tried out for the track team, she wanted to get in shape.

REVISED   Freda tried out for the track team because she wanted to get in shape.

EXAMPLE   I have tried to reason with Melissa about buying a new car that will put her in debt, she is determined to buy the car despite the consequences.

REVISED   I have tried to reason with Melissa about buying a new car that will put her in debt. She is determined to buy the car despite the consequences.

1. Taxes are devouring middle-class incomes people are looking for tax shelters.

2. Please take your tools home today before you do, please clean them well.

3. Tad never stopped to ask the price of cantaloupes at the fruit stand he assumed they were very expensive, he was right.

4. Allie has thirty minutes to read and answer one hundred test questions, she'll have no trouble finishing her mind works like a computer.

5. The tamales in this restaurant are terrible they have a mushy potato filling.

6. Sometimes the combination to the vault works perfectly, it clicks open without a problem other times it doesn't work at all we have to call a locksmith.

7. I'd like to put down a large payment on the braces I'll be getting in October I have the money now I might not have it two years from now when the braces come off.

8. The doctor was weary after doing eight hours of open-heart surgery although he was scheduled to continue on the night shift, he was relieved by his supervisor.

9. Mira has the skill to be a great pianist many people question her dedication, she only practices an hour a day she should be practicing at least five.

10. Fred is always in trouble with his probation officer he continually forgets to check in, Nellie has no problems with hers.

11. Harvey is doing well in plant science although he originally intended to major in business, he may change his major to ag-business, his father, a cotton farmer, will be pleased.

12. The old high school gang broke up after graduation, some of them went away to different colleges others stayed home and went to the local community college others enlisted in the service or went to work at the garment factory.

13. I don't want to go to the movies this afternoon, there is nothing that I want to see.

14. Please borrow all of the modeling clay that you need don't worry about returning it.

15. Samantha got her hair cut and curled at the Hungry Hair salon, then she got a pedicure and a manicure.

ACTIVITY 6

The following passage contains some run-on sentences. Rewrite the passage and correct the run-ons by separating complete sentences or joining them with coordinate or subordinate conjunctions. Separate longer sentences and join shorter, related sentences.

EXAMPLE   The teachers were upset. They had received no raise for three years they decided not to return to school in the fall without a decent contract.

REVISED   The teachers were upset. They had received no raise for three years, so they decided not to return to school in the fall without a decent contract.

Joe was placed in the state penitentiary, he had served time in other places. His first trouble came in grade school. He was caught sniffing glue. He stayed in detention for a night his parents refused to pick him up until morning. Six months later he was back in juvy for stabbing a boy in the shoulder with an ice pick. He got into three more fights with inmates while in detention, he was finally released, his parents had split up neither of them wanted Joe. He was sent to live with an aunt in Grace Falls. He kept out of trouble for over a year until he got involved with some older men. They robbed a liquor store, he drove the car, later they had him delivering drugs because he was a minor. He finally got caught and was sent to detention for two more years. When he got out, he ran away and melted into the street life of the city. His aunt didn't hear about him for two years until she got a call that he had been arrested for assaulting a junkie. He was a month over eighteen, so when he was convicted, he was sent to the state penitentiary, no one from his family visited him.

ACTIVITY 7

If you need more practice correcting run-on sentences, put in periods and capital letters or joining words to either separate or join together the following run-ons.

EXAMPLES

RUN-ON	Matthew likes chihuahuas for companions, he takes four of them on leashes whenever he takes a walk.
REVISED	Matthew likes chihuahuas for companions. He takes four of them on leashes whenever he takes a walk.
RUN-ON	The sofa looks new, it is actually five years old.
REVISED	The sofa looks new, but it is actually five years old.
RUN-ON	Callie is going to town, maybe she can take us with her.
REVISED	Since Callie is going to town, maybe she can take us with her.

1. No one noticed Florence sitting in the corner she had been there for hours.
2. Myron has a winning personality, he can turn his worst critic around.
3. Practice typing without looking at the keyboard you'll learn faster that way.
4. The wind swirled around the outfield it made catching fly balls difficult.
5. The library tapes were battered and torn they had been used for twenty years.
6. Nothing beats the view of the valley from the top of the dam at night it is breath-taking.
7. We'll begin the studio tour at 9:00 please be at the studio by 8:30.
8. A few people left the concert early because of the rain, most people stayed on.
9. Agnes and Morad formed a corporation of two then they filed for bankruptcy.
10. The accident was really no one's fault because of the road conditions no one should be ticketed or sued.
11. I was disappointed by the turnout at the car rally Sunday I had expected a thousand people.
12. No one expected Michelle to get the leading role in West Side Story, she was as surprised as anyone.
13. Lottie sprained her finger in judo practice it swelled and turned purple at the knuckle.
14. Study all the chapters from 1 to 20 for the test, there will be questions from each chapter.
15. Your list of candidates is incomplete the updated list is now available.
16. Linda is my oldest sister, she is thirty-six and lives with her aunt.
17. Marvin is a nervous person he bites his fingernails constantly.
18. Let's go to the movies tonight at the Four-Star Cinema I hear there's a great double feature of horror movies playing.
19. The tumbleweeds blew across the highway and startled a motorist, they stuck in a barbed-wire fence beside the road.

20. All of us can't sit together at one table at the restaurant we will have to split into four groups.

21. Yolanda has been working at the bank for five months, she deserves a raise.

22. The hood of the Oldsmobile was shining it had been freshly waxed.

23. That old fishing knife is too dull to scale and clean the sea bass I've got a sharper one in my tackle box for you to use.

24. The movie about Napoleon wasn't too historically accurate, it starred John Wayne as Napoleon.

25. Make me a batch of gooey chocolate-chip cookies I'll clean up the mess.

■ ■ ■ ■ ■ ■ ■ ■ ■ ■ ■ ■

FRAGMENTS

Here are some common features of *sentence fragments* to be aware of:

1. A fragment is an incomplete sentence. While a sentence expresses a complete idea and makes sense by itself, a fragment makes little sense on its own.

EXAMPLES   The man walking down the freeway.

Because it has been snowing all weekend.

Driving to school in an old Volkswagen bus.

2. A fragment often leaves the reader with an unanswered question.

EXAMPLES   The girl standing in the fountain. *(What happened to her?)*

If you do all your homework tonight. *(What will happen?)*

Whenever I start to apologize to you. *(What happens?)*

3. Fragments often separate thoughts that belong together.

EXAMPLES   *(fragments underlined)*

If you want a ride to school tomorrow. You can give me a call.

I hope the game is over. Before it starts raining hard.

4. Since fragments are incorrect sentence structures that confuse readers, they should be revised to form complete sentences.

EXAMPLE   The girl standing in the fountain.

REVISED   The girl standing in the fountain is cooling her feet.

EXAMPLE   After we pay this month's bills. We'll have little money left for entertainment.

REVISED   After we pay this month's bills, we'll have little money left for entertainment.

Split Complex Sentences

Fragments, like run-ons, come in different patterns. The most common fragment comes from a *split complex sentence*. When the half of the complex sentence beginning with the subordinate conjunction is split from the other half of the sentence, it is a fragment. To correct the problem, the sentence halves need to be joined together to form a complete complex sentence.

Here are some examples of split complex sentences resulting in sentence fragments. The fragment is the group of words beginning with the underlined subordinate conjunction.

EXAMPLES   When the birds left for winter. We missed their singing.

While you were in the air-conditioned store. I waited in the car.

Jodie closed her lingerie shop. Because J. C. Penney's moved in next door.

The calculator will do you no good. Unless it can identify pronouns.

Gilda hates to write papers. Whereas her sister Claudette enjoys writing.

Each group of words beginning with the underlined subordinate conjunction is a fragment. By itself, a fragment makes little sense. To correct the fragments, you should join them with the other halves of the complex sentences. Here are the correctly punctuated sentences.

EXAMPLES   When the birds left for winter, we missed their singing.

While you were in the air-conditioned store, I waited in the car.

Jodie closed her lingerie shop because J. C. Penney's moved in next door.

The calculator will do you no good unless it can identify pronouns.

Gilda hates to write papers whereas her sister Claudette enjoys writing.

ACTIVITY 8

Each of the following groups of sentences contains one fragment beginning with a subordinate conjunction (*when, while, after, unless, because, although, if, since,* and so on). Correct the fragment by adding it to the sentence before or after it that it belongs with to form a *complex sentence.* Copy the other sentence as it appears. *Place a comma after the first half of a sentence if it begins with a subordinate conjunction.*

EXAMPLE   Joe was late for work. Since others were also late. Joe had no problem.

REVISED   Joe was late for work. Since others were also late, Joe had no problem.

1. People are traveling more. Because gas prices aren't increasing. Hopefully, prices won't go up this summer.

2. Before you buy a car at Happy Harry's. Check it out carefully. He sells some real junk.

3. A nuclear accident is always possible. Unless nuclear energy plants are dismantled. Environmental groups continue to protest their existence.

4. Clean out your closet. When you finish. Give me the shirts you've outgrown.

5. The crowds used to be sparse at Minneapolis stadium. People are returning in large numbers. Because the Twins have started winning again.

6. Although the current recession is tough. It doesn't compare to the Great Depression. Ask people who have been through both.

7. Hanna is trusting. Because she believes in people. Her brother is the suspicious one.

8. Thanks for the great breakfast. Before I leave. Can I do the dishes for you?

9. The trip is on. Unless it snows. We'll go if it rains.

10. The choir practiced for hours. They sang the <u>Messiah</u> five times. Before they had finished for the night.

▪ ▪ ▪ ▪ ▪ ▪ ▪ ▪ ▪ ▪ ▪ ▪

ACTIVITY 9

Complete the following complex sentences by adding the second half of each sentence to the half already given. Put a comma between sentence halves if the subordinate conjunction begins the sentences. *Make sure you punctuate the sentences to avoid fragments.*

EXAMPLE   Before you hand in your resignation, <u>have another job lined up.</u>

1. After James took four finals in a row _____ .

2. _____ if you're interested in getting seats for the concert.

3. Before Thelma had a chance to explain _____ .

4. _____ because the rocks were covered with snow.

5. _____ unless you flunk the rest of your tests.

6. While Jacob sat on top of the flagpole _____ .

7. When Loretta cleans out her ears _____ .

8. _____ since no one has the money for a vacation.

9. _____ although I've driven this road many times at night.

10. As the Rolling Stones entered the stadium _____ .

11. Because the lid to the anchovy tin wasn't sealed _____ .

12. After the cannibals finished with the tourists _____ .

▪ ▪ ▪ ▪ ▪ ▪ ▪ ▪ ▪ ▪ ▪ ▪

Missing Subjects and Verbs

A second common sentence fragment has one of its main parts missing, the *subject* or the *verb*. Since a complete sentence requires a subject and verb, if either part or both parts are missing, the sentence is not complete. Fragments with missing subjects or verbs can be corrected by adding what is missing to the sentence.

Here are some examples of fragments with missing subjects and verbs.

EXAMPLES   The girl in the back of the room. *(no verb)*

The reef beyond the bay. *(no verb)*

Relaxed after a hard day's work. *(no subject)*

Enjoying a week's vacation from school. *(no subject or helping verb*)*

A dog sleeping in the shade. *(no helping verb)*

In the back of the old warehouse. *(no subject or verb)*

On the first day of December. *(no subject or verb)*

Each sample group of words is a fragment requiring a subject, a verb, or both. To correct the fragments, the missing sentence part or parts need to be added. Here are the corrected sentence forms, all expressing complete thoughts.

EXAMPLES   The girl in the back of the room is very quiet this morning.

The reef beyond the bay can be very treacherous.

Harry and Eileen relaxed after a hard day's work.

Mabel, Harriet, and Eischen are enjoying a week's vacation from school.

A dog was sleeping in the shade.

In the back of the warehouse is an old U.S. map with forty-eight states.

We will romp in our bathing suits on the first day of December.

ACTIVITY 10

Most of the following groups of words are *fragments*. To correct them, add words that will make the fragments complete sentences. Add subjects, verbs, helping verbs, or any combination that is missing. Mark *C* for complete sentences.

EXAMPLE   The buttermilk in the kitchen.

REVISED   The buttermilk in the kitchen has soured.

---

* Verbs ending in *-ing* require a *helping verb* to be complete. The most common helping verbs with *-ing* verbs are *am*, *is*, *are*, *was*, and *were*.

EXAMPLE   Confused by the loud noise.

REVISED   The child was confused by the loud noise of the downtown traffic.

1. _____ The Goodyear blimp above the stadium.

2. _____ Serving from the left-hand side of the court.

3. _____ The man was happy about getting money back from the IRS.

4. _____ With "Animal" tatooed on her forearm.

5. _____ Sleeping in the hollow of a log.

6. _____ The Buick with the pink and purple stripes is ugly.

7. _____ The ninety-year-old lady on the moped.

8. _____ Bothered by a pulled muscle and a sore toe.

9. _____ On the way home from the zoo, I almost hit a skunk.

10. _____ Against the wishes of his mother, his father, his priest, and his parole officer.

- - - - - - - - - - - -

ACTIVITY *11*

The following paragraph contains a number of fragments. Some are the result of a split complex sentence and others have a missing part. Rewrite the paragraph and correct all fragments by uniting split complex sentences to form complete sentences and by adding words to other fragments that are incomplete.

EXAMPLE   Mabel was interested in fashion merchandising. Because she loved to buy clothes. Expensive clothes in particular.

REVISED   Mabel was interested in fashion merchandising because she loved to buy clothes. She was attracted to expensive clothes in particular.

It was a bad time to be looking for apartments. Because they were scarce and rent was high. A one-bedroom apartment $300 a month. Maria and Henry were hoping to find a two-bedroom apartment. Since she was expecting a baby in April. They needed to live closer to the campus. Because Henry didn't own a car. The only two-bedroom place they found was renting for $350. They decided to take it. Although the payments would be difficult. Could survive until Henry graduated in June. They moved their belongings into the apartment. They felt everything would work out. Unless Henry's grant application was not accepted.

- - - - - - - - - - - -

Left-off Endings

Many sentence fragments come from ending a sentence before it is completed and leaving a group of words cut off as a fragment. In these cases, the correction for the fragment is to add it to the sentence it belongs with by dropping the period and the capital letter.

Here are examples of sentences followed by fragments that have been separated from the sentences. The fragments are underlined. The correct versions follow.

EXAMPLES

WRONG   I had trouble making a decision. That would be best for everyone.

RIGHT   I had trouble making a decision that would be best for everyone.

WRONG   Mae is an interesting person. Who delights in mischief.

RIGHT   Mae is an interesting person who delights in mischief.

WRONG   The room is always comfortable. With its adobe walls and insulation.

RIGHT   The room is always comfortable with its adobe walls and insulation.

WRONG   Manny took my place in the marathon. Which didn't bother me a bit.

RIGHT   Manny took my place in the marathon, which didn't bother me a bit.

WRONG   I love scrambled eggs. Especially with hot sauce or ketchup.

RIGHT   I love scrambled eggs, especially with hot sauce or ketchup.

WRONG   John is a real cowboy. A man with seven hundred head of cattle.

RIGHT   John is a real cowboy, a man with seven hundred head of cattle.

WRONG   I enjoy October. The best month for cool evenings.

RIGHT   I enjoy October, the best month for cool evenings.

WRONG   I've been lonely. Since you left.

RIGHT   I've been lonely since you left.

As you can see, a simple change of punctuation unites the fragments with the sentences they belong with. If you read the sentences aloud, you can usually tell that the fragments belong with the sentences. The groups of words often cut off from the sentence include a variety of prepositional phrases, relative clauses (beginning with *who, which,* and *that*), clauses beginning with subordinate conjunctions, and *appositives,* words that replace and modify the word directly before them (John is a real cowboy, *a man with seven hundred head of cattle.* I enjoy October, *the best month for cool evenings.*).

ACTIVITY **12**

The following groups of sentences contain one fragment each. Rewrite the sentences and correct the fragment by attaching it to the sentence it belongs with.

EXAMPLE   She left home. To live on her own. Her family accepted the decision.

REVISED   She left home to live on her own. Her family accepted the decision.

1. That's a cute terrier. That you got at the animal shelter. Do they have any more?

2. Sally prefers the Honda Prelude. With the sky roof. She wishes she could afford it.

3. Judson had finals this week. He hated his calculus final. A complicated exam with page-long problems.

4. I'm not going to the play. Because you're not going. Please change your mind.

5. Lucy has some problems. With her speaking and writing. She is very bright, however.

6. Watch television tonight. There's a great movie about the 1920s. Which is on channel 52.

7. Alexandra loves listening to Velasquez. A gifted violinist from Brazil. She heard him perform at Carnegie Hall.

8. It was a long and tiring walk. From the cafeteria to the dorms across campus. It took a half hour.

9. Please hand me those books. I am sure they are the ones. That I left in the business class.

10. The farmers grew worried. Because clouds were forming over the mountains. They hoped a wind would blow the clouds south.

■ ■ ■ ■ ■ ■ ■ ■ ■ ■ ■   ■

Fragments with Words in a Series
Another common kind of fragment involves a series of words separated from the sentence it belongs with. The series often provides examples supporting the main point of the sentence. Here are some such sentences and fragments. The underlined series of words are the fragments.

EXAMPLES   John had a boring Saturday. <u>Mowing the lawn, washing the car, and studying for finals.</u>

Millie collected all kinds of things at the beach. <u>Driftwood, shells, seaweed, rocks, and starfish.</u>

You have everything you need for the trip. <u>A tankful of gas, plenty of beer, a raft, and a gallon of suntan lotion.</u>

Maria is everything you want in a tutor. <u>Intelligent, thorough, patient, firm, and caring.</u>

Millie was having a rough semester. <u>Worried about her grades, unsure of herself with strangers, self-conscious about her accent, and harassed by bill collectors.</u>

None of the underlined series of words are sentences. Each makes sense only in relation to the sentence that precedes it, and it provides important examples supporting the main idea. There are two ways to correct the fragments:

1. **Put a *colon* (:), a punctuation mark indicating that a series follows, at the end of the sentence.**

2. **Add introductory words to the series to create a sentence.**

These examples show both correction methods using the sample sentences and fragments.

EXAMPLES   John had a boring Saturday. He spent the entire day mowing the lawn, washing the car, and studying for finals. *(words added to the series to make a complete sentence)*

Millie collected all kinds of things at the beach: driftwood, shells, seaweed, rocks, and starfish. *(colon used to indicate a series of things to follow)*

You have everything you need for the trip: a tankful of gas, plenty of beer, a raft, and a gallon of suntan lotion. *(colon used)*

Maria is everything you want in a tutor. She is intelligent, thorough, patient, firm, and caring. *(words added)*

Millie was having a rough semester. She was worried about her grades, unsure of herself with strangers, self-conscious about her accent, and harassed by bill collectors. *(words added)*

ACTIVITY 13

The following groups of words include sentences and fragments with words in series. Correct the fragments by putting a colon after the complete sentence to join the series with the sentence or by adding words to the series to make it a complete separate sentence. Use the method that seems most effective for each fragment.

EXAMPLE   Rudy was ready to party. Relaxed, in a good mood, and not broke.

REVISED   Rudy was ready to party. He was relaxed, in a good mood, and not broke.

EXAMPLE   Nothing we bought at Big Al's Video worked for long. The tape recorder, the videocassette player, and the Walkman.

REVISED   Nothing we bought at Big Al's Video worked for long: the tape recorder, the videocassette player, and the Walkman.

1. The birds on the lake were a beautiful sight. Geese, cranes, mallards, wood ducks, and herons.

2. Hawaii is a tourist paradise. Beautiful beaches, tropical scenery, volcanoes, luaus, and MasterCard.

3. We couldn't decide what to do with our Saturday afternoon. A picnic at the park, a ride on the subway, a volleyball game, or just loaf around town.

4. The accident was pretty bad. One guy thrown out of the car door and another pinned against the steering wheel.

5. I know what I've got to do this evening. Cram for the history test, review for the French orals, and watch Bugs Bunny cartoons.

6. The chances for a job in the supermarket look good. An opening in the meat department, one in the fresh vegetable section, and an apprentice checker needed.

7. I've never met anyone quite like Laverne. Outgoing yet shy, pretty in a homely way, silly but smart, and generous but very cheap.

8. You can always find Fred at home on weekends. Waxing his Mazda, watching ball games, listening to his stereo, or tinkering with his model airplanes.

■ ■ ■ ■ ■ ■ ■ ■ ■ ■ ■ ■ ■

ACTIVITY *14*

The following passage contains a number of fragments representing the range of problems covered. Rewrite the passage and correct all fragments by changing punctuation or adding words to complete sentences.

EXAMPLE   The service at the restaurant was terrible. Because there was one waitress for ten tables. People got frustrated. Left without ordering.

REVISED   The service at the restaurant was terrible because there was one waitress for ten tables. People got frustrated and left without ordering.

This was the last semester that Charlotte would car pool. Because she had too many bad experiences. She had gotten in a car pool at the beginning of the semester. With three other girls who lived nearby. When Elvira drove, she was always five to ten minutes late. Always with elaborate excuses. Minerva, on the other hand, was always ten minutes early. Tooting her horn and waking up the neighborhood. The third girl was totally unpredictable. Since she relied on her brother to pick her up. One day on time, the next day early, the next day late. Sometimes she wouldn't come at all. Since Charlotte was the only one with first-period classes, the others weren't concerned about the time. Next semester Charlotte will take the bus to school. Even though the bus stop is a mile from her house.

■ ■ ■ ■ ■ ■ ■ ■ ■ ■ ■ ■ ■

When you finish, share your revised passage with classmates. Check for fragments. See how different people corrected the fragments, and share the passages that sound best with the class.

Fragment Review

The following points summarize what you have learned about sentence fragments in this section:

1. A fragment is an incomplete sentence. It does not express a complete thought.

2. Fragments confuse readers by separating thoughts that belong together and by presenting incomplete structures.

3. Most fragments come from splitting complex sentences and punctuating them as separate sentences. The sentence part beginning with the subordinate conjunction is a fragment. Such fragments are corrected by joining them with the other part of the complex sentence.

4. Other fragments lack other parts: a missing subject, verb, helping verb, or subject and verb. These fragments can be corrected by adding the part that is missing to complete the sentence.

5. Other fragments come from splitting a final phrase from the rest of a sentence and punctuating it as a sentence. Such fragments are corrected by attaching them to the sentences they belong with.

6. Other fragments occur when a series of words or groups of words are separated from the sentence they relate to.

EXAMPLE   I enjoy Saturday mornings. Sleeping in late, watching television, and snacking.

These fragments are corrected by joining the series of words to the sentence with a colon (:) or by adding words in front of the series to form a complete sentence:

I enjoy Saturday mornings: sleeping in late, watching television, and snacking.

or

I enjoy Saturday mornings. I like sleeping in late, watching television, and snacking.

ACTIVITY *15*

The following groups of sentences contain one fragment each. Rewrite the sentences and correct the fragments by changing punctuation and attaching them to appropriate sentences or by adding words to the fragments to make them complete.

EXAMPLE   Jules left for school an hour ago. On his new motorcycle. He should have arrived long ago.

REVISED   Jules left for school an hour ago on his new motorcycle. He should have arrived long ago.

EXAMPLE   Because you are new in the neighborhood. Let me warn you about Mr. Twinksler. He mows his lawn in the middle of the night!

REVISED   Because you are new in the neighborhood, let me warn you about Mr. Twinksler. He mows his lawn in the middle of the night!

EXAMPLE   The police are searching for Emily. A tall, thin fourteen-year-old redhead.

REVISED   The police are searching for Emily, a tall, thin fourteen-year-old redhead.

1. Lucille left for Manhattan an hour ago. On the three o'clock train out of Trenton. Calvin will meet her at the depot.

2. I didn't care for the pink sweater. Because it didn't match your burgundy skirt. With something else, it might have looked good.

3. Unless you hear from Josh in the next hour. You can assume he has gone by himself. Don't bother picking him up for the play.

4. Felix is quite a con man. A smooth, fast talker who could charm a crocodile. He'd make a great snake oil salesman for a traveling side show.

5. Freda finally arrived with the lemonade. In the nick of time. Everyone was dying of thirst from the heat and exercise.

6. In case you are looking for a good used refrigerator. Jack's Appliances is having a sale on old Amanas. Most of them have a two-year guarantee.

7. It's nice hearing your voice again after so long. To tell you the truth, I'm a little short of money. Which is the main reason I called you.

8. Claudette was thrilled with her 2.6 grade point average this spring. She needed some good news. Especially after she totaled her car last Saturday.

9. I'm not in the least bit interested in buying an electric ice cream maker. As long as I can turn a crank by hand. I'll stick to the old-fashioned kind.

10. No one wanted to walk in the graduation with Huey. Because he was going to be staggering drunk. He ended up walking with the dean of students.

11. After five years of college in North Dakota, the end was near for Gladys. No more cramming for tests, sitting through boring lectures, or living in the dorms.

12. Howie was anxious to go to the new amusement park in the hills. A giant roller coaster, three log rides, a giant loop-the-loop, and free candy apples.

13. Hal had wanted to join the Marines. Since he was in grade school. His dad convinced him to enroll in the ROTC program at a nearby college.

14. Sue finally saved enough money for a trip to Hawaii. When she got there, she wasn't disappointed. Beautiful exotic plants, warm-water beaches, pineapple plantations, luaus, and college guys everywhere.

15. The bird refuge in the park had a variety of wild ducks. That had flown south for the winter months. There were mallards, wood ducks, teal, and eiders.

■ ■ ■ ■ ■ ■ ■ ■ ■ ■ ■

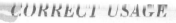
CORRECT USAGE

A writer may make errors within a sentence that distract readers. Many of these errors involve grammar problems, and knowledge of the basic rules of grammar help a writer eliminate such errors. This "Correct Usage" section introduces rules that help you eliminate grammatical problems and give you practice proofreading sentences for errors.

SUBJECTS AND VERBS

As a general rule, every sentence you write contains a *subject* and a *verb*. The *subject* is *who* or *what the sentence is about*, and the *verb tells what the subject is doing* or *joins the subject with words that describe it*. To deal with subject-verb agreement, you need to be able to identify these main sentence parts.

Subject-Verb Identification

The following sentences have their subject underlined once and the verb twice. Notice that in each sentence, the *subject* is who or what the sentence is about, and the *verb* tells what the subject is doing.

EXAMPLES   The <u>dolphin</u> <u><u>leaped</u></u> through the air. *(The sentence is about a* dolphin. Leaped *tells what the dolphin did.)*

The <u>doctor</u> <u><u>made</u></u> house calls. *(The sentence is about a* doctor. Made house calls *tells what he did.)*

The <u>boulders</u> <u><u>tumbled</u></u> down the mountain. *(The sentence is about* boulders. Tumbled *tells what they did.)*

A second way of finding the subject and verb is to locate the verb first and then the subject. To find the verb, look for the *action* in the sentence: running, thinking, talking, looking, touching, and so on. To find the subject, ask, "Who or what is doing the action?" Here are more examples.

EXAMPLES   The <u>raisins</u> <u><u>shrivel</u></u> in the sun. *(The action is* shrivel. *What is shriveling? The* raisins.)

<u><u>Jogging</u></u> <u>builds</u> Jolene's stamina. *(The action is* builds. *What builds stamina?* Jogging.)

<u>Clyde</u> <u><u>hates</u></u> sardines and anchovies. *(The action is* hates. *Who hates?* Clyde.)

ACTIVITY 16

Underline the subject once and the verb twice in the following sentences. Either find out what the sentence is about (the subject) and what the subject is doing (the verb), or look for the action in the sentence (the verb) and find who or what is doing it (the subject).

EXAMPLES   The <u>noose</u> <u>tightened</u> around his neck.

The <u>skier</u> <u>fell</u> off the ski lift.

1. Joann's ankle aches from roller skating.
2. The tarantula crawled inside Felix's sleeping bag.
3. Aunt Nel from Toledo cracks walnuts on her head.
4. Ashes from the volcano covered the city.
5. Knitting relaxes Joseph.
6. Today the stock market dropped to a record low.
7. Sal often thinks about joining the circus.
8. A fire spreading from a tool shed destroyed the family's belongings.
9. The countries in the Middle East negotiated a new peace treaty.
10. The rats chewed through the pantry wall.
11. High interest rates in March and April killed Fred's chances for a loan.
12. The hockey team from Calgary practices at 4:00 a.m. every day.
13. The opportunity for fame escaped Alice.
14. The poetry competition between classes ends today.
15. Ink blots from his fountain pen stained Harvey's shirt pocket.

■ ■ ■ ■ ■ ■ ■ ■ ■ ■ ■ ■

Subject-Verb Agreement

The following basic information will help you understand subject-verb agreement.

1. The subject of a sentence can be *singular* (one of anything) or *plural* (more than one of anything). The plural of most words is formed by adding -*s* or -*es*: *cats, dogs, dresses, boxes.*

2. There are two present tense verb forms: one ends in -*s* and one does not.

3. When you use a present tense verb, you must select the correct form of the verb to agree with the subject. If the subject of the sentence is *singular,* use the present tense verb form that ends in -*s*. If the subject is *plural,* use the present tense verb form that does *not* end in -*s*.

    a. *Singular subject:* present tense verb ends in -*s*.
    b. *Plural subject:* present tense verb does not end in -*s*.

    EXAMPLES   *(subject underlined once, verb underlined twice)*

    SINGULAR SUBJECT   The <u>elm tree</u> <u>sheds</u> its leaves in early December.
    PLURAL SUBJECT   The <u>elm trees</u> <u>shed</u> their leaves in early December.

SINGULAR SUBJECT   Your aunt believes in reincarnation.

PLURAL SUBJECT   Your aunts believe in reincarnation.

4. **Here are the exceptions to the basic subject-agreement rules. With the singular subject pronouns *I* and *you*, the verb does *not* end in -s: I enjoy roller-skating; you prefer skateboarding. Verbs such as *dress*, *press*, *regress*, and *impress* end in -s despite the presence of a plural subject: The Johnson girls dress alike.**

■ ■ ■ ■ ■ ■ ■ ■ ■ ■ ■ ■

ACTIVITY 17

Circle the correct present tense verb form in parentheses that agrees with the subject of the sentence.

EXAMPLES   Your uncle (build, (builds)) huge sand castles.

Your uncles ((build,) builds) huge sand castles.

1. Juanita often (practice, practices) her baton twirling three nights a week.

2. The girls (practice, practices) karate in the school's gymnastics room.

3. My nephew from New Orleans (believe, believes) in extraterrestrial beings.

4. My nieces (believe, believes) that my nephew is crazy.

5. The pole-vaulters from Central College (warm, warms) up for their event by using a trampoline.

6. The high jumper from Drake University (warm, warms) up for her event by doing stretching exercises.

7. The city newspapers that I subscribe to (do, does) a lousy job of covering campus activities.

8. The college newspaper (do, does) a great job of covering city events.

9. That pickle on your hamburger (look, looks) like it's been nibbled on by a rat.

10. Those olives (look, looks) like they've been dehydrated.

11. Your dentist (need, needs) braces on his lower teeth.

12. Most physicians that I know (need, needs) to take better care of their own health.

13. Your success (prove, proves) that hard work sometimes pays off.

14. My recent failures in math (prove, proves) that hard work isn't always enough.

15. A savings account (are, is) one thing I need to open immediately.

16. Savings accounts (are, is) great if you have anything to put into them.

■ ■ ■ ■ ■ ■ ■ ■ ■ ■ ■ ■

ACTIVITY **18**

The following sentences contain *singular* subjects. Notice that the verbs end in *-s*. Rewrite the sentences so that the subjects are *plural*, and change the present tense verb form to *agree* with the plural subjects. To make a singular subject plural, you add *-s* or *-es*. The verb form with the plural subject will not end in *-s*. *Underline the subject and verb as you write the sentences.*

EXAMPLE   The boy looks tired.

                 The boys look tired.

1. The girl in the nursery plays well with her classmates.
2. The boy in the back of the room sleeps a lot.
3. The building looks sturdy for its age.
4. One twin changes moods quickly.
5. The foreign student from Cambodia understands the rules for Monopoly.
6. The answer to the math problem comes slowly to Anna.
7. The lady who brought us flowers works at the nursery.
8. Your sock with the huge hole in the heel needs darning.
9. The neighbor next door to our apartment throws wild parties in the summer.
10. A friend of mine buys leather coats in Venezuela for $35.

■ ■ ■ ■ ■ ■ ■ ■ ■ ■ ■

Subject-Verb Variations

Here are some variations in the subject-verb pattern that often create agreement problems for writers:

1. *Separated subject and verb:* The subject and verb are separated by a group of words, most often a *prepositional phrase*, that confuses the agreement situation. Solution: *Ignore any words between a subject and verb when making decisions about agreement.*

   PREPOSITIONAL PHRASES   *(prepositions italicized)*

after the game	*from* his room
against his will	*in* the boat
among the roses	*into* the water
around the house	*of* the three churches
before the test	*on* the table

behind the batter   *to* the ground
between the lines   *through* the mail
for good mileage   *with* her friends

EXAMPLES   *(subject and verb underlined, prepositional phrases crossed out)*

One ~~of the women teachers~~ smokes a pipe in the lounge.

The aroma ~~of barbecuing steaks~~ nauseates Herman.

Men ~~in the back of the room by the pencil sharpener~~ look threatening.

Each ~~of the sixteen yellow raincoats~~ has a flaw in it.

2. *Sentences beginning with* there *plus a form of* to be: **Sentences beginning** *there is, there are, there was,* **and** *there were* **cause writers problems because the subject comes** *after* **the verb. Solution: Because** *there* **is** *never the subject* **in a** *there + to be* **sentence, locate the subject after the verb and use** *is* **or** *was* **with** *singular subjects* **and** *are* **or** *were* **with** *plural subjects.*

EXAMPLES   *(subjects and verbs underlined)*

There is a snake in the basement.

There are sixteen ways to cook potatoes.

There was no one home at the Garcias'.

There were no Christmas trees left in the lot when I went shopping.

3. *Compound verbs:* **If a sentence has a single subject and two or more main verbs (compound verb), each main verb must agree with the subject.**

EXAMPLES   *(subjects and verbs underlined)*

Mavis jogs to work, does aerobics on her lunch hour, and lifts weights at night.

My uncles make great chili and serve it in old tin cans.

G Street winds around our suburb and then dead-ends by the canal.

Sarah and Clyde love to fight and love to make up even more.

ACTIVITY *19*

Underline the *subject* **in each of the following sentences, and then circle the verb in parentheses that** *agrees* **with the subject.**

EXAMPLE   One of my goldfish (look, (looks)) ill.

1. Sarah and Jesus (dances, dance) smoothly together.

2. No one in the audience (understand, understands) the plot of the Fellini movie.

3. The huge planes (circles, circle) the runway in the fog.

4. The french fries from the Happy Hamburger (is, are) greasy.

5. The children from Grant School (appears, appear) bored after Act One of <u>The Great Anchovy</u>.

6. There (is, are) something about you that I like.

7. After the election, the mayor (hires, hire) his opponent and (divorces, divorce) his wife.

8. Tryouts for the philharmonic orchestra (begins, begin) on Monday.

9. Julia and Fred (seems, seem) surprised by the attention from the press.

10. The students from Sweden and Israel (speaks, speak) and (writes, write) excellent English.

11. In the back of your locker (lies, lie) a pair of stinky sweat socks.

12. The view across the bay from the middle of the bridge (was, were) magnificent.

13. There (is, are) one of the Daffney twins, but I (don't, doesn't) know the whereabouts of her sister.

14. There (is, are) no good reason for you to miss the farewell party for Gonzo.

15. From the looks of your car, it (needs, need) a good wash and wax job.

■ ■ ■ ■ ■ ■ ■ ■ ■ ■ ■

ACTIVITY 20

Fill in the blanks in the following sentences with appropriate *present tense* verbs. Remember, if the subject is singular, the verb ends in -s. If the subject is plural, the verb does not end in -s. Find the subject, decide whether it is singular or plural, and then fill in a verb that agrees. Remember, the subject may come *after* the verb, and a *prepositional phrase* may separate the subject from the verb.

EXAMPLES   Maria *prefers* football.

The Dodgers *dress* like winners.

1. The plane from Des Moines _____ this evening at 10:00.

2. Ben and Clara _____ more money than they need.

3. Beside the building _____ some old oak trees.

4. One of the monsters _____ a whole city.

5. With you around, the minutes _____ like hours.

6. I _____ stuffed from eating all this pizza.

7. There _____ a crowd of people on hand for the boat launching.

8. There _____ just you and I left in the spelling contest.

9. There _____ six different exercises for tightening your stomach muscles.

10. The noises from the swamp _____ spooky.

11. Everyone _____ your famous smile.

12. Cats and dogs _____ each other's company.

13. The ways to success in college _____ Hermie.

14. There _____ flies and grasshoppers in the apple cider.

15. There _____ a pregnant hamster in your bathtub.

. . . .

Subject-Verb Agreement Review
Here is what you have learned about subject-verb agreement:

1. *Present tense* verbs must agree with their subjects.

2. If the subject is singular, the verb ends in *-s* (except for first and second person singular pronouns *I* and *you*).

3. If the subject is plural, the verb does *not* end in *-s* (unless the basic verb form already ends in *-s* as with *dress, mess,* or *confess*).

4. The following indefinite pronouns are always considered singular: *each, every, one, everyone, someone, somebody, everybody, anyone, anybody, no one, nobody.*

5. Many subject-verb problems occur when the word *there* begins the sentence followed by the verb and then the subject. You must look beyond the verb to the subject to determine the correct verb form.

    EXAMPLE   There are many ways to cross the river, but there is only one way to cross the canal.

6. Other subject-verb problems occur when a word *between* the subject and the verb is mistaken for the subject. Any group of words separating the subject and verb has no effect on subject-verb agreement.

    EXAMPLES   The boys who live in the new apartment house at the end of the road walk two miles to school.

    The aroma of barbecued hamburgers cooking over charcoal tempts Harold.

ACTIVITY *21*

Fill in appropriate present tense verbs to complete the following sentences. Determine the verb form by deciding whether the subject is singular or plural. For practice, underline your subjects.

EXAMPLE   One of the doctors *charges* less for a checkup than others in his medical group.

1. Jim and Gracie _____ buying stocks in a local produce company.

2. Our college _____ foreign students from all over the world.

3. Three of the students from Spokane _____ together in the dorms.

4. There _____ remodeling plans for the library next fall.

5. The plants you sent me from Brazil _____ beautiful.

6. Tomorrow _____ hope for everyone.

7. The odor of garbage from the trash cans _____ me.

8. None of the food we ate _____ as good as this chicken casserole.

9. There _____ not been any changes in Rose's condition.

10. By the altar _____ a statue of the Virgin Mary.

11. Someone walking down the corridors _____ gum on her shoes.

12. Nobody that I know of _____ anything but success for Mildred.

13. There _____ a bike and three red wagons in the driveway.

14. Each of the store owners _____ liable for having exposed wiring outside his shop.

15. The map that you gave me of the Caribbean Islands _____ me do my geography homework for Kingsley's class.

16. The weapons on display in the window of the sporting good's store _____ business.

17. Either Teddie or Maria _____ credit for completing the mural.

18. The crook who was captured with his accomplices _____ like my English teacher.

19. Standing in the doorway next to the candy counter _____ Ferdie and Merkle.

20. _____ everybody going to the Roller Derby finals together?

■ ■ ■ ■ ■ ■ ■ ■ ■ ■ ■

ACTIVITY 22

Here is one additional activity with subject-verb agreement for anyone needing it. Select your own *present tense* verbs to fill in the blanks in the following sentences. Locate the subject and underline it, determine whether it is singular or plural, and then use the correct verb form.

EXAMPLES   Rita *enjoys* taking long baths.

One of the men *arrives* late to work every day.

1. The woman I introduced you to _____ in Florida.

2. One of those two chickens _____ a male.

3. The smell of roses _____ Herbie.

4. The view from the tops of those hills _____ magnificent.

5. Freda and Hortensia never _____ over money.

6. The odors that come from the kitchen _____ pleasant.

7. There _____ the most expensive cars in town.

8. Behind the washing machine _____ six newborn kittens.

9. When he is tired, Albert _____ when he walks.

10. The lilacs on the veranda _____ watering.

11. The cost of six pairs of Levi's _____ over $200.

12. The racing car you lent me for a few days really _____ .

13. The salary of professional basketball players _____ that of football players.

14. There by the lily pads _____ a school of bass.

15. _____ John and Sonia going to get married soon?

16. _____ that the outfit you wore on April Fool's Day?

17. Each of the students on the dean's list for two semesters _____ a scholarship certificate.

18. There _____ many ways to leave your lover.

19. December and January _____ months when the crime rate is higher.

20. There _____ to be flies in my gravy!

PAST TENSE VERBS

Not all of your writing is done in the present tense. You use *past tense* verbs when writing about an event that has already occurred, whether it happened a minute or a decade ago. The most common errors involving past tense verbs include leaving off the *-ed* ending on *regular* past tense verbs and using incorrect *irregular* verb forms.

Regular Past Tense Verbs

Most verbs form their past tense by adding *-ed* to the regular verb. Here are examples of regular past tense verbs.

Verb	Past Tense Form	Verb	Past Tense Form
answer	answered	instruct	instructed
ask	asked	kick	kicked
borrow	borrowed	learn	learned
climb	climbed	part	parted
count	counted	question	questioned
detail	detailed	rush	rushed
edit	edited	sail	sailed
fish	fished	scale	scaled
flood	flooded	talk	talked
head	headed	walk	walked

Regular verbs that end in certain letters offer slight variations to the basic *-ed* verb ending.

1. Verbs already ending in *-e* just add the *-d*.

Verb	Past Tense Form
believe	believed
create	created
hate	hated
invite	invited
love	loved
receive	received

2. Verbs ending in *-y* preceded by a *consonant* change the *-y* to *-i* and add *-ed*.

Verb	Past Tense Form
bury	buried
carry	carried
marry	married
rely	relied
reply	replied
tarry	tarried

3. Verbs ending in -y preceded by a *vowel* merely add -ed.

Verb	Past Tense Form
annoy	annoyed
betray	betrayed
delay	delayed
destroy	destroyed
relay	relayed

4. A number of short regular verbs ending in consonants preceded by vowels with a *short vowel* sound (*plăn, bŭg, fĭt*) *double* their last letter before adding -ed.

Verb	Past Tense Form	Verb	Past Tense Form
acquit	acquitted	knit	knitted
admit	admitted	mar	marred
bat	batted	plan	planned
bug	bugged	ram	rammed
can	canned	scan	scanned
cram	crammed	slug	slugged
fit	fitted	tar	tarred

ACTIVITY 23

Write the past tense form for the following regular verbs. Some verbs will add -ed, some will change -y to -i and add -ed, and some will double the final letter and add -ed.

EXAMPLES   slice *sliced*   cry *cried*   plan *planned*

1. betray _____
2. flood _____
3. cite _____
4. learn _____
5. plan _____
6. deny _____
7. marry _____
8. announce _____
9. save _____
10. annoy _____

11. time _____
12. dam _____
13. bury _____
14. believe _____
15. instruct _____
16. reply _____
17. fund _____
18. inflate _____
19. cheat _____
20. hurry _____

21. bellow _____   23. cap _____

22. admit _____   24. decide _____

. . . .

ACTIVITY *24*

The following passage is written in the present tense. Rewrite the passage changing the verbs to the past tense. Make sure to add -*ed* endings to all regular past tense verbs.

EXAMPLE   Gertrude likes mustard on her rice.

PAST TENSE   Gertrude liked mustard on her rice.

Tonight the moon looks strange. Wispy clouds cover its surface, and a huge halo that looks perfectly round encircles it. Moisture drips from the air, and the moon glistens behind the veil of clouds. It appears eerie and beautiful. I watch the moon from my window and then drift to sleep. I enjoy enchanted dreams about hidden moon caves and moonmaids that lure sleepers into their caverns.

When you finish, check your past tense verb endings with a classmate. If you overlooked any, make corrections.

. . . .

Irregular Verbs

Many verbs do not form their past tense with the regular -*ed* verb ending. Instead, they form their past tense in different, *irregular* ways that involve changes within the verb instead of the addition of an ending. Although there are groups of irregular verbs that form their past tense in similar ways, there are no rules to follow like the -*ed* rule for regular verbs; therefore, *irregular verb* forms need to be memorized to use at your command.

The following is a list of frequently used irregular verbs whose forms are often confused. The verbs with similar forms are grouped as much as possible. The last column, "Past Participle," contains the irregular verb forms used with *helping verbs* such as *has, have, had, was,* and *were.* Here are examples of sentences containing the past tense and past participle verb forms:

John flew cross-country in a single-prop Cessna.   *(past tense, action completed)*

John has flown cross-country many times.   *(past participle + helping verb has; action continuing into the present)*

Lillie sang beautifully at the graduation ceremony.   *(past tense, action completed)*

Lillie has sung at many graduation ceremonies   (past participle + helping verb
has; *action continuing in present*)

Lillie had sung at many graduation ceremonies.   (past participle + helping verb
had; *action completed*)

Present Tense	*Past Tense*	*Past Participle*	
become	became	become	
come	came	come	
run	ran	run	
begin	began	begun	
drink	drank	drunk	
ring	rang	rung	
sing	sang	sung	
swim	swam	swum	
fly	flew	flown	
grow	grew	grown	
know	knew	known	
throw	threw	thrown	
burst	burst	burst	
cut	cut	cut	
quit	quit	quit	
set	set	set	
choose	chose	chosen	
drive	drove	driven	
eat	ate	eaten	
get	got	got, gotten	
give	gave	given	
rise	rose	risen	
speak	spoke	spoken	
take	took	taken	
write	wrote	written	
bring	brought	brought	
build	built	built	
catch	caught	caught	
has	had	had	
lead	led	led	
sit	sat	sat	
do	did	done	
go	went	gone	
see	saw	seen	
lay	laid	laid	*(to place or set some-thing down)*
lie	lay	lain	*(to recline or rest)*

ACTIVITY *25*

Fill in the blanks with the correct past tense and past participle forms of the irregular verbs in parentheses. Use the past participle form when a helping verb (such as *has, have, was, were*) comes before it.

EXAMPLES   (get) She has *gotten* good grades on her math quizzes.

(run) George *ran* into a brick wall.

1. (write) Ted has _____ more this semester than ever before.

2. (lead) The winding path _____ to a gazebo among the pines.

3. (drive) You have _____ me wild with your accusations.

4. (sit) Grace _____ on a stump contemplating her future.

5. (eat) Have you _____ the stuffed peppers in the cafeteria?

6. (build) Ted has _____ model planes since he was in grade school.

7. (begin) It has _____ to drizzle outside.

8. (throw) Mia _____ her back out in aerobic dance class.

9. (know) Hal has _____ some very strange people.

10. (set) Judy _____ her collection of figurines on the mantel.

11. (fly) We've _____ with six different airlines.

12. (drink) You have _____ enough coffee to last you a month.

13. (see) No one _____ or heard from Ezekiel for over two months.

14. (choose) You have _____ the most expensive brand of panty hose.

15. (come) By the time Ames had _____ home, everyone was asleep.

16. (become) You have _____ very proficient at archery.

17. (go) Mattie has _____ to collect dry firewood by the lake.

18. (bring) Grover _____ swamp mud in on his shoes.

19. (give) Reading has _____ Louise great pleasure for years.

20. (swim) Have you _____ across the lake by yourself yet?

21. (lie) Yesterday I _____ down at noon and awakened at 6:00 p.m.

22. (lay) Where have you _____ your pipe?

23. (lie) Have you ever _____ in a hammock?

24. (lay) The construction crew _____ five miles of asphalt in a day.

25. (see) Has anyone _____ my red pajamas?

■ ■ ■ ■ ■ ■ ■ ■ ■ ■ ■ ■

ACTIVITY *26*

Here is more practice using irregular verbs. Write sentences using the following irregular verbs in the tenses indicated. Then share your sentences with a classmate and check each other's verb forms.

EXAMPLES

run (past)   Last night John ran past my house at 3:00 a.m.

eat (past participle) You have eaten all of the cherries I was saving for the picnic.

1. fly (past participle)
2. burst (past)
3. choose (past)
4. fly (past participle)
5. drink (past participle)
6. write (past participle)
7. set (past)
8. rise (past)
9. take (past)
10. see (past)
11. lie (past participle)
12. swim (past participle)
13. drive (past participle)
14. become (past participle)
15. ring (past participle)
16. bring (past)
17. lead (past)
18. lay (past)
19. throw (past participle)
20. drive (past participle)

■ ■ ■ ■ ■ ■ ■ ■ ■ ■ ■ ■

ACTIVITY 27

Fill in your own choices of past tense and past participle verb forms to complete the following sentences. If you have trouble with irregular verb forms, refer to the list on page 233. Spell correctly.

1. Freda _____ angry last night when her

   roommate _____ her bed.

2. The Gomez family has _____ all the way from Florida for their son's graduation.

3. It seems that we have _____ out of things to argue about.

4. It _____ raining early this morning.

5. Have you ever _____ as much cider as you _____ last night?

6. Jacqueline _____ across the lake and back in three hours.

7. That fifty-pound pumpkin was _____ with a special fertilizer.

8. Have you _____ the table for lunch yet?

9. I have _____ all along that you were a special person.

10. The balloon _____ high in the air and then _____ on a tree limb.

11. You have _____ to be very obnoxious with your Al Capone impressions.

12. Fran _____ her new car around town and _____ up boys.

13. Your father has _____ , and that is the end of that!

14. Have you _____ good care of your health this semester?

15. The criminal was finally _____ to justice after years of evading the law.

16. Have you _____ all of your math homework?

17. Sammy _____ to the movies last night and _____ Attack of the Killer Tomatoes.

18. Have you ever _____ on a sharp tack that someone _____ on your seat?

19. You have _____ everyone with your time and patience.

20. The new Chevies aren't _____ to last like the older ones.

21. You _____ your history test easily, but you _____ your P.E. physical.

22. They _____ the missing painting and _____ it to its owner.

20. Mr. Harnsby _____ your story about little green men, but I

_____ .

24. Have you _____ your dear mother lately, or have you _____ her?

25. Henrietta _____ a mean saxophone at the party, and everyone

_____ .

26. I _____ to invite you to tea, but I _____ .

27. Trudy has _____ 23 units of pottery classes and has _____ 6 of them.

28. The roses have _____ their flowers because you haven't _____ them.

29. Sam _____ the tree, _____ from a branch, and _____ his tongue out at a sparrow.

30. I have _____ to help you but you haven't _____ , so

I've _____ up hope that you'll ever become a sword swallower.

■ ■ ■ ■ ■ ■ ■ ■ ■ ■ ■ ■ ■

ACTIVITY 28

The following passage is written in the present tense. Rewrite the passage in the past tense by adding *-ed* to regular past tense verbs and by using the correct past tense and past participle forms for the irregular verbs.

EXAMPLE   Clyde buys his shoes at Zody's and wears them for years.

REVISED   Clyde bought his shoes at Zody's and wore them for years.

The campus goes berserk at Halloween. Boys sneak into girls' dormitories, hide in the closets, and scare them when they return from the cafeteria. Students bombard motorists' cars with water balloons, and there isn't a person asleep anywhere on campus. An army of dorm students attacks its rivals across campus. The students capture the dorm president and spray his body with green paint. They steal the dorm banner and hide it in a car trunk. Students from off campus begin a shaving cream war with on-campus students. They quit when the campus police finally intervene at 3:00 a.m. Then everyone is quiet for about a half hour, but the wildness begins again when the police leave.

■ ■ ■ ■ ■ ■ ■ ■ ■ ■ ■ ■

PRONOUN USAGE

Pronouns are among the most useful words writers have at their command. Without pronouns, a paragraph could read like this.

Freda invited Ted and Maria to Freda's home to study. Ted and Maria brought Ted and Maria's algebra books with Ted and Maria, and Freda, Ted, and Maria all sat at the kitchen table and worked on simplifying an algebraic equation. The algebraic equation was very complicated, and Freda, Ted, and Maria worked on the algebraic equation for over an hour. When Freda, Ted, and Maria finally solved the algebraic equation, Freda, Ted, and Maria took a break.

As you can see, without pronouns, the same nouns would have to be used over and over in a boring pattern. Here is the same paragraph, with underlined pronouns substituting for the nouns.

Freda invited Ted and Maria to her home to study. They brought their algebra books with them, and they all sat at the kitchen table and worked on simplifying an algebraic equation. It was very complicated, and they worked on it for over an hour. When they finally solved it, they took a break.

Pronoun-Antecedent Agreement

Pronouns are used to replace nouns that don't need repeating in a sentence or paragraph. To use pronouns most effectively, follow these basic conventions:

1. **Replace a word with a pronoun instead of repeating the word unnecessarily.**

   AWKWARD   The building lost the building's roof in the tornado.

   BETTER   The building lost its roof in the tornado.

   AWKWARD   Betty was going to be late for class, so Betty called her teacher.

   BETTER   Betty was going to be late for class, so she called her teacher.

2. **Be sure a pronoun agrees in number and gender with the word it replaces (its *antecedent*). For example, if an antecedent is singular and female (*Betty*), the pronouns replacing it must be singular and female (*she, her, hers*). In the following examples, the subject is underlined twice; the pronoun is underlined once.**

   EXAMPLES

   A student in dental assisting must take 12 units of science if she wants to get a degree. *(The antecedent student is singular, so the pronoun she referring to student is also singular.)*

   One of the boys is missing his watch. *(The antecedent one is singular, so the pronoun his referring to one is also singular.)*

   Women should never downgrade their abilities. *(The antecedent women is plural, so the pronoun their referring to women is also plural.)*

   Jays are beautiful birds. They are a brilliant blue color in winter. *(The antecedent jays is plural, so the pronoun they referring to jays is also plural, even if it is in a different sentence.)*

9. Use the pronoun forms that agree with different antecedents:

a. singular female antecedent *(woman, Barbara): she, her, hers, herself*

b. singular male antecedent *(man, Roscoe): he, him, his, himself*

c. singular genderless antecedent *(book, desk): it, its, itself*

d. singular male/female antecedent *(a person, a student, one): he or she, his or her, himself or herself, oneself*

e. plural female antecedent *(girls, women): they, them, their, theirs, themselves*

f. plural male antecedent *(boys, men): they, them, their, theirs, themselves*

g. plural genderless antecedent *(trees, boxes): they, them, their, theirs, themselves*

Be aware of other antecedent situations:

a. others + yourself *(John and I, the class and I): we, our, ours, ourselves*

b. person spoken to *("Mary," "Felix"): you, your, yours, yourself*

c. yourself: *I, me, my, mine, myself*

The following sentences show a variety of pronoun-antecedent agreement situations (the pronoun is underlined, and an arrow is drawn to the antecedent):

Rita lost her wallet, and she had twelve credit cards in it.

A twenty-dollar bill is lying on the kitchen table, and it has been there for a week.

Jack, Jonathan, and Sylvester all took their SAT test last Saturday.

Marian and I always take our dirty clothes to the dormitory laundry service.

Clyde doesn't believe that he can maintain his current 3.4 GPA.

Thelma, you look stunning in your pink taffeta dress.

The students all took their compasses with them on the backpacking trip.

A student should always lock his or her car when it's in the parking lot.

ACTIVITY 29

Substitute an appropriate pronoun for each word that is repeated unnecessarily in the following sentences, making sure that the pronoun agrees with its antecedent.

EXAMPLE   Mary brought Mary's baby brother with Mary to class Monday.

REVISED   Mary brought her baby brother with her to class Monday.

1. That building should have been torn down years ago. That building is a terrible fire hazard.

2. Gretchen used to weigh over 190 pounds, but now Gretchen is down to 130.

3. Marian and I used to shop at Macy's, but Marian and I don't shop there anymore.

4. The teachers at the high school are getting old, and the teachers seem bored with the teachers' jobs. A lot of the teachers should retire.

5. That blister on your heel looks sore, and that blister is going to get worse if you don't put medication on that blister.

6. Thelma should do Thelma a favor and get some sleep for a change.

7. John and I don't consider John and me close friends, but John and I do share a lot of interests.

8. My English book got my English book's cover torn off of my English book. Now my English book's pages are starting to come unbound.

9. The new movie playing at the Bijou is frightening. The new movie involves deranged killers on the loose on a college campus, and the college campus looks a lot like Hillcrest Community College.

10. Small earthquakes hit the valley a number of times last month, and although the small earthquakes caused little damage, the small earthquakes kept all of the neighbors on edge. Some of the neighbors are thinking about moving.

■ ■ ■ ■ ■ ■ ■ ■ ■ ■ ■ ■

Here is a list of *indefinite pronouns* that are always considered *singular* and therefore always require *singular* pronoun references:

anybody	everybody	nothing
anyone	everyone	one
each	everything	somebody
either	nobody	someone
every	no one	something

The following examples of pronoun-antecedent agreement involve *indefinite pronouns*. This is probably the most troublesome agreement situation because the incorrect plural pronoun references don't *sound* wrong to many people. Here are the correct and incorrect forms.

EXAMPLES

INCORRECT   Everyone should bring their books to the room.

CORRECT   Everyone should bring his or her* books to the room.

---

*Singular antecedents of unspecified gender traditionally took singular masculine pronoun references. Today, however, it is customary to refer to such antecedents with "he or she," "him or her," "his or hers," or "himself or herself." (A student should do *his or her* homework before *he or she* gets too tired.) Because "he or she" or "him or her" becomes awkward if overused, use a *plural* antecedent when possible in speaking about a general group: "Students should do *their* homework before *they* get too tired."

INCORRECT	Each person should finish their homework before taking a break.
CORRECT	Each person should finish his or her homework before taking a break.
INCORRECT	No one did their best in the marathon because of the oppressive heat.
CORRECT	No one did his or her best in the marathon because of the oppressive heat.
INCORRECT	Somebody must have completed their art project before the contest deadline.
CORRECT	Somebody must have completed his or her art project before the contest deadline.

ACTIVITY 30

Fill in the blanks in the following sentences with pronouns that agree with their antecedents. Circle the antecedent for each pronoun.

EXAMPLE   The (mind) can snap if too much stress is placed on __it__ .

1. The opossum hangs upside down beside _____ mate.

2. The man who won the canned hams should bring _____ car to the alley.

3. Each of the women works for _____ room and board.

4. A woman from the Bronx left _____ purse in a Manhattan theatre.

5. One of the trucks lost _____ brakes. _____ careened downhill.

6. Those bags she carries weigh a ton, and _____ are huge.

7. Pronouns should always agree in number with _____ antecedents.

8. A person should never press _____ luck.

9. Every one of the politicians made a promise that _____ couldn't keep.

10. The geraniums are losing _____ flowers very early.

11. John told me that it didn't matter to his instructors if _____ came to class late if _____ homework was completed and _____ maintained an A average on all quizzes.

12. One of the male monkeys in the middle cage kept spitting on _____ sister who shared a swing with _____ .

■ ■ ■ ■ ■ ■ ■ ■ ■ ■ ■ ■ ■

ACTIVITY *31*

For more practice with pronoun-antecedent agreement, fill in the blanks in the following sentences with pronouns that agree in number with their antecedents. Circle the antecedent for each pronoun.

EXAMPLE   People can usually be trusted if *they* are given responsibility.

1. The old shack lost _____ tin roof in the hurricane.

2. Each of the girls has a room to _____ in the bungalow.

3. Two men from New Zealand left _____ passports at the airport.

4. A student needs to set _____ priorities straight before _____ can do well in college.

5. Every one of the geraniums got _____ bloom at the same time.

6. Hawaii is a favorite vacation spot for Japanese tourists. _____ is _____ island home away from home, and _____ flock there by the thousands.

7. Humans are _____ own worst enemy in destroying _____ environment. _____ must reverse the destructive process _____ have initiated.

8. Maria did _____ math totally by _____ for the first time in _____ life, and _____ was very proud.

9. A person in need of financial help should consult an expert, and _____ should stay away from well-meaning friends no better off than _____ is.

10. Each cadet was instructed to do _____ own locker inspection, and no one was to leave the barracks before _____ had finished _____ chores.

11. The watches that I bought from the catalog have all lost _____ plastic covers because _____ weren't properly attached to the faces.

12. Skateboards are being seen on college campuses again. _____ lost _____ appeal to students in the late seventies, but now _____ are back in vogue as a means of transportation.

13. Either Sarah or Brunhilda left _____ beaker in the chemistry lab.

14. The presents that you bought me for my birthday lost _____ charm

when I heard you paid for _____ with my credit card.

15. The women who got the best bargains at the garage sale did _____

shopping before 7:00 a.m., and the rest of us were left with what

_____ had picked over.

■ ■ ■ ■ ■ ■ ■ ■ ■ ■ ■ ■

ACTIVITY *32*

Rewrite the following paragraph and change any pronoun that doesn't agree with its antecedent. Make any corresponding verb changes that the pronoun changes make necessary.

EXAMPLE

College students need to begin looking for summer work by Easter. If he waits any later, he will be competing with the high school student who usually doesn't begin their job hunting until May.

REVISED

College students need to begin looking for summer work by Easter. If they wait any later, they will be competing with the high school student who usually doesn't begin his or her job hunting until May.

A person who reads the newspaper has an advantage over one who doesn't. First of all, they are better informed about what's going on in the world and at home. Second, they are in a better position to take advantage of financial bargains, whether it is a furniture discount found in a going-out-of-business ad or a lower home refinancing rate found in the business section. Third, people who read newspapers find much of their conversation in it. He is a better informed, more interesting communicator, and, consequently, he tends to be viewed as more intelligent than his nonreading friends. Finally, if a person reads the newspaper daily, they do more reading than 95 percent of the American population, which has to be an advantage.

■ ■ ■ ■ ■ ■ ■ ■ ■ ■ ■ ■

Subject Pronouns
The following information will help you use the correct subject pronoun forms in your writing:

1. Subject pronouns are always the same: *I, he, she, we, you, it, and they.*

2. The following pronouns are *not* used as subjects: *me, him, her, us, them, myself, herself, himself, ourselves, yourself, themselves.*

3. The most common subject pronoun errors involve compound subjects:

EXAMPLE

John and me went skating. Mary and him are a couple. The Ludlow family and them met for brunch. Felix, Katerina, and her look great together.

4. A good technique for selecting the correct pronoun form with compound subjects is to consider the pronoun by itself. For example, in the sentence "John and me went skating," would you say, "Me went skating"? In the sentence "The Ludlow family and them met for brunch," would you say, "Them met for brunch"? The incorrect forms stand out badly by themselves, and the correct forms—*I* and *they*—sound correct.

EXAMPLES

INCORRECT	Jonathan, Syd, and me like tuna sandwiches.
CORRECT	Jonathan, Syd, and I like tuna sandwiches.
INCORRECT	Samantha and him are excellent mechanics.
CORRECT	Samantha and he are excellent mechanics.
INCORRECT	Fran's mother and her don't want to go shopping in the rain.
CORRECT	Fran's mother and she don't want to go shopping in the rain.
INCORRECT	Alice, Alex, and them did well on the fitness test.
CORRECT	Alice, Alex, and they did well on the fitness test.

ACTIVITY 33

Fill in the blanks in the following sentences with correct subject pronouns. Use the pronouns *I, he, she, you, it, we,* and *they.* Do not use object pronouns such as *me, him, her, us,* and *them.* Try to use all of the different subject pronouns available.

EXAMPLE   Harold and *I* are good friends.

1. Marie and _____ could have built a better float with more time.

2. The Greens and _____ left for the mall an hour ago.

3. _____ and _____ have been feuding all semester.

4. John and _____ will wait for the storm to clear, but Sam and _____ must leave now.

5. My brother and _____ are twins.

6. Sally's mother and _____ are great at attracting crowds.

7. Jackie, Fran, and _____ shared a room in the boarding house.

8. Their family and _____ budget their money poorly.

9. The cat, the alligator, and _____ had a decent time together.

10. Andy, Francis, Homer, _____ , and _____ got free tickets to the High Energy concert.

. . . .

ACTIVITY 34

Underline the correct subject pronoun in each of the following sentences.

EXAMPLES   Sue and (I, me) belong to the same business sorority.

I don't think that you and (she, her) really hate each other.

1. The Smiths, the Gonzales, and (we, us) will meet at the bottom of the mountain.

2. Shirley, (he, him), and (I, me) are studying together tonight.

3. Fred and (they, them) quit their jobs on the same day.

4. Do you think that Gladys, Thelma, and (she, her) are triplets?

5. I'm tired of wandering around the museum, but Gwen and (they, them) certainly aren't.

6. Are you and (they, them) still obligated to attend the supermarket opening?

7. Matty and (I, me) don't have anything in common.

8. Phil, my brothers, and (I, me) went ice skating at Mill Pond.

9. (We, Us) and (they, them) are archrivals in bocci ball.

10. (She, Her) and (he, him) don't see eye to eye on anything.

. . . .

ACTIVITY 35

Some of the following sentences contain subject pronoun errors that need correcting. Rewrite any sentence with a pronoun problem and replace

the incorrect pronoun with the correct subject pronoun form. If the sentence is correct, mark *C*.

EXAMPLE   Howard and me don't care about going to the play tonight.

REVISED   Howard and I don't care about going to the play tonight.

1. I believe that Phyllis and him don't care much for each other's company.

2. Gertie and me don't care about going to visit the museum today.

3. Do you think that Sarah, Henry, and me have a chance in the math contest?

4. Mr. Sanchez and him don't seem to get along at all.

5. Your mother and I have had a long talk about your wonderful grades.

6. Do you know whether Karen and he are coming to the house for dinner?

7. My dog Clyde and me go for long walks on Saturdays.

8. Henry and her go bicycling at the stadium on weekends.

9. Tad, Sam, Sue, Mary, Mick, and me all have short names.

10. Freddie and I are leaving when Melissa and her arrive.

■ ■ ■ ■ ■ ■ ■ ■ ■ ■ ■ ■ ■

Pronoun Shifts

A problem some writers have with pronouns is shifting unnecessarily from one pronoun to another within the same paragraph. The following paragraph contains a number of confusing pronoun shifts:

I prefer taking a semester load of around 12 units. Twelve units usually means you have four classes, and that is the maximum that one can effectively study for at a time. If I take 15 units or more, you have to study for so many classes that you do none of them justice. So most students prefer a 12-unit load although it may take you a bit longer to graduate.

In the sample paragraph, the writer switches from *I* to *you* to *one* to *I* and *you* again. The switching is unnecessary and confusing for readers. Here is the same paragraph with the switching eliminated:

I prefer taking a semester load of around 12 units. Twelve units usually means I have four classes, and that is the maximum that I can effectively study for at a time. If I take 15 units or more, I have to study for so many classes that I do none of them justice. So I prefer a 12-unit load although it may take me a bit longer to graduate.

Here are some basic suggestions for avoiding needless pronoun shifting in your writing:

1. **As a general rule, use the pronoun that you begin with through-out the paragraph. (See the previous sample paragraph.)**

2. **Change pronouns only as you bring in new people to your writing.**

> EXAMPLE   I was alone and bored all day until Henry came over after dinner. He also brought his brother William along, and <u>we</u> all watched TV until midnight.

3. **Avoid using different references to "people in general" within the same paragraph;** *one, a person, people, you.*

EXAMPLE

<u>A person</u> needs to be himself. If <u>you</u> spend your life being what other people think you should be, <u>one</u> ends up with no identity. Once <u>people</u> can say, "This is who I am--take me or leave me," <u>a person</u> can have the peace of mind that only comes with being <u>yourself</u>.

REVISED

You need to be yourself. If you spend your life being what other people think you should be, you end up with no identity. Once you can say, "This is who I am--take me or leave me," you can have the peace of mind that only comes with being yourself.

ACTIVITY 36

Rewrite the following sentences, correcting any unnecessary shifts in pronouns or related words (*a person, people*).

EXAMPLE   You can do anything that a person sets his mind to.

REVISED   You can do anything that you set your mind to.

EXAMPLE   I love popcorn, so I always take a big bag with us to the drive-in.

REVISED   I love popcorn, so I always take a big bag with me to the drive-in.

1. Freda lectures people on the evils of drinking, and one practices what one preaches.

2. I really enjoy morning exercise, for it makes you feel great all day.

3. You can do extremely well on your math test if a person really tries.

4. Marian hasn't been feeling well lately because one has failed to take one's thyroid medication.

5. I'm extremely fond of Clarence, and people have a great time together watching Roller Derby.

6. You can succeed at anything you attempt if one perseveres long enough.

7. Students who enroll late in courses have a tendency to drop, for a student is a step behind to begin with.

8. I am going to eat at the El Rancho tonight, for we love their buffet.

. . . .

ACTIVITY *37*

Rewrite the following paragraph and correct any *unneeded* shifts in tense.

I never enjoyed weight lifting on my own. It was boring, tiring, and somewhat dangerous. If you tried to lift too much, you ended up with two hundred pounds of weight lying on your chest. Then my neighbor, Joe Pulito, started coming over and lifting with me, and you began enjoying it. We spotted each other for safety, and you encouraged each other to lift more reps and more weight. Weight lifting became a game for me, and I enjoy it as long as you have someone to lift with. If you plan on lifting, I'd suggest having a partner.

■ ■ ■ ■ ■ ■ ■ ■ ■ ■ ■ ■

ACTIVITY *38*

Correct any *unnecessary* pronoun shifts in the following paragraph. Some changes in pronouns will be appropriate.

Watching music videos on MTV can be addictive. I started watching them when our dormitory got cable hookups. First, I watched an hour or so in the early evening. Then I started watching them whenever I came back to our room between classes. Pretty soon we had MTV on from early afternoon until 11:00 or 12:00 at night. You can really get hooked on the constant music and the videos, an endless series of surrealistic fantasies. One can also get way behind in one's studies when the videos take over. The only way I could quit watching MTV was to have our cable hookup removed, so that is what we did.

■ ■ ■ ■ ■ ■ ■ ■ ■ ■ ■ ■

PUNCTUATION AND SPELLING

One last step in checking your draft is to look for punctuation and spelling errors. You may have already corrected some of these errors proofreading your drafts for other problems. Now you want to be sure that you haven't overlooked any misspelled words or any punctuation that needs to be added or deleted. This "Punctuation and Spelling" section makes you aware of common problems and gives you practice proofreading essays to identify and correct the problems.

COMMA USAGE

This first section introduces the most common uses of the *comma*. As with all punctuation, commas are used in sentences to make writing easier for

readers to follow. You place commas where readers should pause before continuing the sentence and where they could become confused if words were run together. Three of the most common uses for commas are presented in this section: between words in a series, in compound sentences, and after introductory groups of words.

Commas in Series

If you have three or more words or groups of words in a series, they should be separated by commas. Words in a series are usually joined by conjunctions such as *and*, *but*, and *or*. Here are some examples of series of words with commas separating them.

EXAMPLES   I enjoy hiking, fishing, and reading. *(three words in a series joined by and)*

Marie usually goes jogging in the morning, after lunch, after work, or before going to work. *(four groups of words joined by or)*

George is excited about the debate, prepared to argue his case, and determined to do well. *(three verb phrases joined by and)*

Taking a shower, brushing her teeth, ironing her blouse, and eating cornflakes are part of Monique's morning schedule. *(four subjects joined by and)*

ACTIVITY 39

Put commas in the following sentences to separate words in a series. If a sentence does *not* have a series of at least three items, don't put in any commas.

EXAMPLE   I'll take ketchup, mustard, and hot sauce on my potatoes.

1. Hang-gliding parachuting and flying are three things Harvey is not interested in.
2. Take the mail to the post office buy ten air-mail stamps put the stamps on the letters and mail them to Australia.
3. You can find Minerva in the library in the cafeteria in the bookstore or in the parking lot with Fred.
4. The test will have true-and-false questions essay questions multiple-choice and matching.
5. The students in rooms 32 33 36 and 39 are excused for today.
6. I want to walk out of here and never come back.
7. The students who were absent yesterday the students who failed the last test the students who didn't turn in a term paper and the students who have lost their books will receive no cookies today.
8. I want a car that is dependable gets good gas mileage has plenty of room looks sporty goes 100 miles an hour and costs under $2,000.

■ ■ ■ ■ ■ ■ ■ ■ ■ ■ ■ ■ ■

Commas in Compound Sentences

As you learned in the section on compound sentences, a comma goes before the conjunction that joins the two halves of a compound sentence. Here are some compound sentences with the commas inserted and the conjunctions underlined.

EXAMPLES   I'd like to go to the concert tomorrow, <u>but</u> I don't have a ride or any money.

I'll go to the concert tomorrow, <u>and</u> you can give me a ride and pay my way.

I could go to the concert tomorrow, <u>or</u> I could stay home and write my history paper.

I'll go to the concert tomorrow, <u>so</u> now you don't have to worry about going alone.

ACTIVITY 40

Write compound sentences using the following conjunctions, and put a comma before the conjunction. *Make sure each compound sentence has a complete sentence on each side of the conjunction.* Write on the topics provided.

EXAMPLE   **a sentence about hamburgers using *and***
I like eating hamburgers more than hot dogs, and I like them the best at the Dog House.

1. a sentence about pizza using *but*
2. a sentence about teachers using *or*
3. a sentence about love using *and*
4. a sentence about donkeys using *so* (meaning *therefore*)
5. a sentence about muscles using *but*
6. a sentence about ears using *and*

Share your sentences with classmates. Check the use of commas in compound sentences, and make sure there is a complete sentence on each side of the conjunction. Share the more interesting sentences with the class.

■   ■   ■   ■   ■   ■   ■   ■   ■   ■   ■

Commas After Introductory Words

Many sentences begin with an introductory group of words that is followed by a pause before the reader continues. A comma is placed at the end of the introduction signaling the pause to the readers. Here are some examples with introductory words underlined.

EXAMPLES   If you have finished taking out the garbage, please give me some help with the laundry.

Since we have begun the new chapter in our history text, I have read over 75 pages.

Looking at his watch every minute, Charlie waited for his blind date.

Alarmed at how quickly his hair was falling out, Marvin bought a hat.

Shouting at the top of her lungs, Alicia attracted the sheriff's attention.

In the middle of his greatest season, Joe Jones broke his passing arm.

On your way out of the auditorium, please lock the double doors.

As you can see, the group of words following each introduction is a *complete sentence*. The introductory words often provide information about the *subject* of the complete sentence. Notice the types of words that begin the introductory words: subordinate conjunctions (*if, since*), *-ed* and *-ing* ending words (*looking, alarmed, shouting*), and prepositions (*in, on*).

ACTIVITY 41

Punctuate the following sentences correctly by putting a comma after each introductory group of words.

EXAMPLE   Down river where the channel narrows, there's a pool full of catfish.

1. In spite of all the work we've done we still must work all night to finish the float.
2. After George lifted 200 pounds over his head he went to the doctor.
3. Shocked by what she saw on the screen Melissa stormed out of the theatre.
4. Waiting until the last minute to decide Hank finally enrolled at Memphis State.
5. Asleep for most of the class Hanna was roused by the sound of her name.
6. Because you have worked so hard in this class take a day off.
7. On your way to the meeting tonight pick up something to use for a gavel.
8. On a bet from her roommates Harriet hung from the balcony by her teeth.
9. If you are interested in getting tickets to next Tuesday's concert you should call today.
10. Although the fog was thick thousands of motorists braved the bad weather.

ACTIVITY *42*

Insert commas in the following sentences where they are needed in series, in compound sentences, and after introductory words or groups of words.

EXAMPLE   In the back of the bus, we found snakes, frogs, and lizards.

1. Andretti barreled down the straightaway braked on the curve and punched the gas on entering the backstretch.
2. Stealing chickens trespassing hunting on private property and tying cats' tails together were charges brought against Akins.
3. In the back of my mind I remember having traveled this stretch of Texas before.
4. Judith wanted to go on a hayride but she was allergic to hay.
5. In spite of everything you've heard about Claudine she's really a dangerous person.
6. We can cut the firewood this afternoon after school or we can wait and cut it on Saturday morning.
7. Because you have been so faithful to the team you've earned the Most Inspirational Chess Player award.
8. It's raining too hard to pick strawberries behind the house so let's do it another time.
9. After we take the subway to Main Street let's walk up to 55th and Broadway.
10. Our plans are to meet at Maria's go to the dance in one car eat at Feducci's go back to Maria's for our cars and drive home.
11. That small mangy feisty flea-bitten cat is all mine.
12. Practicing for the piano concert on Friday Marian got blisters on her thumbs pinkies and index fingers but that didn't prevent her from playing beautifully at the concert.

■ ■ ■ ■ ■ ■ ■ ■ ■ ■ ■ ■

ACTIVITY *43*

In the following sentences, insert commas between words or groups of words in a series, after introductory groups of words, before the conjunction in a compound sentence, and before and after relative clauses beginning with *who* or *which*. See pages 81 and 82 for a review of relative clause punctuation.

EXAMPLES   In the dead of night, Carrie snuck out of her bed. *(introductory phrase)*

You are welcome to ride in my van, but it is going to be very crowded. *(compound sentence)*

Tomorrow we'll vacuum the rug, clean the walls, and water the plants. *(groups of words in a series)*

1. While you were getting a suntan I was cooped up in the library.

2. In the back of his mind Wallace knew that he was under suspicion for the robbery.

3. To know you're doing poorly to continue missing class to ignore your homework assignments and to flunk your final exam put you in a deep hole.

4. Frances will never walk to school again because it took her over three hours this morning.

5. Instead of working on our algebra let's finish our graphic drawings.

6. Bothered by the heat Calvin strapped a fan to his head put ice cubes down his pants and wore fishnet tops.

7. Unless you plan on spending more than one night in Antwerp I'd advise you to stay at the boarding house on Sixth Street for ten dollars.

8. Angered by her teacher's indifference Sally worked extra hard to get his praise but nothing she did seemed to matter to him.

9. When you are ready to make the dressing I'll go downtown and buy the eggs milk bread crumbs and seasoning that you need.

10. George Gomez who works for Bank of America is running for mayor of Stillwater.

11. In spite of her poor showing in the debate Terry entered the district competition and she surprised everyone by placing second in extemporaneous speaking third in humorous oration and first in biographical sketches.

12. Biology 102 which is offered at 8:00 a.m. daily has a prerequisite of Biology 101.

. . . .

Overusing Commas

Commas are very useful in sentences for separating words and identifying pauses that make the sentences easier for the reader to follow. However, when you become more aware of commas, there is often a tendency to overuse them. Too many commas can ruin the flow of a sentence for the reader. This usually occurs when a writer goes beyond a few basic rules for comma placement and decides that if a few commas are good, a lot of commas are probably better. This is seldom the case.

The most common misuse of commas is before the conjunction *and*. Here are the uses for a comma before *and*.

1. A comma is required before the *and* that joins the halves of a compound sentence.

2. A comma should be used before the *and* joining a series of three or more words or word groups.

3. A comma should *not* be used before an *and* that joins only *two* words or word groups or before an *and* where the second part of the sentence has no subject.

The following examples show correct and incorrect uses of commas.

EXAMPLES

CORRECT   John has been driving a tractor since he was eight, and at fourteen he was already driving eighteen-wheel truck rigs. *(Comma comes before the* and *joining the halves of a* compound sentence.*)*

INCORRECT   John has been driving a tractor since he was eight, and has been driving eighteen-wheel truck rigs since he was fourteen. *(There should be no comma before* and *because this* isn't *a compound sentence; there's no subject in the second part of sentence.)*

CORRECT   I'll take tomatoes, ketchup, mustard, mayonnaise, and dressing on my hamburger. *(Comma comes before the* and *in a series of three or more words or word groups.)*

INCORRECT   I'll take tomatoes, and ketchup on my hamburger. *(There should be no comma before an* and *joining only two words or word groups.)*

ACTIVITY *44*

Place commas in the following sentences according to the rules you have learned about commas before in compound sentences, between words or word groups in series of three or more, *after* introductory groups of words, with relative clauses and appositives, and in compound-complex sentence combinations. However, don't put commas incorrectly before *and* if it joins only *two* words or word groups or if the sentence isn't compound.

EXAMPLE   In the early morning hours Mary prowls the house and waits for dawn to break.

REVISED   In the early morning hours, Mary prowls the house and waits for dawn to break. *(comma after introductory phrase)*

1. John and Henrietta decided to jog to school and back three times a week.

2. John Helen and Henrietta decided to jog to school and they later decided to also jog back home.

3. Before you try the cornflakes in the cupboard check the packaging date on the box and see how old they are.

4. Samantha really enjoys playing strange characters in plays because the parts are so different from her personality.

5. After Gladys fixed the radiator hose on her Plymouth the fan belt and the smaller radiator hose broke.

6. Working on his stamp collection and watching old "Cisco Kid" reruns on TV are Albert's pastimes and he ignores everything else around him for weeks at a time.

7. For the week-long field trip to Death Valley we'll need picks and shovels tents and eats food and water and heavy jackets.

8. Harvey left third base at the crack of the bat and raced for home plate well ahead of the ball.

9. From the looks of that cut on your head and your bruised knees you'd better see a doctor and do it fast!

10. Louise and Mavis invited Teddie and Rumford to the Lucky Horseshoe Casino and then didn't show up.

11. If I had a dime for every time you had an excuse for being late for work I could retire early and live like a king.

12. Allyson thought about attending Mumsford College and even sent in an application but at the last minute she decided to attend a business college.

13. Rex Garcia who was born in Santa Fe, New Mexico, is now the mayor of his hometown.

14. When I returned to my apartment I found Marian Weber an old high school friend waiting for me outside.

15. I wanted to sit in a floor seat at the Tina Turner concert but since all floor seat tickets are sold I'll settle for a balcony seat which costs $15.

* * * * * * * * * * *

Comma Review

Remember these basic uses for commas:

1. **Separate three or more words or groups of words in a series with commas.**

   I am going to bake a cake, hire a band, blow up balloons, and give you a birthday party you won't forget.

2. **Place a comma before a conjunction joining halves of a compound sentence.**

   I am very tired of pulling weeds, so I am going to get some weed killer instead.

3. **Place a comma after an introductory group of words.**

   Before you decide against voting for O'Banion, consider his record on women's rights. In every vote taken in the assembly on a women's rights issue, he has voted the liberal position.

4. **Place commas around an appositive. (See page 121 for review.)**

   Josephine Moranda, a ticket taker at the Grandview Cinema, has seen The Rocky Horror Show forty-seven times.

5. **Place commas around a relative clause in a complex sentence when the modified word is named or clearly identified. (See pages 81 and 82 for review.)**

Ms. Fairchild, who ran for board of supervisors last spring, was just indicted for income tax evasion. The indictment that she received alluded to $50,000 of unreported income. That income, which she made on the college lecture circuit, didn't appear on her 1040 tax form.

6. **Use commas in compound-complex sentence combinations as you would in regular compound and complex sentences.**

When we left for the basketball game last night, we forgot our tickets, so we drove forty miles for nothing and came home.

Jonathan isn't really interested in graduating this semester, and because he already has a great job waiting for him in his father's lumber business, he may never graduate.

7. **Don't misuse commas, particularly before an *and* joining two words or two verb phrases.**

WRONG   We left for Shreveport at 6:00 a.m., and arrived at 2:00 p.m.

WRONG   Shelly and I bought Steve, and Carl a box of oranges, and a box of apples.

ACTIVITY 45

Put commas in the following sentences where they are needed. Don't put in commas unnecessarily.

EXAMPLE   I enjoyed my dinner last night but the dessert a rich custard made me sick.

REVISED   I enjoyed dinner last night, but the dessert, a rich custard, made me sick.

1. When Bernie steps up to the plate the outfielders move to the right.

2. In spite of his spotty record on welfare reform I'll still vote for Smith a man of great integrity.

3. Take out the garbage feed the dogs wash the car vacuum the carpet mop the floor and then wake me from my nap.

4. I'm not leaving anything up to Henrietta for she has a very short memory.

5. Although you have accomplished a lot in life the best still lies ahead for you.

6. Winnie works at Dairee-Delight on weekends and holidays.

7. Cletus a 280-pound mailman is a gentle cheerful person.

8. Allie Gomez who lives at the end of the block is a tireless worker for the poor.

9. The Bank of America building that stood on the corner was destroyed in the earthquake.

10. Of all of the classes that Maggie took she felt that her human relations course was the most helpful the most interesting and the easiest.

11. Rita finished her lessons early and took a walk around the plaza with her dog.

12. You Tammy Womack are a talented clarinetist but you need to practice your upper register more.

13. In the nick of time Fred remembered about the English quiz and crammed for a half hour.

14. Before arriving at work Matilda had already fixed breakfast for four done a load of wash ironed two dresses and finished a crossword puzzle.

15. After Helena completed her job application she eyed the other candidates a group of intelligent-looking people.

16. I'm not excited about running for a class office at college but if someone wanted to help me organize a campaign I'd at least consider running.

17. The top of the Empire State Building which is one of the tallest buildings in the country sways in a strong wind.

18. When Mildred Berry walks into a room everyone notices her for she is six feet tall wears four-inch spiked heels and dresses in black leather.

19. If you want my opinion on where to live I'd suggest renting a room at the Theta sorority house which is across the street from campus for the rent is reasonable the girls are friendly and the location is convenient.

20. I was halfway through the intersection before the light turned yellow but a Nashville policeman a guy with squinty eyes and a low forehead pulled me over and gave me a ticket for running a red light.

* * * * * * * * * * * *

SEMICOLONS AND COLONS

The semicolon (;) and colon (:) allow writers to vary their sentence structure and add flexibility to their writing. A review of the uses for each punctuation mark follows.

1. *Semicolon:* **joins two complete sentences that are related in meaning and that are reasonably short (used as an alternative separating sentences with a period or joining sentences with a conjunction).**

   EXAMPLES   Marion should be at the check-out counter any minute; her ten-minute break is almost over.

   Hank's health is his number one concern; nothing else seems important right now.

   Melissa should never have tried to run a hard mile without warming up; she knows better.

2. *Colon:* (a) used after a *complete thought* to indicate that a series of items follows.

   EXAMPLES   We need the following utensils for the picnic: knives, forks, spoons, spatulas, and a cheese grater.

   Sandra has the characteristics of an outstanding athlete: intelligence, dedication, coachability, goal orientation, and confidence.

3. *Colon:* (b) used after a *complete thought* to highlight a single item that follows.

   EXAMPLES   There's one virtue that Peter definitely lacks: patience.

   The answer to Maria's financial problem is obvious: find a better job.

   As a camp counselor, you've made one thing apparent: your concern for troubled children.

   I've got something that you need: the keys to the house.

ACTIVITY *46*

Add semicolons and colons to the following sentences where they are needed. Put a *C* in front of each correctly punctuated sentence.

EXAMPLE   You show a real aptitude for computer programming; you have a promising future.

1. ____ There's one class in college I've had trouble passing physiology.

2. ____ I know how to get from our dormitory to the downtown library I went there several times last semester.

3. ____ Everyone fails occasionally don't get discouraged.

4. ____ Freda replaced her computer's floppy disk system with a hard disk drive the new system is much faster and stores more information.

5. ____ Millicent has been taking aerobic dance four times a week for four years she started when she was forty-five years old.

6. ____ One attribute comes to mind when considering golfer Jack Nicklaus's years of unparalleled success mental toughness.

7. ____ The chain saw equipment in the garage should include two 16-inch Weber chain saws, a bag of extra chains, a gallon of gasoline, three cleaning rags, and four pints of chain saw oil.

8. ____ My aunt's cat Tiger is a fearless fighter her other cat Chubby prefers hiding behind the washing machine.

9. ____ Gretchen has increased sales for the Hartford Insurance office she took over for her father by doing two things doubling the advertising budget and tripling the number of "cold calls" done by agents.

10. ____ In Sweden, all day-care center workers are required to have college degrees in the United States, there are no such requirements.

11. ____ Five major movies have been made about the Vietnam War however, only one movie, *Full-Metal Jacket*, depicted an inductee's training prior to going to Vietnam.

12. ____ I'll see if I can get these chores done before noon mowing the lawn, weeding the flower beds, and trimming the front hedge.

13. ____ There are going to be thirty huge speakers on stage at the Journey concert therefore, we can sit at the back of the arena and still hear very well.

* * * * * * * * * * * * *

ACTIVITY 47

For practice, write five of your own sentences that need semicolons and five more that need colons, and punctuate them correctly. (Use the words *however* and *therefore* after the semicolons in at least two sentences, and write some sentences in which the colon is followed by a single word and others in which it is followed by a series.)

* * * * * * * * * * * * *

QUOTATION MARKS

In any paper you write, you may on occasion want to include the specific words that someone said to add interest to your essay. Another time you may want to quote an expert on a subject to provide support for a position you've taken. To show that a person is "talking" in your paper, you need to do two things:

1. Put *quotation marks* (" ") around the spoken words.
2. Make reference to the person speaking.

Here are some examples of direct quotations correctly punctuated.

EXAMPLES   John said, "Where are you going with my hammer?"

"I don't want to go shopping in these curlers," said Harriet.
Alvin interrupted Mary by saying, "Stop telling those flattering lies about me."

My mother said, "You have always had a bad temper. Remember the time you threw your brother out the window?"

"I want you to go," Mike insisted. "We need you to liven up the party."

"Alice's biggest weakness," her sister admitted, "is that she can't say 'no.'"

Here are the basic rules for punctuating *direct quotations*, as demonstrated in the example sentences, and a word about *indirect quotations*.

1. Quotation marks go around only the spoken words.

2. Quotation marks always go *outside* of end marks.

3. The reference to the speaker may come at the beginning, in the middle, or at the end of a quote. A comma always separates the reference to the speaker from the quote itself.

4. If a quote contains two or more sentences together, the quotation marks are placed in front of the first sentence and after the last sentence only.

5. A comma comes after the last word in a quotation only if the sentence continues after the quote. Otherwise, an end mark is used.

6. If the reference to the speaker is in the middle of a quotation, the quoted words on both sides of the reference are in quotation marks. (See the last two example sentences.)

7. When you change speakers in a paper, you usually begin a new paragraph.

8. Direct quotations are the exact words of the speaker. An *indirect quotation* tells what the speaker said *as told by the writer:* Jack said that he needs a second job; Mary told me that she was tired of school. Indirect quotations are *not put in quotation marks* because they are not the words of a speaker.

ACTIVITY 48

Most of the following sentences are direct quotations that need punctuating with quotation marks. Punctuate the quotations correctly following the rules just given. If a sentence is an *indirect quotation*, don't put it in quotes.

EXAMPLE   If you don't stop biting your nails, you'll draw blood said Claire.

REVISED   "If you don't stop biting your nails, you'll draw blood," said Claire.

1. Hank said Please bring me a glass of Alka-Seltzer.

2. The trouble with school said Muriel is the classes.

3. I know what I'm going to do after my last final whispered Allyson.

4. Freda admitted I have very oily hair. I have to wash it twice a day.

5. That's a beautiful ring exclaimed Bob Where did you buy it?

6. No one said Millie is leaving this house. We have a mess to clean up!

7. Charlotte said that her nephew from Miami would arrive by bus.

8. Teddy said My niece will be on the same bus as your nephew.

9. Maria said that you would help me with my algebra.

10. Will you please help me with my lab report for botany? asked Freddie.

. . . .

ACTIVITY 49

For additional practice, punctuate the following quotations correctly by inserting all punctuation and capital letters necessary. Don't put quotation marks around indirect quotes.

EXAMPLE   Mark replied I could have run faster if I had leaned into the curves.

REVISED   Mark replied, "I could have run faster if I had leaned into the curves."

1. Thelma asked why have you been hanging out with such ornery fellows, Clyde

2. They are no more ornery than I am Clyde replied

3. But they are making moonshine Thelma said and selling it to the school boys

4. They make a little shine admitted Clyde but it's the best around

5. And who are those wild girls they run around with Thelma asked

6. Clyde laughed those are just their cousins from Taber Corners

7. You're starting to sound and act just like those boys Thelma scolded

8. Thank you said Clyde I take that as a compliment

. . . .

ACTIVITY 50

For practice punctuating quoted material in your writing, make up a conversation between two people who are having an argument about something: a brother and sister, husband and wife, two friends, two strangers, a student and teacher, a boss and employee, a boyfriend and girlfriend. They may be arguing about anything: the weather, politics, a grade, a raise, money, behavior, or any subject you choose.

When you write your conversation, place quotation marks around the spoken words and make reference to the two speakers so that readers always know who's talking.

SAMPLE CONVERSATION BEGINNING

"We're overdrawn at the bank again this month," said Margaret.

"How can we be?" Hank asked. "We should be <u>saving</u> money on the salary I'm making."

"You don't realize how much of your check goes to monthly bills," said Margaret. "After I pay the rent, the gas and electric bills, the bank loan, and buy groceries for the month, we have only $150 left to live on."

. . . .

ACTIVITY 51

Write your own dialogue between two or three people who are judging a contest: Miss America, Mr. America, a hog-calling contest, a frog-jumping contest, a bubble-blowing contest, a diving contest, or a musical competition. Share their remarks about the contestants with your readers.

SAMPLE BEGINNING

"That triple somersault that Jones did was worth at least an 8," Herbert said.

"Well, I gave it a 6 because he made too much splash," replied Marya.

"It's impossible to do that dive without making a splash," said Herbert. "He entered feet first."

"It's not impossible at all," said Marya, "if he had pointed his toes. He looked like a frog when he entered."

"A frog!" yelled Herbert. "I'd like to see you do a triple somersault and make that small a splash. What makes you such an expert?"

"I'm as much of an expert as you are," said Marya. "They pulled me out of the same P.E. class they pulled you out of to judge this silly event."

"Yeah, but you'll have to admit judging Olympic diving is better than being in P.E. class," replied Herbert.

"Shut up," said Marya. "The Yugoslavian is about to do a three and a quarter corkscrew with a reverse twist."

. . . .

APOSTROPHES IN POSSESSIVES

One of the most frequently omitted punctuation marks is the apostrophe that is needed in words that are *possessive*. A word that is *possessive* is usually followed directly by something *belonging to it*. Here are some sentences with the possessive words correctly punctuated with apostrophes. The possessive words are underlined.

EXAMPLES   My mother's brother owns a fruit stand in the country.

Today's weather looks menacing with those dark clouds in the east.

I am going to Celia's surprise party tomorrow night.

The men's room at the Forum is flooded.

My three brothers' cars are all 1974 Plymouths.

The ladies' club holds its meetings at the Howbarth Tavern.

As you can see, the word directly following the possessive word belongs to it: mother's *brother*, today's *weather*, Celia's *surprise party*, men's *room*, brothers' *cars*, and ladies' *club*. Notice that sometimes the apostrophe comes before the -s and sometimes it comes *after* the -s. Here are the rules for showing possession:

1. *Singular possessive word:* Add apostrophe and -s to the word:

   a boy's dog, the tree's bark, May's hair

2. *Plural possessive word:* Add the apostrophe *after* the -s:

   three boys' dogs, all the trees' bark, many girls' hair

There are two exceptions to the possessive rules:

1. Plural words that form their possessive *without* adding -s (*man/men, woman/women, child/children, goose/geese*) are punctuated as *singular* possessives (-'s): men's hats, women's shoes, children's lessons, geese's feathers.

2. Possessive pronouns such as *yours, theirs, his, ours,* and *hers* do *not* require *apostrophes* since the form of the pronoun itself indicates possession.

ACTIVITY 52

Put apostrophes in the following possessive words to show singular and plural possessive forms.

EXAMPLES   a dog's life

the boys' club

1. the banks vault
2. a childs prayer
3. my uncles wife
4. six countries treaties
5. thirty books covers
6. the geeses feathers
7. a mans opinion
8. omens strength
9. twenty schools fight songs
10. four doctors nurses
11. Tuesdays child
12. the wars effect

. . . .

ACTIVITY *53*

Write your own sentences showing the possessive relationship that is given for each sentence. Follow the rules for adding -'s or -s'. Make sure that the possessive word is followed by the thing belonging to it.

EXAMPLE   a dog belonging to Mark

REVISED   Mark's dog is a cocker spaniel.

EXAMPLE   the bones of all the dogs in the neighborhood

REVISED   All of the dogs' bones are hidden in the lot behind my house.

1.   the hamster belonging to Mary
2.   the snow of this morning
3.   the lockers belonging to the men
4.   the right to an education belonging to a student
5.   the socks belonging to your grandmother
6.   the station wagons belonging to six families
7.   the great force of the ocean waves
8.   the diagnosis of a doctor

Share your sentences with a classmate. Check each other's uses of possessive words. Are the apostrophes in the right places? Does the thing belonging to the possessive word follow it? Be prepared to share your sentences with the class.

. . . .

CONTRACTIONS

A contraction is a word formed by combining two words with an apostrophe inserted to replace the omitted letters. The most common

contractions combine pronouns with verbs (*I'm, he's, you've, we're*) and verbs with the word *not* (*isn't, wasn't, don't, won't, aren't*).

Here are examples of common contractions and the word pairs from which they are formed.

I'm	I am	aren't	are not
you're	you are	wasn't	was not
he's	he is	weren't	were not
she's	she is	don't	do not
they're	they are	doesn't	does not
we're	we are	won't	will not
he'll	he will	wouldn't	would not
we'll	we will	hasn't	has not
they've	they have	haven't	have not
I've	I have	there's	there is
it's	it is	here's	here is
isn't	is not	who's	who is

ACTIVITY 54

Write contractions for the following pairs of words. Don't forget the apostrophes.

EXAMPLE   he is   *he's*

1. they are _____

2. it is _____

3. do not _____

4. does not _____

5. she is _____

6. I am _____

7. there is _____

8. they have _____

9. will not _____

10. are not _____

11. has not _____

12. you are _____

■ ■ ■ ■ ■ ■ ■ ■ ■ ■ ■ ■ ■

ACTIVITY *55*

Put apostrophes in all of the contractions and possessive words that require them in the following sentences.

EXAMPLE   Theyre not going to the firemens ball Friday.

REVISED   They're not going to the firemen's ball Friday.

1. The chipmunks buried a years supply of nuts in the trees hollow.

2. Were supposed to be at the Smiths home for dinner, arent we?

3. The womens tennis team and the mens team were defeated in the leagues championships.

4. Havent you found your sisters new sweater or your four brothers fishing poles yet?

5. Megs response to Jacks question wasnt at all surprising to the groups leaders.

6. Cant you figure a way to curb Fredas appetite for anchovy pizza and lasagna?

7. No ones frame of mind is any better than Howies when he isnt drinking.

8. The dogs and the cats arent supposed to be in Mr. Grumbleys study.

9. The governments belief in the economys recovery isnt accepted by Willies grandfathers.

10. Youve had a difficult time with Newtons law of gravity, havent you?

■ ■ ■ ■ ■ ■ ■ ■ ■ ■ ■ ■

COMMONLY MISSPELLED WORDS

Misspelled words account for the largest number of writing errors. Spelling errors are a nuisance to the reader, and final drafts should be free of them. While spelling is a minor problem for many writers, it is a big problem for others. This section introduces some of the most commonly misspelled words and gives you a few basic spelling rules to follow; however, if you have serious spelling difficulties, you might seek further assistance from your instructor.

The following is the first of a number of spelling word lists that will appear throughout this section. Each list groups words that follow similar rules.

Spelling List One: "ing"-Ending Words

beginning	kidding	putting	stopping
boring	letting	riding	studying
coming	living	running	swimming

dying	planning	sitting	taking
flying	playing	slipping	writing
hitting			

Words ending in *-ing* are frequently misspelled. Here are the basic rules that will help you decide what to do when adding *-ing* to a word.

1. Verbs ending in *-e:* Drop the *-e* and add *-ing (boring, coming, riding, raking).*
2. Verbs ending in *-y:* Keep the *-y* and add *-ing (studying, playing, flying).*
3. Verbs ending in a *short vowel** followed by a single consonant: Double the last letter and add *-ing (beginning, hitting, kidding, letting, planning, running).*
4. Verbs ending in a *long vowel†* followed by a consonant: Add *-ing,* but do *not* double the final letter *(dreaming, eating, sleeping, cheating).* Note: Writers have few problems with this rule, so the words were not included in this spelling list.

ACTIVITY 56

Following the spelling rules for adding *-ing* to words, add the *-ing* ending to the following words from Spelling List One.

1. come _____   5. study _____   9. ride _____   13. live _____

2. hit _____   6. run _____   10. stop _____   14. begin _____

3. play _____   7. write _____   11. bore _____   15. swim _____

4. plan _____   8. kid _____   12. put _____   16. let _____

■ ■ ■ ■ ■ ■ ■ ■ ■ ■ ■

ACTIVITY 57

Write eight sentences using two different *-ing* words from Spelling List One in each sentence, and make sure to spell the words correctly. Underline the list words used.

EXAMPLE   <u>Coming</u> to school every weekday for twelve years becomes <u>boring</u>.

■ ■ ■ ■ ■ ■ ■ ■ ■ ■ ■

---

* Short vowel sounds are found in words like *hăt, kĭd, Frĕd, hŏt,* and *bŭt.*
† Long vowel sounds are found in words like *hāte, kīte, frēe, hōle,* and *būtte.*

Here is the second list of words that writers frequently misspell. Each list contains words that are similarly misspelled.

Spelling List Two: "ie" and "ei" Words

achieve	field	neither
believe	friend	receive
deceive	grieve	relief
eight	height	review
either	neighbor	their

As you can see, each of these words contains either an *ei* or an *ie* vowel combination. Many writers misspell these words by turning the two letters around. Here are the basic rules for when to use *ie* and when to use *ei*.

1. In most words, the *i* goes before the *e unless* it follows the letter *c*. Then the *e* goes before the *i*, as in *receive, deceive,* and *perceive*.

2. If the *ei* has a *long a vowel sound*, the *e* comes before the *i*, as in *neighbor, eight,* and *freight*.

3. You need to memorize some exceptions to the *i* before *e* rule: *height, either, neither*.

ACTIVITY *58*

Write eight sentences using any two of the Spelling List Two words in each sentence. Use all fifteen words in the eight sentences. Spell the words correctly.

EXAMPLE   You can <u>achieve</u> more in life if you <u>believe</u> in yourself.

. . . .

ACTIVITY *59*

For fun and spelling practice, see how many of the Spelling List Two words you can use in a *single* sentence. Then try to use the rest of the List Two words in a *second* sentence. Look for connections among the words before you write your first sentence.

EXAMPLE   I <u>believe</u> I can <u>achieve</u> much in life and <u>deceive</u> <u>neither</u> <u>neighbor</u> nor <u>friend</u>.

. . . .

The words in Spelling List Three are grouped together because writers often misspell them in the same manner: by leaving out a letter.

Spelling List Three: Left-out Letters

again	opinion	stereo
always	restaurant	straight
clothes	schedule	surprise
familiar	separate	whether
February	several	which
finish	similar	while
interest	sophomore	

Thus, *again* is spelled *"agin,"* *February* is spelled *"Febuary,"* *interest* is spelled *"intrest,"* *clothes* is spelled *"cloths,"* or *whether* is spelled *"wether."* The letters are often left out because of the way many people pronounce the words. Three-syllable words such as *interest, restaurant, sophomore,* and *several* are often pronounced and spelled as two-syllable words: *in-trest, rest-rant, soph-more,* and *sev-ral.* The *wh-* words are frequently pronounced and spelled without the *h* sound: *"wether," "wich,"* and *"wile."* Because there is no spelling rule to cover the range of List Three words, you will need to memorize them. The best tip for helping you learn them is to *pronounce* the words correctly so that you won't leave out letters by omitting syllables or sounds.

ACTIVITY 60

Write ten sentences including two different Spelling List Three words in each sentence. Use the words in any order you wish, and spell them correctly. Underline the spelling words.

EXAMPLE   I <u>always finish</u> my English assignments five minutes before class.

▪ ▪ ▪ ▪ ▪ ▪ ▪ ▪ ▪ ▪ ▪

Spelling List Four contains words that are grouped together because they all contain double consonants that can cause confusion. The writer is not always certain which letters to double. Unfortunately, there is no rule similar to the rules covering words in List One and List Two to tell you which letters to double. The words in List Four need to be memorized so that their correct spelling is easily visualized. Because these words are commonly used, you should know them well by the time you complete this course.

Spelling List Four: Double-Letter Words

across	dinner	parallel
arrangement	embarrass	success
attitude	immediate	surround
business	impossible	terrible
different	occasion	tomorrow
difficult	occurred	

ACTIVITY *61*

Write nine sentences using any two of the Spelling List Four words in each sentence. Use all seventeen words in your sentences.

EXAMPLE   Sarah made a <u>business arrangement</u> with her banker for a loan.

Spelling List Five contains words that end in *-ly.*

Spelling List Five: "-ly"-Ending Words

actually	finally	lovely
busily	fortunately	naturally
completely	hungrily	really
easily	lively	unusually
especially	lonely	usually
extremely		

Writers who misspell *-ly* words get confused about whether to drop a letter before adding the *-ly* or whether to add an extra *-l* to form an *-lly* ending. The following simple rules should clear up the problems.

1. Add *-ly* to the root word. Do *not* drop the last letter of the word (*lovely,* not *lovly, fortunately,* not *fortunatly*). An *-lly* ending is used only when the root word ends in *-l* (*real/really, unusual/unusually, natural/naturally, actual/actually*).

2. If a root word ends in *-y,* change the *-y* to *i* and add *-ly (busy/ busily, easy/easily, hungry/hungrily*).

ACTIVITY *62*

Add *-ly* to the following root words following the rules just covered for adding the *-ly* ending.

EXAMPLES   clumsy *clumsily*

sane *sanely*

1. natural _____

2. live _____

3. hungry _____

4. special _____

5. busy _____

6. unusual _____

7. real _____

8. fortunate _____

9. lone _____

10. complete _____

11. actual _____

12. final _____

13. easy _____

14. love _____

■ ■ ■ ■ ■ ■ ■ ■ ■ ■ ■

ACTIVITY 63

Write seven sentences including two different -*ly* words from Spelling List Five in each sentence. Use the words in any order you wish.

EXAMPLE   Fortunately, we finally arrived at the concert.

■ ■ ■ ■ ■ ■ ■ ■ ■ ■ ■

SPELLING REFERENCE LIST

The following list includes more than one hundred of the most frequently misspelled words. You may use it as a convenient spelling reference when proofreading your drafts for errors. You may also want to select five to ten words per week to work on until you can spell every word on the list correctly.

accommodate	apparent	business
achievement	appearance	certain
acquaintance	approach	chief
acquire	argument	comparative
actual	attendance	conscience
against	beginner	controversy
alleys	believe	convenience
amateur	benefit	criticism
amount	boundary	dealt

dependent	knowledge	possess
describe	laid	practical
despair	led	preferred
disappoint	leisure	prejudice
disease	license	preparation
divine	loneliness	principal
efficient	loose	principle
embarrass	lose	privilege
exaggerate	luxury	probably
exercise	maintenance	procedure
existence	marriage	prominent
expense	meant	promise
experience	mere	psychology
explanation	naturally	pursue
extremely	necessary	really
fascinate	ninety	receive
forty	noticeable	recommend
friend	obstacle	repetition
government	occasion	sense
grammar	occurrence	separate
guarantee	operate	shining
height	opinion	similar
heroes	original	studying
huge	paid	success
ignorant	parallel	surprise
imaginary	particular	tries
immediately	performance	truly
independent	personal	villain
intelligent	physical	weather
interest	piece	whether
interrupt	planned	writing

There/Their/They're

The words *there*, *their*, and *they're* are frequently confused. Once you understand the use of each word, you will have little trouble distinguishing among them. However, you should always proofread your drafts for *there*, *their*, and *they're* errors because they appear occasionally in most writing.

Here is the meaning of each word.

THERE an introductory word often preceding is, are, was, and were
(*There* are five goldfish in the pond. I think *there* is room for you in the bus.)

a location
(Your books are over *there*. *There* are the books I've been looking for.)

THEIR possessive pronoun (belonging to them)
(*Their* car was vandalized. Joo took *their* picture.)

THEY'RE contraction for *they are*
(*They're* going to get married on Sunday. I think *they're* beautiful slides of Rome.)

ACTIVITY 64

Fill in the blanks with the correct word: *there, their,* or *they're*. Select the word or words that fit each sentence.

EXAMPLES   *They're* going to break the snail-eating record.

Their patience is waning.

There are four hummingbirds in the bird bath.

1. _____ are thousands of wheat fields in Kansas.

2. _____ webbed feet help mallards cruise across the pond.

3. _____ an unusual breed of turkey.

4. _____ is a need for voters to mail _____ ballots by June.

5. _____ coming at 9:30, but _____ will be no one home.

6. _____ new sofa will be at _____ house by morning.

7. Plant the marigolds _____ , _____ , and _____ .

8. _____ learning algebra faster than _____ cousins did.

9. Is _____ a phone in _____ store?

10. _____ taking _____ time in _____ .

- - - - - - - - - - -

ACTIVITY 65

Write your own sentences using *there, their,* and *they're* as directed.

EXAMPLE   **a sentence beginning with *their***

Their schedules for the fall semester are full of errors.

1. a sentence beginning with *there*
2. a sentence beginning with *their*
3. a sentence beginning with *they're*
4. *there* and *their* in the same sentence
5. *there* and *they're* in the same sentence
6. *their* and *they're* in the same sentence
7. *their*, *there*, and *they're* in the same sentence
8. *there* three times in the same sentence.

■ ■ ■ ■ ■ ■ ■ ■ ■ ■ ■ ■

ACTIVITY 66

Here is more practice using the words *there*, *their*, and *they're* correctly. Remember, *there* is an introductory word or shows location, *their* is a possessive pronoun (belonging to them), and *they're* is a contraction for *they are*. Fill in the correct form in each blank in the following paragraph.

EXAMPLE   *Their* shoes are new, but *they're* not bragging about it.

_____ is no doubt that Henrietta and Hank are nervous taking the test.

_____ hands are shaking, and _____ frowning intently.

_____ pencils are moving rapidly over the test booklet. _____

backs are hunched in effort. _____ working at a feverish clip, but

_____ is a good chance they won't finish. It is a long and difficult test.

_____ are one hundred multiple-choice questions and five essay questions.

Finally, Henrietta and Hank stop at the bell, put _____ pencils down, and

relax _____ minds. They've done _____ best, and

_____ satisfied.

■ ■ ■ ■ ■ ■ ■ ■ ■ ■ ■ ■

Confusing Duos: List One

A number of word pairs often confuse writers. These "confusing duos" can slip erroneously into anyone's paper. The problem is not misspelling a word but using the wrong word in the wrong place. Here are some of the more commonly confused pairs with some information to help you tell them apart. (This is the first of two lists of "confusing duos.")

ACCEPT	**to receive** (I accept your gift. Joy accepted the award.)
EXCEPT	**to exclude, leave out** (Everyone is going bowling except Millicent.)
A	**comes before words beginning with a** *consonant* (a book, a slug, a dog, a cat)
AN	**comes before words beginning with a** *vowel* **or** *vowel sound* (an apple, an orange, an answer, an herb)
ADVICE	**what is** *given* **to someone** (Joe gave me some very good advice about my major.)
ADVISE	**the verb meaning to give advice** (Joe advised me to major in computer technology.)
AND	**conjunction joining words or groups of words** (George is going, and so am I.)
AN	**comes before words beginning with a** *vowel* **or** *vowel sound* (an apple, an orange, an answer, an herb)
ARE	**present tense of** *to be* **for plural subjects** (The gifts are on the table.)
OUR	**possessive pronoun, belonging to us** (Our plans are uncertain. We'll go our separate ways.)
IT'S	**contraction for** *it is* (It's going to snow today. It's a rough exam.)
ITS	**possessive pronoun** (The tire lost its tread. Its flowers are drooping.)
KNOW	**to have knowledge, to understand** (I know the answer. He knows his limits.)
NO	**none, negative** (No one minds. There is no smoking in the library. I say "no.")
MINE	**possessive pronoun, belonging to me** (That book is mine. Mine is the red jacket.)
MIND	**to behave, to oppose** (The dog minds well. I mind your eating my lunch.)
PAST	**time gone by** (In the past, you have always done well. Your past is your business.)
PASSED	(You passed my inspection. His fever passed hours ago.)

■ ■ ■ ■ ■ ■ ■ ■ ■ ■ ■ ■

ACTIVITY 67

Fill in the blanks with appropriate words from the list of confusing duos.

EXAMPLE   *No*   one cares where we sleep tonight.

1. Mattie paid _____ way into the park last night.

2. For breakfast I'd like _____ apple, _____ omelet, and _____ banana.

3. Everyone seems to be having a good time at the party _____ you.

4. If Shandra takes my _____ , she'll forget about working.

5. Do you know why _____ so foggy this month?

6. We are planning to spend _____ honeymoon in Tulsa.

7. I don't _____ if you borrow my sweater tomorrow.

8. I enjoyed studying with you this morning, _____ I hope we can do it again.

9. Fenway was too tired to be good company to _____ guests.

10. Do you _____ if we take up where we left off yesterday?

11. Jack would _____ you to take _____ aspirin and _____ hot bath.

12. Your case is _____ exception to _____ rule.

■ ■ ■ ■ ■ ■ ■ ■ ■ ■ ■ ■

Confusing Duos: List Two
Here is a second group of confusing word pairs to add to your list.

CHOOSE	**present tense verb** (I <u>choose</u> the present with the green bow.)
CHOSE	**past tense of *choose*** (Yesterday I <u>chose</u> to stay home from work.)
QUIT	**not to finish, to give up** (John <u>quit</u> his job with General Motors.)
QUITE	**completely, wholly** (Are you <u>quite</u> certain of the time? That was <u>quite</u> a show.)
QUIET	**opposite of noisy** (Please be <u>quiet</u> in the hospital. I would like a <u>quiet</u> moment.)
THIS	**singular word that identifies or locates** (<u>This</u> is a great story. <u>This</u> table is new.)
THESE	**plural of *this*** (<u>These</u> are the best stories I've read. <u>These</u> tables are new.)
TO	**preposition of many uses** (We went <u>to</u> the game. Look <u>to</u> your leader. Sheila belonged <u>to</u> the Modernes. <u>To</u> my knowledge, no one is missing.)

TOO	**also, in excess** (We are going to the game <u>too</u>. You have done <u>too</u> much work for one person.)
WERE	**past tense form of** *to be* **with plural subjects** (They <u>were</u> here a minute ago!)
WHERE	**indicates location** (<u>Where</u> are you going? Do you know <u>where</u> the dishes are?)
THROUGH	**preposition of movement or passage** (<u>Through</u> the years, you've grown more lovely. We glanced <u>through</u> the book.)
THREW	**past tense of** *throw* (He <u>threw</u> the ball through the window. Mildred <u>threw</u> out her boyfriend.)
YOUR	**possessive pronoun, belonging to you** (<u>Your</u> books are a mess.)
YOU'RE	**contraction for** *you are* (<u>You're</u> the first person to call since the trial.)
THEN	**indicates time** (<u>Then</u> you can go home. I did my work, and <u>then</u> I slept.)
THAN	**indicates comparison** (You are smarter <u>than</u> I am. I saved more money this year <u>than</u> last.)

ACTIVITY 68

Fill in the blanks in the following sentences with appropriate words from the list of confusing duos.

EXAMPLE   Last night you *chose* to be by yourself.

1. _____ pickles from Julio's Deli are the spiciest I've eaten.

2. _____ do you think _____ going with my ant-eater?

3. _____ dog was found in the neighbor's flower garden.

4. I am not _____ ready to _____ on the project.

5. _____ _____ you when we needed relief?

6. I think _____ taking _____ test too seriously.

7. Jody went _____ the races three hours _____ early.

8. I enjoy a _____ evening at home listening to _____ records.

9. I hear _____ not sure _____ _____ tapes

_____ left at school.

10. We went _____ the motions of reading our lines, but we didn't

_____ have the feeling needed _____ move our audience.

11. Fred felt better _____ he had expected after the race, but

_____ the exhaustion started setting in.

■ ■ ■ ■ ■ ■ ■ ■ ■ ■ ■

ACTIVITY 69

Here is a list of all the confusing duos covered in this section. Using the words correctly, write one sentence for each confusing duo. Underline the words.

EXAMPLES   **your/you're**

You're going to the library, but your brother isn't going.

are/our

Are you going to take our advice about taking vitamin C?

1. **choose/chose**
2. **quit/quite/quiet**
3. **this/these**
4. **through/threw**
5. **to/too**
6. **were/where**
7. **your/you're**
8. **there/their/they're**
9. **accept/except**
10. **a/an**
11. **an/and**
12. **advice/advise**
13. **are/our**
14. **it's/its**
15. **know/no**
16. **mine/mind**

17. past/passed

18. then/than

▪ ▪ ▪ ▪ ▪ ▪ ▪ ▪ ▪ ▪ ▪ ▪ ▪

ACTIVITY *70*

For more practice with all the confusing duos, fill in appropriate words in the blanks from the list of confusing duos you just used in Activity 69.

EXAMPLE   I don't _mind_ if you haven't _passed_ any courses.

1. _____ you sure you left _____ wallet over

   _____ ?

2. If the choice were _____ , I'd _____ _____
   orange binder.

3. _____ car was stripped of _____ _____
   accessories.

4. Take my _____ and watch _____ _____
   going.

5. Do you _____ the difference between _____ tangerine

   and _____ orange?

6. _____ the years, _____ grades have improved

   and _____ haven't.

7. Will you please _____ _____ award from

   _____ club?

8. _____ going to _____ us to forget _____
   problems.

9. _____ is _____ way _____ going

   on _____ honeymoon,

10. Jack _____ _____ tantrum when everyone was

    invited _____ him.

11. _____ shirts and _____ jackets have been

    _____ hard times.

12. Sammy _____ his job _____ _____

_____ offer from _____ old friend.

13. _____ you at the party _____ they _____

everyone in the pool in _____ clothes?

14. Please be _____ because I _____ that some people

aren't _____ _____ with _____ tests.

15. _____ raining outside, so we should take _____ taxi

to _____ destination.

Acknowledgments

Page 24: Paul Kaser, "Cross Country Skiing," is reprinted by permission of the author.

Page 26: Megan Bell, "Writing Music," is reprinted by permission of the author.

Page 28: Sam Negri, "Loafing Made Easy," is from *The New York Times*, July 12, 1980. © 1980 by The New York Times Company. Reprinted by permission.

Page 54: Floyd Dell, "We're Poor," is from *Homecoming: An Autobiography* by Floyd Dell. Copyright 1933, © 1961 by Floyd Dell. Reprinted by permission of Henry Holt and Company, Inc.

Page 56: David R. C. Good, "Science," is reprinted by permission of the author.

Page 58: Maxine Hong Kingston, "The Woman Warrior," is from *The Woman Warrior* © 1975, 1976 by Maxine Hong Kingston. Reprinted by permission of Alfred A. Knopf, Inc.

Page 88: Donald Murray, "Victims of the Age of Prosperity," is from *The Boston Globe*, September 15, 1987. Reprinted by permission of the author.

Page 90: Mary Mebane, "Black Wasn't Beautiful," is from *Mary* by Mary Mebane. © 1981 by Mary Elizabeth Mebane. All rights reserved. Reprinted by permission of Viking Penguin, a Division of Penguin Books USA, Inc.

Page 92: Thomas French, "Long Live High School Rebels," is from *The St. Petersburg Times*, November 22, 1987. Reprinted by permission of the publisher.

Page 129: Suzanne Britt, "Neat People vs. Sloppy People," is reprinted by permission of the author.

Page 131: Margaret Atwood, "Canada Through the One-Way Mirror," is from *The Nation*. © 1986 by The Nation Company, Inc. Reprinted by permission of the publisher.

Page 133: Yi-Fu Tuan, "American Space, Chinese Place," © 1974 by *Harper's Magazine*. All rights reserved. Reprinted from the July issue by special permission.

Page 150: Dan Wightman, "Winners, Losers, or Just Kids?" is from the *Los Angeles Times*, July 25, 1979. Reprinted by permission of the publisher.

Page 158: Grant Hendricks, "When Television Is a School for Criminals," is from *TV Guide* Magazine. Copyright © 1977 by Triangle Publications, Inc.

Index